KEEPING IT UNREAL

SEXUAL CULTURES

General Editors: Ann Pellegrini, Tavia Nyong'o, and Joshua Chambers-Letson
Founding Editors: José Esteban Muñoz and Ann Pellegrini

Titles in the series include:

The Tragedy of Heterosexuality
Jane Ward

Times Square Red, Times Square Blue
Samuel R. Delany

Private Affairs: Critical Ventures in the
Culture of Social Relations
Phillip Brian Harper

Tropics of Desire: Interventions from
Queer Latino America
José A. Quiroga

Our Monica, Ourselves: The Clinton
Affair and the National Interest
Edited by Lauren Berlant and Lisa A.
Duggan

Black Gay Man: Essays
Robert F. Reid-Pharr

Queer Globalizations: Citizenship and
the Afterlife of Colonialism
Edited by Arnaldo Cruz-Malavé and
Martin F. Manalansan IV

Queer Latinidad: Identity Practices,
Discursive Spaces
Juana María Rodríguez

Love the Sin: Sexual Regulation and
the Limits of Religious Tolerance
Janet R. Jakobsen and Ann Pellegrini

Boricua Pop: Puerto Ricans and the
Latinization of American Culture
Frances Négron-Muntaner

Manning the Race: Reforming Black
Men in the Jim Crow Era
Marlon Ross

In a Queer Time and Place: Transgender Bodies, Subcultural Lives
J. Jack Halberstam

Why I Hate Abercrombie and Fitch:
Essays on Race and Sexuality
Dwight A. McBride

God Hates Fags: The Rhetorics of Religious Violence
Michael Cobb

Once You Go Black: Choice, Desire,
and the Black American Intellectual
Robert Reid-Pharr

The Latino Body: Crisis Identities
in American Literary and Cultural
Memory
Lázaro Lima

Arranging Grief: Sacred Time and the
Body in Nineteenth-Century America
Dana Luciano

Cruising Utopia: The Then and There
of Queer Futurity
José Esteban Muñoz

Another Country: Queer
Anti-Urbanism
Scott Herring

Extravagant Abjection: Blackness,
Power, and Sexuality in the African
American Literary Imagination
Darieck Scott

Relocations: Queer Suburban
Imaginaries
Karen Tongson

Beyond the Nation: Diasporic Filipino Literature and Queer Reading
Martin Joseph Ponce

Single: Arguments for the Uncoupled
Michael Cobb

Brown Boys and Rice Queens: Spellbinding Performance in the Asias
Eng-Beng Lim

Transforming Citizenships: Transgender Articulations of the Law
Isaac West

The Delectable Negro: Human Consumption and Homoeroticism within US Slave Culture
Vincent Woodard, Edited by Justin A. Joyce and Dwight A. McBride

Sexual Futures, Queer Gestures and Other Latina Longings
Juana María Rodríguez

Sensational Flesh: Race, Power, and Masochism
Amber Jamilla Musser

The Exquisite Corpse of Asian America: Biopolitics, Biosociality, and Posthuman Ecologies
Rachel C. Lee

Not Gay: Sex between Straight White Men
Jane Ward

Embodied Avatars: Genealogies of Black Feminist Art and Performance
Uri McMillan

A Taste for Brown Bodies: Gay Modernity and Cosmopolitan Desire
Hiram Pérez

Wedlocked: The Perils of Marriage Equality
Katherine Franke

The Color of Kink: Black Women, BDSM, and Pornography
Ariane Cruz

Archives of Flesh: African America, Spain, and Post-Humanist Critique
Robert F. Reid-Pharr

Black Performance on the Outskirts of the Left: A History of the Impossible
Malik Gaines

A Body, Undone: Living on After Great Pain
Christina Crosby

The Life and Death of Latisha King: A Critical Phenomenology of Transphobia
Gayle Salamon

Queer Nuns: Religion, Activism, and Serious Parody
Melissa M. Wilcox

After the Party: A Manifesto for Queer of Color Life
Joshua Chambers-Letson

Sensual Excess: Queer Femininity and Brown Jouissance
Amber Jamilla Musser

Afro-Fabulations: The Queer Drama of Black Life
Tavia Nyong'o

Queer Times, Black Futures
Kara Keeling

Queer Faith: Reading Promiscuity and Race in the Secular Love Tradition
Melissa E. Sanchez

Archiving an Epidemic: Art, AIDS, and the Queer Chicanx Avant-Garde
Robb Hernández

Frottage: Frictions of Intimacy Across the Black Diaspora
Keguro Macharia

Becoming Human: Matter and Meaning in an Antiblack World
Zakiyyah Iman Jackson

The Sex Obsession: Perversity and Possibility in American Politics
Janet R. Jakobsen

Keeping It Unreal: Black Queer Fantasy and Superhero Comics
Darieck Scott

For a complete list of books in the series, see www.nyupress.org.

Keeping It Unreal

Black Queer Fantasy and Superhero Comics

Darieck Scott

NEW YORK UNIVERSITY PRESS

New York

NEW YORK UNIVERSITY PRESS
New York
www.nyupress.org

References to Internet websites (URLs) were accurate at the time of writing. Neither the author nor New York University Press is responsible for URLs that may have expired or changed since the manuscript was prepared.

Library of Congress Cataloging-in-Publication Data
Names: Scott, Darieck, author.
Title: Keeping it unreal : Black queer fantasy and superhero comics / Darieck Scott.
Description: New York : New York University Press, [2021] | Series: Sexual cultures |
Includes bibliographical references and index.
Identifiers: LCCN 2021011567 | ISBN 9781479840137 (hardback ; alk. paper) |
ISBN 9781479824144 (paperback ; alk. paper) | ISBN 9781479810956 (ebook) |
ISBN 9781479811694 (ebook other)
Subjects: LCSH: African American superheroes. | African Americans—Race identity. |
Fantasy—Social aspects. | Fantasy comic books, strips, etc. | Fantasy literature. |
Queer theory.
Classification: LCC PN6714 .S384 2021 | DDC 741.5/352996—dc23
LC record available at https://lccn.loc.gov/2021011567

New York University Press books are printed on acid-free paper, and their binding materials are chosen for strength and durability. We strive to use environmentally responsible suppliers and materials to the greatest extent possible in publishing our books.

Manufactured in the United States of America

10 9 8 7 6 5 4 3 2 1

Also available as an ebook

To my mother, father, and my sisters

CONTENTS

Introduction: Fantastic Bullets   1

1. I Am Nubia: Superhero Comics and the Paradigm of
   the Fantasy-Act   47

2. Can the Black Superhero *Be*? Blackness vs. the Superhero   89

3. Erotic Fantasy-Acts: The Art of Desire   173

   Conclusion: On Becoming Fantastical   221

   Acknowledgments   239

   Notes   241

   Index   255

   About the Author   267

Introduction

Fantastic Bullets

> But nothing can't stop you from wishin'. You can't beat no-
> body down so low till you can rob 'em of they will.
> —Zora Neale Hurston, *Their Eyes Were Watching God*

> You might not like bein' who you are, but you better start
> likin' it
> Because you sure can't be nobody else
> In other words: I can't be you—ain't no way, yeah—you can't
> be me
> Well, that's how it is, sisters and brothas
> . . . .
> It's the Law of the Land.
> —The Temptations, "Law of the Land"

> She told them that the only grace they could have was the
> grace they could imagine. That if they could not see it, they
> would not have it.
> —Toni Morrison, *Beloved*

These are parlous times. As they ever were.

And to be honest, I want out.

When I began thinking about this book some years ago, I supposed that it would be an extension of my previous book *Extravagant Abjection*. There I had been drawn to delve literary representations (in both literature proper and in theory) of how blackness is born out of abjection— how, in other words, dark-skinned bodies and the minds that live them are tortured and all-but-destroyed to create "black people," which/who then become available to "white people" as cheap, disposable economic, political, cultural, and psychic resources. My interest was in showing that these literary representations of black abjection provide universal accounts of existential, historical, psychological—and, by implication, political—qualities or truths: that we are all at base always abject, abject to histories that we cannot unmake or ever fully know, abject to our dependence on the frailties of language and on our brains' fear-drenched perceptions of our environments; yet that, precisely in this always-already abjection, precisely in its formless, frightening unshapeliness, we can discover capacities to make and to shape, to flee and to create. And blackness is one mode, perhaps one of the modern world's primary modes, to access both the abjection of Homo sapiens and abjection's unexpected power.

For this book, I thought I would investigate the flipside. *Keeping It Unreal* was to examine representations of blackness in fantasy-infused genres such as superhero comic books, erotic comics, and fantasy and science-fiction genre literature, and to theorize therefrom how fantasies of black power and triumph fashion theoretical, political, and aesthetic challenges to—and respite from—white supremacy and antiblackness. This is still my general aim. But, as should be no surprise (though it was a surprise to me), my initial motivation was shaped, not altogether consciously on my part, by the context of its times, which like any present moment appears to be eternal rather than the decidedly historical relic it swiftly becomes. It made a certain fundamental sense to think about fantasies of black power during the presidency of Barack Obama: yes, it's true that the image and fact of a black man holding the office created to administer a slaveholding republic did not, of course, realize at last dreams deferred, as pessimists and the many events that never fail to give comfort to pessimism proved every single day of Obama's eight years in office. But the Obama phenomenon did reveal that there were indeed things largely undreamt of in many of our philosophies, and it showed to some of us how strangely cautious we might have been in imagining the possibilities of black folks and the possible ways blackness can signify. The various phenomena for which Obama is a synecdoche gave to some of us the not-unpleasant defamiliarizing feeling that we had been cramped and defensive and afraid even in our black interiors.

Suddenly in sites where we gather to play pretend, such as the two-dimensional plains of superhero comics (a place you'll often find my mind tarrying), you could glimpse black supermen never before seen. Riding tall and powerful like the figures whose role and stature in the dominant culture's stories might lead them to be described as "white knights," you could see all-powerful black men in Marvel Comics' *Adam: The Legend of Blue Marvel* (2008–9) and DC Comics' *Final Crisis* (2008–9). Their nigh-heretical—and sadly evanescent—appearance revealed that the whiteness of the white knight was not without a crucial racial dimension and that we never really conceived of a superhero without imagining *his* imaginary whiteness (figures 1.1–1.4).

Figure 1.1. In Grant Morrison's *Final Crisis*, a clearly Obama-inspired president of an alternate United States on an alternate Earth reveals that he is that world's Superman. (*Final Crisis* #7, 2009; Doug Mahnke, artist)

Figure 1.2. Blue Marvel, a black male character in Marvel Comics possessed of DC Comics' Superman powers. (*Might Avengers* #3, 2013; Salvador Larocca, artist)

Figure 1.3. Grant Morrison's *Final Crisis* black Superman. (*Final Crisis* #7, 2009; Doug Mahnke, artist)

Figure 1.4. Two splash-page drawings of a black Kryptonian character from *Earth-2*— yet another black Superman. (Tom Taylor, writer; Nicola Scott, artist)

The shift between then and the time of writing this book in 2019 and 2020 seemed epochal. From the first black president to an all-but-openly white supremacist one who surrounds himself with advisers who are latter-day Nazis, accomplished in one traumatic step in November 2016—thus revealing, as we scarcely needed reminding (though evidently this understanding is so fragile that *they* needed a very dramatic reminder), that, as Ralph Ellison fictively demonstrated, the whiteness of the White House is not only or even mostly a description of the color of its paint.

Of course, like many such apparently radical breaks, this shift was in truth both more gradual and more predictable than it felt. The vicious attitudes and venal interests taking the guise of political forces that have decreed we will all have to live with the damage Trump has done did not and could not spring fully grown from the soil as though they were the soldiers of Cadmus. Those interests were visibly gathering adherents and actively plotting Trump's or some other avatar's rise in 2012 and indeed in 2009 during the apogee of national Obama-love. (Probably they are grooming his successor or plotting his resurrection at the time of this writing.) And as Ibram X. Kendi warned, "Everyone who has witnessed the historic presidency of Barack Obama—and the historic opposition to him—should now know full well that the more Black people uplift themselves, the more they will find themselves on the receiving end of a racist backlash."[1] We might then understand that we are in fact living the changing same and that it's not so much a matter of things outside our doors making an ominous change but of us having to shift what we pay attention to when we go out there.

But though the world probably hasn't really changed that much since I first began thinking of this book, and its changes such as they are might readily have been foreseen, it has nonetheless changed enough to make my interest in fantasies of black power and triumph look very different than it did circa 2011. Now such fantasies look as though they're debris of a ship exploded at sea, or like a door or a window to another realm in spacetime I'd much much rather be in. They begin to look like a survival guide or a survival device in parlous times, like they provide an answer to a newly urgent question (which probably should have been just as urgent without the necessity of referring to Satan du jour by its proper name): "How and where do I find some happiness and justice in an age of mass idiocy, willful destructiveness, and wanton injustice whose avatar is the odious 2016 Electoral College winner Donald Trump?"

* * *

One of my favorite comments by one of my favorite artists in the world provides a pleasing example of what compels me about the subject of fantasy. I've had it in mind during all the thinking and writing of *Keeping It Unreal*. This favorite artist is the Spanish cinema auteur Pedro Almodóvar. What I love about Almodóvar is of course his films. But not only that. I love something he's said, a certain savage sentiment he's articulated, which I both share and to which I aspire. This sentiment resonates because Almodóvar may be the most globally recognized artist and public figure associated with *la movida*, the cultural efflorescence that took place in Spain after the fascist dictator Francisco Franco's death in 1975.[2] Critic Pauline Kael quotes Almodóvar in 1987 saying, "My rebellion is to deny Franco. . . . I refuse even his memory. I start everything I write with the idea 'What if Franco had never existed?'"[3] This lovely bit of bravura is not a quip but seems to have served as a kind of artistic orientation for Almodóvar during the creation of his early films, as he has articulated the same point in similar terms several times. In an interview with Frédéric Strauss about his film *Live Flesh* (1997), Almodóvar discusses the differences between his later and earlier films thus: "Things change over time. . . . Twenty years ago, my revenge against Franco was to not even recognize his existence, his memory; to make my films as though he had never existed."[4]

The project of this book, written at last in parlous times, is a project close to my heart—revenge, of the early-Almodóvarian sort: revenge against the 2016 Electoral College-winner (and 2020 election denier) Satan and all he represents and embodies and furthers; the revenge of artistic or art-imitative refusal of memory; or the revenge of the artistic creation of memories for which there is as yet no historical correlate.

What if there were no racism or antiblackness or sexism or misogyny or homophobia or classism or ableism or transphobia or any of the horribly effective ways the modern world has found to create disposable people? What does that world look like? Even just a slice of it—say, a day in someone's life, a biography of one person? What if we imagined a history in which racism ended? Or in which, à la Almodóvar, Trump never existed, or if he did exist, he is as distant and forgotten as the once-great Helvius Pertinax? (Yes, I've deliberately chosen a Roman emperor whose tenure in that august office was about four months and of whom only classical historians know anything at all and of whose name I had zero knowledge until I picked up my classical dictionary as I wrote.)

As a novelist, I like to follow early Almodóvar: my current projects involve writing a fantasy-genre series of novels about just such a world, one where there's such a thing as race but some key pieces of how we think about it and live it somehow went happily missing—and, hence, where the Trump phenomenon could never have existed at all.

But as a scholar, I want to think about and to elaborate such an artistic mission, to theorize it and give some account of it. Is there *really* (as it were) anything significant to note about the activity of fantasy—specifically fantasizing against the powers that be, fantasizing against antiblackness? About not just wishing but concertedly thinking and creating the likes of Franco away? And if so (naturally my answer to the previous question, having bothered to write this book, must be yes), what is significant about it?

We rarely call anyone a fantasist, and if we do, usually the label is not applied in praise, or even with neutrality, except as a description of authors of genre fiction. In the same 1987 review of Almodóvar's *Law of Desire* in which Kael quotes him, Kael declares, "*Law of Desire* is a homosexual fantasy—AIDS doesn't exist. But Almodóvar is no dope; he's a conscious fantasist . . ."[5] Kael's review is in very high praise of Almodóvar's film. But her implicit definition of "fantasist" via the apparently necessary evocation of its opposites—Almodóvar is *not* a dope, Almodóvar *is* conscious—suggests that garden-variety fantasists and whatever silliness they get up to have little to recommend them, and in any case are not worthy of critical attention.

We have already seen that Kael is right and that Almodóvar was indeed quite conscious of the project of his fantasy: the erasure of Franco. But my mind is drawn to different judgments from those implicit in Kael's understanding of fantasists and to other questions.

When is any elaborated fantasy *not* conscious, and when is such a fantasy *not* responsive to and *not* somehow working with the material consequences of the political and historical events and conditions we understand to be "real" and that we understand to be the object of serious, meaningful inquiry? Might conscious, responsive working be what fantasy is and does? And does not, or might not, a fantastic gesture like refusing the memory of Franco operate suggestively, even in something so apparently trivial as filmic entertainment, in ways that exceed the specific dream-world content of the elaborated fantasy? (For one thing, a world without AIDS isn't just a "homosexual" fantasy alone, as it may have appeared to Kael in 1987; it is a fantastic goal and desire of millions on the globe who are not remotely identified with gay European and North American worlds.)

Almodóvar meticulously, laboriously chose not to remember Spain's recently (at the time) entombed fascist history and not to acknowledge AIDS's deaths and illness, in the world-construction represented in his art. These are the foundational moves of an imperious act of creation. They may seem specious and unsustainable—rather as if he were building a house on top of a hole he'd dug into the earth. But such gestures mimic—with far different purposes and presumably less consequential effects—the world-building moves of political hegemonies: erasing through the tricks of naturalization whole swathes of history or intentionally failing to render historical events lived in the past; not acknowledging the deaths and suffering of any whom it deems its enemy or its instrument. In this light, Almodóvar's fantasy is work *with* what we call reality and an assault *on* the injustices and tragedies of the reality that always abuses us.

What is fantasy? Or to be more precise, what do I mean when I write "fantasy" and describe it as revenge? In this book, I plan to keep my attention on artistic work—primarily textual and visual, and/or literary—that bears hallmarks that categorize it in genres of fantasy or the fantastic: thus, primarily, comic books, with references to one unavoidable movie and a scattering of mentions of sci-fi and fantasy genre fiction or speculative fiction. These artistic works are bound to fantasies in our minds—what we might call psychic fantasy or psychological fantasy—via a heavily congested but fast-moving two-way highway. Artistic works are the products of psychic fantasies of the artist, distributed and shared, entered into and contributed to, and in immeasurable, countless ways changed by, the audiences of the works. These works stimulate, influence, shape all the various individual minds and psyches that encounter them.

In theorizing about what-fantasy-is, I will be shuttling rapidly back and forth between arts and minds, oft times hovering over one end of the traffic only to need to jet as quickly as possible to the other. This means, I think, that what I am calling "fantasy" describes both the process and its product: fantasizing and fantasies themselves. I'm generally less interested in the origins of fantasies or the whys of fantasy. I'm beginning with the premise that fantasy—especially where fantasy has the kind of political valence I'm interested in, and especially as such fantasy impinges on how we view or how we imagine or how we live with blackness—arises from somebody's interest in a better world, with variable meanings attached to what counts as better and what is the compass and content of the world that the fantasy seeks to escape from, improve, or obliterate.

What do I mean by "fantasy"? To extend the highway metaphor, there are other important locations—often they pose as *one* singular location, though this apparent coherence is a ruse—that fantasy crisscrosses and traverses, where fantasy exits to arrive and from which fantasies summon us to depart. And, to mix the metaphor and perhaps shatter it altogether, this location casts its shadow over fantasy, and yet fantasy is also a powerful device by which we perceive or map it. This metaphorical location is reality. In the case of Almodóvar's fantasy, this would be a person and a period and a catalogue of terrible acts: the *real* General Franco under whose grim aegis so many dead bodies and lost freedoms entered the necropolis of time.

Simple semiotics tells us that all terms are at least partly defined by what they do not signify. Indeed every term charged with meaning elicits the ghost of its supposed opposite, which haunts it with double and contradictory meaning (this is one reason why the coherence of reality, at least as linguistically described, is always something of a ruse). But "fantasy" is a more directly comparative term than many, and its ghost is quite tangible. The core meaning of "fantasy" is drawn from its contrast with what it, precisely by such contrast, helps constitute: reality. So puissant is this particular not-so-ghostlike ghost that "fantasy" is a term that I think I can say is implicitly disparaging in the English language: its supposed opposite is the noble standard, fantasy the shunned and ridiculed deviation.

Hence the outrage here of a seminal thinker in literary criticism about fantasy, Rosemary Jackson, writing about fantastic literature. Composed deep in the bowels of time that was 1981, Jackson's screed hardly seems less relevant now than it would have been fifty years before she wrote the words:

> An implicit association of the fantastic with the barbaric and non-human has exiled it to the edges of literary cultures. Novelists redeploying some fantastic elements, such as Dickens, Gogol, or Dostoevsky, have been placed differently from Jane Austen, George Eliot, or Henry James, in the establishment of a canon of "great" literature, whilst Gothic novelists, Sade, M. G. Lewis, Mary Shelley, James Hogg, R. I. Stevenson, Calvino, have been relatively neglected. . . . In so far as it is possible to reconstruct a "history" of literary fantasy, it is one of repeated neutralization of its images of impossibility and of desire—both in the trajectories of the literary texts themselves and in the criticism which has mediated them to an intellectual audience.[6]

"Fantasy" is still more pejorative when its odor is detected infiltrating realms beyond literature and art. Here is my favorite thinker, Frantz Fanon, in the famous "On Violence" chapter of *The Wretched of the Earth*, cataloguing the necessary elements of transition from colonized stupor to revolutionary awakening that he observed in anticolonial struggles in Algeria and throughout Africa in the 1950s:

> After years of *unreality*, after wallowing in the most extraordinary phantasms, the colonized subject, machine gun at the ready, finally confronts the only force which challenges his very being: colonialism. And the young colonized subject who grows up in *an atmosphere of fire and brimstone* has no scruples mocking *zombie ancestors, two-headed horses, corpses woken from the dead*, and *djinns* who, taking advantage of a yawn, slip inside the body. The colonized subject *discovers reality* and transforms it through his praxis.[7]

This epistemic scaffold disparaging fantasy is especially persuasive when it helps build an antiracist political argument like Fanon's. In such arguments—powerful, enthroned by the lessons of bitter experience, by the horrifying testimonies of injustices both brutal and subtle, and given a crown of thorns by common sense—the "fantastic" is marked and defined by what we *know* to be its immense distance from relentless material realities, such as the pervasive endangerment and devastation of black people's lives and the abyssal disparities between black and nonblack (especially white) populations in wealth and the exercise of political power.

Indeed a central component of what makes fantasy fantastic is that fantasies actively occlude the perception of these very material realities. Blackness as a racial, existential, social, and political category is often analytically understood in critical race scholarship to be a project underwritten and sustained by pernicious fantasy: by these lights, the notion that the human species can be intelligently apprehended as belonging to different "races" is a cunning deception (accreted over time) enabling the divide-and-conquer operations of enslavers and colonizers. Thus blackness, as an invention of the fantasy that there are races, acquires meaning primarily through cruelly tendentious misreadings of histories and bodies. No one makes this argument better than Fanon: blackness as an imposition of fantasy on social reality facilitated the creation of a class of readily identifiable slave labor; and blackness was historically crucial in establishing a boundary definition and status marker for the emerging "human" post-1492, thus strengthening the (nonblack) human's claim to political citizenship in a global world structured by the nation-state, capitalism, colonialism, and modernity.

Racial fantasy in these senses secures material practices of economic exploitation and anchors psychic processes of differentiation and identification: it is a political tool of subjugation par excellence, efficiently organizing economies and social groupings and seductively demanding that all individuals and collectives take up—and *believe*—racialized terms of self-definition as the price of social belonging and of economic as well as psychic well-being.

This fundamental understanding naturally leads critical race scholarship mostly to condemn or to dismiss fantasy, especially in relationship to blackness, as useless at best or at worst as sinister and harmful. "Fantasy" then is a term discrediting ideas or political programs or narratives, a way of saying that something fails to meet the need to establish a just social world; or it is a way of describing how injustices are perpetuated in false or duped perceptions of the world. The implication is that if our perceptions were purged of the distorted shapes into which fantasies of race and blackness skew them, we would have a more accurate and very possibly more just social world.

What is fantasy? Or to be more precise, what meanings of fantasy—especially as it appears in the struggles against antiblackness and racism, in the advocacy of queerness and the fight against homophobia—am I trying to rescue "fantasy" from or to complicate?

Fantasy is misperception. Fantasy is *not* knowing or failing miserably to know whatever we are trying to know: it is a retreat from or a refusal of knowledge. Fantasy is inaccurate in relationship to the real. "Fantasy" is a word for what is not happening, what we are not doing, or what is at best merely the precarious inchoate precursor of a doing. Fantasy as an object of intellectual analysis names the antithesis or serves as the antonym of authentic relations to the temporal past (history) and the temporal present (reality) and has meager, if not dangerously opiate-like, purchase on the temporal future.

The most trivializing common notion of fantasy entails the idea that it's about childish or naive wish fulfillment. Lauren Berlant says in *Cruel Optimism*, "fantasy recalibrates what we encounter so that we can imagine that something or someone can fulfill our desire."[8] I quote this definition almost at random (the sentence leapt to my attention as it was quoted by one of my former dissertation students) to indicate the pervasiveness of an understanding of fantasy as suspect deception, as diversion from reality.

Hence, again, Rosemary Jackson:

> When fantasy has been allowed to surface within culture, it has been in a manner close to Freud's notion of art as compensation, as an activity which *sustains* cultural order by making up for a society's lacks. Gothic fiction, for example, tended to buttress a dominant, bourgeois, ideology, by vicarious wish fulfillment through fantasies of incest, rape, murder, parricide, social disorder. Like pornography, it functioned to supply an object of desire, to imagine social and sexual transgression.[9]

Jackson is talking about the fantastic in literature rather than identifying fantasy in politics and social life as Berlant is, but her grievance is with the logic of a critical approach to fantasy that obtains—and reigns—over both domains. The lubricious fit between the critique of literary genre fantasy and the critique of political fantasy suggests that these otherwise-disparate kinds of fantasy are not unconnected—if not quite sisters, then cousins at least. The literary fantastic and political fantasy both answer desire (fulfilling desire, supplying its object), but sadly in a kind of pathetic, stupid way, such that under the bright light of critique, these desires appear more like spasms than motives, the products of infantile consciousness rather than maturity.

I align in sympathy with Jackson, at least as far as the direction of her grievance. But Jackson doesn't disagree that "vicarious wish fulfillment" is at best of little use and at worst pernicious. For her, fantasy is indeed worthy of mockery if it's like pornography, engaging in what is implied to be the de minimis activity of "imagin[ing] social and sexual transgression." Of course, as someone who engages with porn studies, I have learned to apply pressure to this kind of easy dismissal of "low" culture and believe that it is precisely such formulations that cry out to be leveraged. Is "vicarious wish fulfillment" and merely imagining social and sexual transgression so fully compatible with or assimilated into sinister projects of sustaining of cultural order or pacification of resistance to that order? Do these phrases describe all that such activities entail? Is fantasy "compensation" only or even primarily a stabilizing, pacifying force?

To ask these questions as though Jackson in her ventriloquy of her opposition or Berlant in her offhand disdain would answer resoundingly in the affirmative is disingenuous, I admit. It's clear enough that the opposition being set up between resisting and sustaining is too easy and simply can't hold up in any absolute way: a work of art or of imagination is almost always too incoherent and variegated within itself to either *only* resist or sustain the cultural order, and in any case, nothing that resists is without a fundamental relation to that which it challenges, since the very hegemony it opposes supplies its terms and its content. And this is to hold at bay whether or to what extent the cultural order is ever successfully an *order* at all, much less an abiding one. The critical positions I'm using Jackson to identify and Berlant to represent would agree that our discursive universe and the reality it interacts with and in part constitutes is layered, contradictory, and complex. As Jackson acknowledges while she argues that *no*, fantasy *is* worth our attention and does do something serious, "To attempt to defend fantasy as inherently transgressive would be a vast, over-simplifying and mistaken gesture."[10]

Yet dependent though these questions may be on a bit of caricature and straw-man legerdemain, they do serve to focus my interest. Even apart from these simple provisos, I want to locate, track, and/or theorize the incoherences and perhaps not-altogether-assimilable effects of wish fulfillment and imagination as they are manifested in fantasy literature and comics, in their relation to black and queer politics. If fantasy doesn't as a logical matter *only* sustain the unjust status quo that decrees blackness and queerness must occupy lower rungs on its hierarchy, and if therefore we can surmise that fantasy as an experiential matter seems to do something that asks for an account, what might we say that fantasy "does," or what might we say that fantasies "are"?

* * *

What is fantasy? The understanding that fantasy is about stabilizing and pacifying is an understanding that supposes fantasy functions like a fetish. The general use of the term "fetish" in criticism of art/literature and in politics is borrowed largely from its coining within psychoanalytic theory and within Marxist theorizations. To say "fetish" is, again, to describe a logic. To make brief work of a subject that is ridiculously vast—but that I have every intention of corralling and holding in tight constraints throughout *Keeping It Unreal*—we might say that a fetish is a substitute that does the work that synecdoche does in rhetoric and poetics. The fetish substitutes for something experienced as missing, covering over a perceived lack by reference to some ostentatious figure that serves to re-create the whole, and yet that never ceases to remind us that it is makeshift and that thus the whole is lost. The fetish is the part that doesn't fully fit and that shows us we can never have the whole, but paradoxically by calling attention to its substitutive properties, it summons into nigh-tangible experiential reality the ideal of wholeness.

Fantasy as fetish describes what fantasy is, or how it plays a part in modes of living or structures of power when we talk about "national fantasy" (the fantasy that we are part of a nation) or "racial fantasy" (the fantasy that we belong to a race or races).

Additionally we know, or we suppose we know, what a sexual fetish is and that, whatever we suppose a sexual fetish to be—chiefly it's some sort of sexual interest very unlike your own—a sexual fetish is invested with, permeated by, made up of "sexual fantasy": an erotic attachment to various "parts," which in the emphasis that erotic investment confers on them evoke and subsume the "whole" of the attachment itself—leather, an ankle, a comic-book superhero costume, streams of piss, copious body hair.

At the same time, "sexual fantasy" itself is yet another instance of fetishism's logic, since the function of the fetish in sexual fantasy is to confer on the fantasizer a kind of "control" and "fulfillment" that are (false) mental and bodily experiences of "wholeness." Indeed, "sexual fantasy" might be a term related to sexual fetish in at least bidirectional synecdochical ways, just as in common usage a sexual fetish is the exemplar of fetishism. Concomitantly, we can see "sexual fantasy" at the root of, and as an exemplar of, how fetishism functions in national and racial fantasy—thus naming the sexual or psychosexual dimensions of both national and racial fantasies.

Here I wish to submit the formulation of fantasy as fetishistic to somewhat hostile pressure. Though I am sure that fetishistic logic informs and perhaps governs how we tend to critically approach fantasy, especially when we think about fantasy politically or in its social(izing) operations, I am not sure fetishism *is* the correct identification of the logic of fantasy.

Over the course of the next several groups of paragraphs, I want to try a thought experiment to help me think about fantasy.

(1) Here is a list of familiar fantasy plots. Let us think of them as fantasy propositions. These are descriptions of literary or paraliterary genre fantasies, innovated by particular creators, reproduced and distributed in media of mass entertainment, primarily books and comics, but also movies. Following the caricatures I've been using, we can imagine that these are the sorts of fantasies that Rosemary Jackson is talking about (she isn't, actually, but never mind that). I'll call this Set A:

A kind-hearted, slightly cowardly, well-to-do bachelor in a rural and suburban country finds a powerful magical ring; this ring was long ago forged by a devious and evil semidivinity, and now the semidivinity wages a war to recapture his ring and to subjugate the world with its powers; but the bachelor discovers reserves of indomitable courage within him as he embarks on an incident-filled, terrifying quest to destroy the evil ring and thwart its master's plans of world domination, accompanied and assisted by his dear friends—a great wizard, an elf, a dwarf, and an exiled king aiming to regain his rightful throne. . . .

A child from a planet far away populated by a species exactly like northern Europeans on Earth escapes his home planet's fiery destruction in a tiny spaceship ark built by his genius father. The spaceship ark lands in Kansas, where a kindly childless couple adopt him. As he grows into an adult, the alien discovers that on Earth he can fly, has great powers of strength and speed and magnificently heightened senses, is invulnerable to harm, and can burn through the hardest substances with mere sight; possessed of these powers and more, the alien fights for the values that his adoptive parents taught him: truth, justice, and the American Way. . . .

A bespectacled, bullied high school nerd gets bitten by a radioactive spider and gains superhuman strength, agility, reflexes, and senses to combine with his scientific genius; he sets out to make money as an entertainer, but when a thief whom he refused to aid the police in apprehending murders his beloved uncle, he learns that with great power comes great responsibility, and dedicates himself to fighting crime. . . .

A bespectacled boy with a scar on his forehead grows up in suburban England, under the neglectful and sometimes brutal care of his aunt and uncle, who despise him; a mysterious stampless letter arrives at his house, and soon he learns that he is a wizard, the child of two wizards murdered by a powerful, evil wizard who also tried to kill the boy, but failed; the boy is brought to a school for wizards and witches, makes lifelong friends, learns magic and more about his heritage, and engages in a protracted battle with the homicidal evil wizard, who pursues the boy with relentless enmity and activates a plan for world domination. . . .

A rich boy's parents are murdered before his eyes by a mugger; with his wealth and his rage as unlimited resources, the boy as he matures into a man, trains his body and mind to the pinnacle of human perfection, and, adopting the guise of a frightening creature of the night, wages a personal war against the mentally disturbed criminals that regularly terrorize his city, aided by a succession of young apprentice crime-fighters. . . .

A young woman blessed by the Greek gods with gifts of superhuman strength, speed, and intelligence comes of age on an isolated island populated by immortal warrior women; when an American pilot crash-lands on the island where no man has walked before, the young woman wins a contest of skills to return with the pilot to the United States, aiming to heal the wrongs of a violent, unjust world as the champion of her people's complex philosophy of peace and equality achieved via martial skill, warrior courage, and coded BDSM practices.[11]

(2) Next, following is a list of fantasies of an altogether different sort—the kinds of fantasies my caricature of Lauren Berlant refers to: political fantasies, national fantasies, social fantasies, the fantasies that thread their way through and sometimes frame our daily lives. These, being descriptions of collective fantasies without singular or clear narrative focus, appear more in the form of statements of fact than as fictive plots; but this does not make them any less—or any more, for that matter—fantasies. (Or at least I'll say so provisionally.) I'll call this set of fantasy propositions Set B:

The United States is an example of a democracy and a republic. A republic is a form of democracy. In republican representative democracy—or to use a somewhat out-of-fashion but more accurate term, in *indirect* democracy—groups of actual people's interests are represented by delegates whom these actual groups of people carefully vet and approve and send to the capitals of their towns, cities, regions, and nations to govern them on their behalf—which makes it then a form of *self*-government. . . .

There is a deity of definable attributes, with a name or set of names by which the deity can be addressed, and this deity is much like a member of the human species but infinitely wiser and more powerful. This deity created the entire universe with all its galaxies and quasars and black holes and white dwarf stars and gas-cloud planets, and yet the deity is also simultaneously deeply interested in prescribing various, sometimes all, aspects of human existence and behavior here on Earth, such as what kind of sex we have and with whom and what we eat and on what days and at which times. Moreover, it is possible to fully comprehend exactly what this deity desires of us regarding our eating and sexual habits, because the deity has revealed itself to select human beings, and these select intermediaries have written down the deity's instructions. This universal deity rewards good people and punishes bad people; sometimes this deity sends droughts, floods, earthquakes, diseases, plagues, and so on as forms of punishment for wicked people, as a reminder of the deity's power and as a nudge to wicked people to change their ways. A public, repeated statement of one's submission to this deity or one's dedicated involvement in the practices prescribed by this deity is both expected and demanded. And concomitantly it is expected and understandable, if not required, that people who assert their allegiance to one such deity should torture, murder, or otherwise castigate and subjugate those people who assert their allegiance to *another* such deity (even if the competing deities are very similar); or should so treat those people who are loyal to the same deity but according to some markedly different interpretation of the deity's or the deity's prophet's instructions; or should so treat those few who believe in no deity at all. . . .

It is not really possible (nor is it desirable) to live too closely with people who are too different; compatibility indicated by sameness is most desirable in social life. Sameness makes us safe. Difference makes us uncomfortable and threatens us. The languages people speak are significant measures of the differences between us. What set of genitals and/or body types each individual is born with is a very significant measure of the differences between each of us and everyone who is or was not born with a similar set of genitals and/or body types. The continuum of skin "colors" manifested in the human species is significant: thus, a very, very significant measure of difference between groups of people—and the key to all kinds of distribution of social goods—is "race." We all know exactly which race is which and who belongs to which, and in the rare instances that we don't know, it is because something unsettling or freaky has occurred or we have been deceived or there has been some unwonted "mixture" between our otherwise clearly distinct races. . . .

It is reasonable to inquire into the sexual habits and experiences of other people, even if—perhaps especially if—we are not having and never will have sex with any of these other people. This is because sexual habits and experiences are very, very important measures of difference and of sameness, and much depends on assessments of the sexual lives of other people. When we assess people's morality, their goodness or badness as human beings, we can and should be mostly concerned with their sexual habits and experiences—or, as is often the more accurate description, with what we *think* we know about their sexual habits and experiences, since we have not and probably never will have sex with the vast majority of the people whose morality we judge, ever. . . .

Adults naturally partner with each other as two-person couples, and coupledom intrinsically involves a mutual promise not to use one's genitals or other body parts in any kind of sexual, romantic, or pleasure-generating way with someone not part of the two-person couple. Thus, the most important part of other people's sexual habits and experiences that we want and need to know has to do with whether these other people are somehow using their genitals or bodies with someone who is not their spouse or publicly recognized partner: this is called cheating, and the very worst, most hurtful and destructive thing you can do in your two-person couple is to fail to submit to your spouse's or partner's de facto ownership of your genitals and/or pleasure-producing body parts. . . .

There exist entities called nations, which consist of hundreds of thousands, if not tens of millions or billions, of persons. These nations, or nation-states, have histories, cultures, geographies, and people(s) with putatively similar characteristics that set them apart from all other nations, including the nations with which they share borders (borders being the natural demarcation lines between nations). However, not all of the members of a given nation, sadly, are the same, which is a source of vexation and a cause of intranational violence for all the reasons stated earlier. As in the case of our declared allegiances to deities with different names, it is expected and understandable, if not required, that persons who are members of one nation should torture, murder, and otherwise castigate and subjugate persons who are members of other nations—or should so treat members of their "own" nation whose difference from the nation's image of itself is self-evident. . . .

It is expected and understandable that for each of us, the people whom we most care about and who most care about us are those most closely genetically related to us, whom we call our "family"; it is also expected and understandable that we mistrust, or dislike, those who are not most closely genetically related to us. Moreover, determining who is genetically "close" as opposed to "not close" to us requires no skill in genetics; figuring out who's family is very easy. . . .

(3) I admit that rage underwrites my list of the fantasies of Set B. But even allowing for having let the list get away from me, my point

is that although Set A lists different *kinds* of fantasies than Set B, both sets enumerate fantasies. While we can't say that the relation between the sets is strictly causal one way or the other, we can certainly say that they do nevertheless *relate to* each other; and it isn't unreasonable to suppose that the propositions of A, being initially the products of individual minds engaged in creative imagination, *refer and/or respond to* the propositions of B, which are collectively imagined and thus provide significant elements of the social and political contexts in which the initial producers of A are ensconced and from which those producers and their products therefore cannot be extricated.

It is moreover precisely by positing the items on each list as *propositions* that they are revealed as having in common the character of fantasy. According to *The Oxford Dictionary of American English*, among the meanings of the noun form of "proposition" are,

> 1. The action or an act of propounding or proposing something for consideration; something proposed for consideration. . . . A question proposed for solution, a problem, a riddle. . . . 2. The action or an act of representing or displaying something. . . . 3. a. A statement, an assertion; the making of a statement about something; *spec.* in Logic, a statement expressed in a form requiring consideration of its truth rather than its validity. . . . b. Logic. Either of the premises of a syllogism, *esp.* the major premiss. . . . 4. A scheme or plan of action put forward, a proposal. . . . 5. Math. A formal statement of a truth to be demonstrated (a theorem) or of an operation to be performed (a problem) (freq. including also the demonstration).

A proposition has *yet to be demonstrated* to be true, in logic or math; a proposition is *to be considered*. A proposition is not as yet, and may not ever be, proven to be true, actual, real. A description of a—perhaps *the*—fundamental character of fantasy, when we can see fantasy as proposition, is its provisional unreality, its demonstrable failure to be demonstrated. We cannot demonstrate satisfactorily the concerns God has with our eating habits, let alone the deity's existence; nor can we show that there is a person who has been bitten by a radioactive spider who is currently swinging, or has ever swung, from Manhattan rooftops. Fantasy as proposition, or propositions in the aspects they share with fantasies, describe a relation to, an orientation in thought and/or action toward, something for which no sense physical or psychic provides consistent evidence of its existence: you cannot see it, you cannot hear it or taste it or touch it or smell it, nor does it impinge in any direct way on your emotions, but you're sure it's there. This describes what exists "in"—which is really to say what exists *as the substance of*—our minds.

The unkind synonym for "fantasy," then, might be "lie," for the substance of fantasy is its insubstantial untruth.

A warning that we're about to get a little dizzy: this is a good place, maybe, to experience the effect of fantasy, which disturbs our perception of what's real but is probably not so great for thinking productively about fantasy's definitions. With this caveat, onward: What is the real that fantasy defines itself in contradistinction to? The conundrum is that fantasy can be said to have no existence at all, because fantasies are not real—though immediately things get tricky: fantasy does not exist, though it is the opposite of and therefore a guarantor of reality (by, according to simple Aristotelian logic, providing the exemplar of what reality is not). Everything that exists can only be accounted as existent by virtue of its being real—which is of course a tautology.

If that which guarantees reality does not exist, does this not weaken reality's claim to exist? Hegel, in his fable of the rise of consciousness in a social relation, supposed that the social relationship between two consciousnesses, each vying to establish its existence for itself, would via a life-or-death struggle become a hierarchical relationship: the lord and bondsman, or master and slave. The lord/master "is the independent consciousness whose essential nature is to be for itself, the other [the bondsman/slave] is the dependent consciousness whose essential nature is simply to live or to be for another."[12] This resolution is, however, inherently unstable. The master could not forever maintain its precedence over the slave, since it was the slave's acknowledgment, after being subjugated by the master, of the master *as* master that secured mastery. Since the slave's subjugation rendered him instrumental to the master, his existence inessential, he could not ultimately serve as the master's guarantor. "The unessential consciousness is for the lord the object, which constitutes the *truth* of his certainty of himself. But it is clear that . . . the object in which the lord has achieved his lordship has in reality turned out to be something quite different from an independent consciousness.

What now really confronts him is not an independent consciousness, but a dependent one. He is, therefore, not certain of *being-for-self* as the truth of himself. On the contrary, his truth is in reality the unessential consciousness and its unessential action."[13]

As we know all too well, in the series of binary analyses endemic and arguably foundational to the epistemologies of the modern world's European colonizers, the binaries continually recur to hierarchies of master-slave rather than to equalities: white-black, man-woman, no less than reality-fantasy. But the central fulcrum cannot hold, and rough beasts ever slouch back to the site of the apotheosis that was supposed to have banished them. Substitute "reality" for "lord" in the previous quotations, "fantasy" for "bondsman." How real is the real if fantasy is its opposite?

We can be further distracted here, in that the attempt to render a more accurately descriptive account of fantasy—what fantasy does, how it operates, in lived experience—must also shed some light on those imaginary aspects of various real *facts*: of blackness, of race, of gender, of sexuality, of ability, and beyond. In finding ways to use fantasy, we also take great note of how fantasies use us to build the prisons of our reality. For an incisive instruction on how this works with regard to blackness, look back for a moment to Fanon. Here in *Black Skin, White Masks*, we find Fanon companionably mocking ostensibly liberatory iterations of blackness in the Negritude movement and also in Langston Hughes's "The Negro Speaks of Rivers":

> The Negro, alerting the prolific antennae of the world, standing in the spotlight of the world, spraying the world with his poetical power . . . I embrace the world! I am the world! The white man has never understood *this magical substitution*. The white man wants the world; he wants it for himself. He discovers he is the predestined master of the world. He enslaves it. His relationship with the world is one of appropriation. But there are values that can be served only with my sauce. As a magician I stole from the white man a "certain world," lost to him and his kind. When that happened the white man must have felt an aftershock he was unable to identify, being unused to such reactions. *The reason was that above the objective world of plantations and bananas and rubber trees, I had subtly established the real world. The essence of the world was my property. Between the world and me there was a relation of coexistence.*[14]

That is, the false image, the fantasy, of "the Negro" produced out of histories of enslavement and colonization in part makes the modern world; thus the world *is* in part that false image, is a fantasy, produced out of those true histories. This sinister sleight of discourse and reality may be backed up by countless acts of violence and intimidation, countless bullets and links of chain. But the fundamental tool of fantasy is thought, and a different thought—perhaps a thought freed from what it has been constrained to know as "real"—may find some leverage for conducting the magic trick for a different set of results, if it is accompanied by the transformative powers of repetition (and probably some bullets, too). Reality—certainly the reality we interface through our social relations, through our cultures, through our languages—is unfinished and ever will be. In fantasy, we may detect reality's future shapes as well as its present habitability.

Obviously, realness as the antithesis of fantasy has no necessary connection with materiality, nor is the real limited to its being available to the physical senses: we can testify that consciousness is real without being material—even if Jean-Paul Sartre, philosopher of existentialism, points out that consciousness is "nothing" and that it "annihilates" the world in which it is enmeshed by positing itself as separate from that world and removing itself from the immediate immersion in the world, he says that consciousness "exists" a body. Consciousness is real because our embodied selves experience it, and the same can be said of love and pain. In this sense, then, fantasy *is* real, and *exists*, in the same manner as consciousness and love are and do—indeed, both consciousness and love might easily be said to be made up, as it were, of fantasy.

We need only notice this labyrinth's twists and snares, though; we don't have to go inside. The general functionality and unknowable layout of the ideal labyrinth—its character—is itself a guide to understanding that the relationship between *fantasy/propositions/lies* and *reality/actuality/truth/the world* is not unlike the relationship we have seen between Set A and Set B:

Both former and latter define themselves in opposition to one another; *and* the terms of Set A are set by Set B even as the former contradicts the latter; *and* Set B is fundamentally informed by Set A in that human perception and experience of Set B do not happen without the significant contribution of Set A as an organizing structuring of Set B—

such that all these contradictory assertions are right, and such that while fantasy ≠ reality and Set A ≠ Set B, the sum, measure, and content of neither can be fully distinguished from the other.

(4) Set A lists lies we pay money to read or to see performed and let play in our minds. Set B lists lies we live by. If both Sets A and B are a list of lies, it follows that there should be no restraint on making up other lies, as there should be no restraint, logically speaking, on the range or kinds of fantasies that any of us might entertain.

Next, then, are some counters—or, strictly speaking, counterparts—to the recognized fantasies listed earlier. We can think of these as another list of propositions, which could be either individual or works of art— fantasy art, which individuals or groups of individuals "propose" as an act of creation, and which audiences, readers, revisers (such as fan fiction) communities engage with and engage in:

A bespectacled, bullied high school nerd gets bitten by a radioactive spider and gains superhuman strength, agility, reflexes, and senses to combine with his scientific genius; he sets out to make money as an entertainer, but when his unarmed half brother is killed by police in an incident in which he fails to intervene, he learns that with great power comes great responsibility and dedicates himself to protecting people of color in his city from dirty cops and a corrupt system of justice. . . .

A child from a planet far away populated by a species exactly like southern Africans on Earth escapes his home planet's fiery destruction in a tiny spaceship ark built by his genius father. The spaceship ark lands in Mississippi, where a kindly childless couple adopt him. As he grows into an adult, the alien discovers that on Earth he has great powers of strength, speed, flight, invulnerability, and sense perception; possessed of these powers and more, the alien fights for the values that his adoptive parents taught him: justice for the poor and downtrodden, societal healing from the fatal wounds of slavery and Jim Crow, establishing the American Dream for all. . . .

A kind-hearted, slightly cowardly, well-to-do bachelor from the suburbs finds a powerful superscience device called a Cosmic Cube, created by an evil-genius Nazi war criminal who intended to use it to establish the world domination of an eternal Fourth Reich. The Nazi genius wages a war to recapture the Cube, but the bachelor discovers reserves of courage and indomitable willpower within him as he embarks on an incident-filled, terrifying quest to master the Cube's powers and, with the guidance of a wizardly immortal warrior woman from an island of Amazons, learns to use the Cube to eliminate poverty, bigotry, exploitation, and war from all human societies and to heal the damage that humans have done to the biosphere, aided by his dear friends, a diverse group of freedom fighters and activists. This I'll call Set A(x).

Set B(x): Racial, gender, and sexual difference are insignificant differences, so much so that "race," "gender," and "sexuality" have no meaning beyond neutral descriptions, of admittedly loose accuracy, of a person's genetic heritage or aggregation of physiognomic traits. Or there is racial, gender, and sexual difference and they are significant, but such differences have no bearing on or even statistical correlation with differences or hierarchical distributions of political power, economic wealth, and mental and physical health and life chances. Or, perhaps best yet, there *was* such a thing as racism and sexism and homophobia, and so on, and these differences once upon a time had meaning, but now they are historical circumstances having no greater bearing on daily life or even what we study in history than the facts that the Khazars once dominated Silk Road trade or that Vikings raided Paris off and on for a couple of hundred years more than a millennium ago or that probably there was once an ancestral species to which the organisms that would later evolve into humans and cephalopods both belonged. . . .

Sexual, romantic, familial relationships between humans imply no necessary hierarchy of power between the partners or members: they have no necessary or preordained choice of partner(s) designated by such partner(s)' gender, race, and so on, and such relationships do not have any necessary preordained number of partners or members. Nothing in such wholly voluntary partnerships or families entails anyone's ownership or control of liaisons of any kind outside the partnership or family. The two necessary aspects of these partnerships or family-memberships are that all involved have agreed to enter them and to re-negotiate them as desired and that all bear significant responsibility for the care of any children that may result from, or have been adopted into, the family-partnership collective.

(5) For me, there's a certain zesty excitement in the simple act of committing to laptop-screen and paper the fantasies in the *x* sets. Partly the excitement arises from combining of fantasy typologies, something

akin to a genre crossing that violates conventions. Chiefly my excitement arises from the recognition, in embarking on this crossing, that these genre markers are conventions governing *what it is possible even to imagine*: recognizing in the act of surpassing them that somehow the logics of these typologies have loomed larger than mere fences of convention and its habits-cum-rules. Somehow they have felt like walls, walls almost as tangible as the structures of the "built environment," walls I'm in the process of hurdling.

Even positing the *x* sets is no simple endeavor, not nearly as easy as we presume that creating with no greater tool than our neuronal activity ought to be and usually is (or is it?). The counterpropositions themselves are endangered by failures of imagination or by the difficulties of sustaining imaginative sparks.

Frankfurt School philosopher Ernst Bloch trumpets the indelibility of the utopian imagination during a public talk with Theodor Adorno in 1964. There Bloch insists that even when mired in the most intractable materialist perspective, where to call something "utopian" is an insult (like calling something a "fantasy" is to ridicule its content), an "it-should-be" desire for other than the unjust present troubles the seemingly all-conquering capitalist monolith.

"If we had not already gone beyond the barriers, we could not even perceive them as barriers," Bloch avers (and gets Adorno's assent). "The fact that there is such a sensitivity about an 'it-should-be' demonstrates that there is also utopia in this area where it has the most difficulty," and, "I believe utopia cannot be removed from the world in spite of everything."[15]

Here I think of utopia as the kind of fantasy I want to nurture; and I am convinced, or wish to be convinced, of Bloch's insight. But the fact that it isn't as easy to imagine the counterpropositions I've listed or to sustain them once imagined, even with no necessity of transforming them into consensus reality, is worrying. Maybe utopia cannot be removed, but it can be and is constantly harried to the threshold of vanishing. (Bloch himself teaches us this.)[16] For example, it is significant to me that my revision of the comic-book Superman fantasy (apart from my alien visitor's demographics) is actually pretty close to what Superman's creators, Joe Shuster and Jerry Siegel, committed to paper. Their Superman leapt tall buildings in the late 1930s in order to defeat the likes of corrupt politicians, manipulative war-profiteer capitalists, and a mine owner who put profit before the safe working conditions of his miners, and to save an impoverished juvenile offender from the harsh penalties of a criminal justice system that was indifferent to his social circumstances. Why did this Superman give way to the icon of an Eisenhowerish "American Way"? And how do we produce an account for the effects or importance, if any, that flow if we recover the spirit of the original or, alternatively, if we consider the factors that produced this putatively childish and literally paper-thin imaginary character's strangely political evolution? How might typology-combining fantasies such as those in x effect both the production and dissemination of fantasy genre art and entertainment and the lived realities of our ever-unhappy politics?

I am interested, too, in why within the "privacy" of my own fantasies, I can't or I don't imagine myself having privileges that accrue to white bodies. That is, why can't I on the imaginary plane both "be" black and imagine myself replete with the powers of whiteness?

Such a fantasy might well involve imagining myself as colorless—as in the famous, and curious, clinical anecdote reported by Fanon: "For the Antillean the mirror hallucination is always neutral. When Antilleans tell me that they have experienced it [the encounter with the mirror-image described by Jacques Lacan as the Mirror Stage], I always ask the same question: 'What color were you?' Invariably they reply: 'I had no color.' . . . It is not I as a Negro who acts, thinks, and is praised to the skies."[17]

Or I could fantasize that I've been chemically transformed, as in George Schuyler's bitterly funny 1931 *Black No More*.

Yes, I shouldn't have to follow either dubious example. But I *don't* do *either*, nor do I seek any third avenue. It should be possible to fantasize the privileges of whiteness within my own mind—we are, after all, each the protagonist of a drama playing out for the sole audience of ourselves (and sadly, even while we interact with a host of others, that's too often *all* we're doing). But I can't seem to accrue them to my own self-imagined avatar once I acknowledge race—and apparently I never fail to acknowledge it—as an explicit factor.

These observations are an indication that even if utopia cannot be removed and if barriers are already bowled over by our capacity to imagine barriers as barriers, the power of these barriers is in large part preemptive. Barriers to imagination are powerful because they tilt against our ability to notice that they *are* barriers and our ability to count as worthwhile an investment in possibilities of living unconstrained by those barriers. These barriers are not merely mistakes of mind, but structures of epistemology and hermeneutics bearing down on and constraining our existence. Thus pushing past them requires heavy counterweights.

Fanon in the final flourish of *Black Skin, White Masks* describes a measure of that weight, and he intimates to us that the distinctions we might assume between the merely psychic/psychological and the materially hefty body, between imagination and reality, are the very substance of what disables us. "I find myself one day in a world where things are hurtful; a world where I am required to fight," Fanon writes. "If the white man challenges my humanity I will show him by weighing down on his life with all my weight of a man that I am not this grinning *Y a bon Banania* figure that he persists in imagining I am. . . . I must constantly remind myself that the real *leap* consists of introducing invention into life."[18]

It may be objected that Fanon is here, as he often is in *Black Skin*, deeply rhetorical. But Fanon's point is that the object of his critique—the blackness (read: inhumanity, abjection, etc.) of his body—is itself *made up* of rhetoric wedded to image, is figural, is fantastical, in such a way that merges nigh imperceptibly into the "weight" of bodies and existence (life).[19] Blackness is "lived experience" but fundamentally an occulted experience, where by "occulted" I refer metaphorically to astronomical occultation and more literally to the word's meaning as "hidden."

So why might it be difficult, effortful, vexed, for creators of fantasies (including me) to envision rich fantasies of, say, black privilege? Or, à la Siegel and Shuster, are such fantasies in fact *not* difficult to imagine? Are they rather laboriously censored by the fine machinations of systems of exploitation and oppression-for-the-benefit-of-a-few that constitute and control the distribution of ideas, narratives, and images in human communications defined by commerce?

Following the breadcrumb trails to the dead ends of collective-cum-personal imagination—and making the effort to vault over them—is what interests me here. Perhaps a consideration of these difficulties tells us something about how we get to living happier politics, making *these* fantasies = reality. In envisioning such combinations, how better might we understand the relationship (assuming there is any) between the two types of fantasy?

Such questions, with admitted tendentiousness, lead to my reframing of fantasy into what I want to call, provisionally, *fantasy-acts*. This reframing pulls us away from thinking of fantasy as essentially passive and pacifying, from damning it because it is not strongly material or demonstrably powerful. *Fantasy-acts* allows that *fantasy is without the weight or carry or power of "reality," but* it also reminds us that *fantasy has* some *accountable weight or carry or power, so that we have to call fantasy an existent or an act of some kind.*

And if this is true, what can we say is the "weight" of these fantasy-acts?

An important part of the answers to these particular questions lies with Lacan's vital observations of the inextricability of self from language, that vast collective impersonal Other that speaks us into being and authors our (delusions of) self-authorship. But we need not only find this wisdom in Lacan (since I've already once announced the avoidance of labyrinths). In the phenomenology of Zen Buddhist thinking, we might find a plainer pathway:

> Where does the person we take ourselves to be come from in the first place? Apart from our parents' genes and their support and care, and society and all it produces for us, there's the whole network of conditions and circumstances that intimately makes us what we are. How about our thought and feeling? Where does it come from? Without words to think in, we don't think, we don't have the emotions and feelings that are shaped and defined by our words. Did we invent this language that constitutes ourselves? No, it is the product of untold numbers of speakers over untold numbers of generations. . . . Literally every thought in our minds, every emotion that we feel, every word that comes out of our mouth, every material sustenance that we need to get through the day, comes through . . . the interaction with others.[20]

So every fantasy is the product of untold numbers of fantasizers over untold numbers of generations and our interactions with those untold numbers in their myriad forms. For reasons we have yet to fully examine—or to take a stab at greater accuracy, for reasons I've not myself explored to my satisfaction—these generations of fantasizers (whose number probably *can* be told, dating from circa 1492) have not sustained an imaginary of blackness triumphant, blackness redeemed, blackness powerful.

One reason, to be sure, we can understand by again following Fanon: blackness is a category of subhumanity created to subject its bearers to the control and desire of others thus created as white. Hence we can see that blackness highlights and arguably exaggerates the abject universal of the human condition (again, we are always already abject to language, abject to the histories that precede us and determine us). Or we might pose the relation in this way, that blackness does the cultural (as well as the economic, social, political, psychological, and psychic) work of signing, of *bearing* the abjection that the human—ascending to that position by dint of creating blackness—pretends—lies—fantasizes—that it can slough off. If this is so, the historical conditions giving rise to blackness place an inherent—and severe—limit on the degree to which blackness can be imagined in relation to triumph or power. Blackness as abjection is obviously blackness as antithetical to fantasies of power; one needs a subjected blackness, or something else doing blackness's work, to fantasize power at all. (We can of course complicate this a great deal if we reconsider what "power" is—which is the subject of *Extravagant Abjection*.)

Does, then, enjoying fantasy, utilizing its powers—the ability to render fantasy as an *act*—require privilege? It seems not unreasonable given all I've discussed to suppose that a fantasy-act requires first the privilege that comes with insulating oneself from "harsh realities," the luxury available only to those living in the relative comfort of economic security, those graced to pass their days physically unmenaced. My call for the uses of fantasy might easily appear to be counterproductive or diversionary in the case of blackness, indeed in any situation where survival of the body is at stake. By analogy, it seems nearly axiomatic to dismiss as frivolous, say, an interest in beauty or aesthetic concerns when you are faced with the immediate *physical* need to abolish conditions of structural impoverishment or to counter state terror and slow genocide by police action. These of course are primary conditions of black communities in many, if not most, places in the world. So is it the case, looking along the axis of relations between fantasy and reality as they graph with racial positioning (as we might in a graph with gender positioning, etc.), that blackness marks you as the one fantasized *about*, the *object* of fantasy, *subjected* to and by fantasy, thus never empowered to fanta*size*?

Two replies to these questions—related to each other and yet pushing in opposite ways, both concordant and discordant—suggest that fantasy is not solely the province of dominance and hegemony, even though it's also true that fantasy cannot wholly escape dominant sectors of societies or the hegemonies that rule them:

On the one hand, fantasy defines reality by serving as the limit of the real; and the same processes that make fantasy also underwrite the real—that is, the processes of human consciousness that make a meal out of the worlds that flood our human senses. The latter, as I've noted, tells us that what is real and actual is also—and to an extent that is so great that we cannot disentangle this process from reality—real*ism*: which is to say that the real is comprised of constructs produced and repeated by our ancestors' (both genetic and cultural) perceptions of their environments, as well as our accession to (our abjection to) repetitions and revisions of those perceptions.

Our chief access to reality is through the sense-data-distorting mechanisms of our brains; we are immersed in reality through this primary mediation. Only in extreme cases, when factors in our environment act with the greatest force and violence, are we directly subject to reality: a tornado or a hurricane wind is strong enough to pick us up and move us, but otherwise we are not directly subject to the wind—rather, nerve endings in our skin, in our noses, our ears, transmit the data of the wind's presence to our brains. Reality is never without this *perceptual realism*.

Perceptual realism is rarely (perhaps never?) without its cultural component. Thus we can say that there is a history, a catalogue of ancestral and present action, for what we deem to be *real*—and too, for what in light of what we deem real, what we deem to be *possible*. By extension, we can surmise that since the unreality of fantasy serves to establish the limit of the real and the possible, the contents of fantasies serve to reinforce foregone conclusions about the range of possibility: one great weapon in the arsenal of epistemology-as-power is then being able to dismiss as impossible a wide range—perhaps an infinite range—of "possibles" under the denigrated term "fantasy." Perceptual realism is political realism (and it is no coincidence that both real*isms* become most "real" when they impress themselves on us most violently: when the wind flings you against the rocks, when the lion's fang sinks into your flesh, when the bullet enters your brain or the chain attached to the bracelets at your ankles tugs).

This is why Bloch and Adorno in their 1964 conversation can agree that there is a clear interest that has prevented the world from being changed into the possible: we are each of us born into a world already enslaved by its realisms, by its versions of the real.

It follows, however, that fantasy functioning as reality's antonym also potentially unmasks the politics of reality-which-is-really-realism. Here is Adorno rejoining Bloch:

> My thesis . . . would be that all humans deep down, whether they admit this or not, know that . . . it could be different. Not only could they live without hunger and probably without anxiety, but they could also live as free human beings. At the same time, the social apparatus has hardened itself against people, and thus, whatever appears before their eyes all over the world as attainable possibility, as the evident possibility of fulfillment, presents itself to them as radically impossible. . . . I would say that this is due to the evident possibility of fulfillment and the just as evident impossibility of fulfillment only in *this* way, compelling them to identify themselves with this impossibility and make this impossibility into their own affair. In other words, to use Freud, they "identify themselves with the aggressor" and say that *this should* not be, whereby they feel that it is precisely *this* that *should be*, but they are prevented from attaining it by a wicked spell cast over the world.[21]

In this sense, fantasy's activity is partly the recovery of the possible, the *action*—even if not remotely on par with the range of violence available to reality's actions—of forging some kind of *realization of the possible*; it is a push back against the tyranny of history.

Here, then, fantasy is not solely a property of, say, whiteness. Says Bloch, "It is impossible to be at the outer margins of the status quo without the 'dream of a thing' being irregularly glimpsed."[22] This "dream of a thing" refers to Marx railing against mysticism yet being evocatively gnomic in an 1843 letter. Marx writes, "Our program must be: the reform of consciousness not through dogmas but by analyzing mystical consciousness obscure to itself, whether it appear in religious or political form. It will then become plain that the world has long since *dreamed of something* of which it needs only to become conscious for it to possess it in reality."[23]

We might begin a consideration of fantasy-acts with observations concerning the fantasy of one consciousness, one person. Here are premises: the sole inalienable possession I "have" is my self, if by "self" we mean my thoughts and feelings, both those that are recognized and those that go unrecognized, and if by "thoughts" and "feelings," we maintain an awareness of their existence in and as an amalgam of all the physical cells of the organism that is called the body. *Only I* am the locus of my particular thoughts and feelings; and so far as we can tell, only I in the whole history and unhistoried two-hundred-thousand-year past of human beings has experienced the particular combination of *my* thoughts and feelings. I have no instrument whereby I experience or encounter the world beyond myself but my self (my thoughts and feelings); therefore, the world is not the world to me but is the world as filtered through my self, this one self that no other being has ever "had" or, so far as we know now, will ever have in the future—and nothing will escape this or change it. If this is true, then whatever you or anyone else thinks or feels about what I think and feel cannot be known or experienced and must then be of negligible consequence.

But these thoughts and feelings, it should be objected, do not really "come from" me but from discourse, from the Lacanian Other, as I noted earlier. We cocreate each other's world; you create mine as I create yours. Our forebears, who never have to answer for their crimes nor will ever be given adequate witness to their suffering, cocreated the worlds we live.

Yet even so, we are not telepaths. As a consequence of this limitation, you will never know with any certainty what I think or feel, and I will never know what you think or feel. You can, if you like, tell me what you want me to think or feel, but you can't ascertain the success of your command. This is an incontrovertible fact of human existence, of human species-being, an artifact of consciousnesses embedded in and as our separate bodies. Whatever we do or intend in the vast web of our various communications and relations, we must always fail to achieve telepathy (so far); and put differently, as the Temptations once sagely reminded us, any aspiration to be someone else (better, richer, more beautiful), or to overtake someone else to render them into slavish reflections of our masterful ideal selves or solely as instruments of our will, is doomed to failure.[24]

In this, which is where fantasy lies and what it is—the perhaps-predetermined-but-anyway-inaccessible-to-others play of the mind—we can discern a fundamental resistance to domination. I'm taking the leap to say that in fantasy lies, inherently, resistance: it may well be resistance to things that politically or spiritually we would prefer there be no resistance to—a resistance to recognizing the degree to which our lives are mangled by exploitative forces, a resistance to living in the moment. In these lights, fantasy appears in its typical guise as agent of domination and tool of deception. But I want to turn this mask inside out: fantasy *might* be under any number of circumstances an agent of domination and deception, but a priori, it is the stuff of resistance. "But nothing can't stop you from wishin'. You can't beat nobody down so low" that they can't *wish*. Surely, yes, such resistance fails when the body/mind that enacts it is killed or beaten or tortured or starved into a cognizance of nothing other than bare survival—and these are common hallmarks of those of us embodied under the sign of blackness. But it is resistance nonetheless.

What, then, compels me about thinking blackness in relation to fantasy? A possibly paradoxical or counterintuitive move in consideration of what fantasy is, or how fantasy works or what fantasy does, is to give way to the assumption that, on the one hand, fantasy *does nothing*.

On the other hand, positing fantasy as *fantasy-acts* breaks down "does nothing" in the following way: fantasy's admittedly largely immaterial "doing" is the creation of the nonactual—such that "doing" is the mining of the possible latent in the actual, or the denomination and use of what does not exist as a resource; and the "nothing" is the nonactual. The "does nothing" of fantasy-acts is the apparently insubstantial process of creating a nonactual world.

This description of negligible action borrows from the (annoying) ubiquity of current critical and commercial coinage of "world-building" when assessments are made of the strength of any given fantasy-genre literary work. It's worth noting that such world-creation is modeled on, or surely provides the model for, what we imagine or believe is the divine act par excellence. Surely some element of what fantasy *is*, is *not waiting* for our compatriots or our species to come to their senses and discard the lies we currently live by (and frequently kill for) in favor of a better set of lies we might prefer. A fantasy-act is, again, comparative in content: it is *not* waiting. The fantasizer, which we can think of either as an individual or as works of fantasy art that individuals or groups of individuals "propose" as an act of creation and that audiences, readers, and revisers (fan fiction) communities engage with and engage in, recognizes that the achievement of a just real world is exceedingly complicated and hard. More to the point, the fantasizer recognizes that the wait will be exceedingly long and probably futile, since even if the arc of the moral universe bends toward justice, (1) none now living will live to see it get there and (2) the greater likelihood based on history and current trends is that our species will render the environment we depend on for life inhospitable to our continued existence and, like some compulsive serial killer stranded on a desert isle, our species will slowly strangle itself to death.

In response, the fantasizer/fantasy, not-waiting, decrees in Jehovian fashion, "Let it be" to some world not our own.

We might think then of "fantasy" as a kind of placeholder term for the disavowed anxieties of authorship concerning the ineffectual nature of writing or creating art, the unavoidable and perhaps necessary distance between the written (or published) word or the artwork and the social and material relations that it describes: the lag, or lack of cause-effect temporal relationship, between discourse and discursive effects: the failure of the writer or artist to effectually traverse that paradox of doing and being that is described in the lines from Genesis, "in the beginning the word was with God." In this sense, then, fantasy recuperated takes us into both the dreams of and the frustrations of dreams unrealized of godhood.

The project of this book is to identify some examples of these fantasy-acts, these counterpropositions—Bloch would describe them as imaginative anticipatory illuminations of utopian humanity—and yet also explore the pitfalls and difficulties of sustaining the imagination of them, to strengthen the unreal power of fantasies not by assessing the imminence of their realization in the material and political, but by examining and theorizing them as the acts that I believe they are.

Thus we can begin to feel the *weight* of the fantasy-act and to see where fantasy might align with the antiracist or anti-antiblackness projects of cultural and political blackness. *Black* fantasy as I'm interested in it here *realizes the possible(s)* of blackness that reality declares *should not be*, transforming "irregular glimpses" of a radical impossible that we know *should be*—and yet that, for the apparently exigent sake of "keeping it real," we refuse to know.

What the shape or the content of such a *realization* of the unreal is I'll endeavor to theorize in the following chapters. For the moment, I want to think about the shape and content of this unreal black possible:

An unreal, antireal fantasy blackness is freed from the shackles of perceptual and political realism—or at least it's able to anticipate shaking off those shackles. An unreal fantasy blackness signifies, is lived, feels different from real blackness. We may suppose that this unreal blackness strays far from the narrow monoliths of the blackness we know too well, in number—the range of possible unreal blacknesses is far wider than we can readily guess—as well as content. A "real nigga" under the terms of unreal blackness will probably be difficult to recognize. Perhaps Lennon and McCartney's line will describe this personage: "Got to be good looking 'cause he's so hard to see." Perhaps the primary work of black fantasy will be finding the brushstrokes, the words, the media in which to portray its possibility.

Ursula K. Le Guin's provocative story "The Ones Who Walk Away from Omelas" (1973) is probably most often read as a discomfiting riddle about the morality of utilitarianism. Omelas is a fantasy city or country where everyone lives happily. Unfortunately this universal happiness depends on the lifelong misery of one child. The causal relationship between the child's unhappiness and everyone else's commonplace ecstasy is never explained in the story, but arguably the story's conceit is all the more convincingly "realistic" for its lack of explanation. Surely we *expect* happiness to be bought by *someone's* misery? No explanation needed—an assumption Le Guin cleverly begins to expose.

But what gets me excited about the story is the challenge it throws down to our imagination (a challenge that the story deliberately fails to live up to). Describing Omelas, Le Guin's narrator says,

As they did without monarchy and slavery, so they also got on without the stock exchange, the advertisement, the secret police, and the bomb. Yet I repeat that these were not simple folk, no dulcet shepherds, noble savages, bland utopians. They were not less complex than us. The trouble is that we have a bad habit, encouraged by pedants and sophisticates, of considering happiness as something rather stupid. Only pain is intellectual, only evil interesting. This is the treason of the artist: a refusal to admit the banality of evil and the terrible boredom of pain. If you can't lick 'em, join 'em. If it hurts, repeat it. But to praise despair is to condemn delight, to embrace violence is to lose hold of everything else. We have almost lost hold; we can no longer describe a happy man, nor make any celebration of joy.[25]

This claim about the treason of art is too harsh, I admit, if I take it up and make it into a critique of African Americanist scholarship and intellectual endeavor. But it is not wholly inapt. Certainly regarding what we canonize and teach under the rubric "African American literature" and even "Afro-diasporic literature," the description has a ring. For a literature defined by the near unanimity of its voices agitating, analyzing, narrating, and narrativizing political projects of emancipation and antiracism, too great an attention to delight and joy and happiness seems a political betrayal. It isn't a matter of needing to claim interest or to stave off boredom: for us, only the description of injustice, of torture, murder, intimidation, enslavement, rape, dispossession, is political, is exigent, is *real*. Yes, of course, we can recognize and take seriously representational and analytical strategies of humor and satire, descriptions of resistant cultural practices, locations of temporary marronage. But who has described, without irony or shame, a black happy person? In the light of harsh realities, who has the time? Who has the *right*? I'm so accustomed to investigating, if not exactly praising, despair, pain, and evil that if a description of black happiness appeared somewhere, I missed it. And if it appeared somewhere, it was a challenge to the very conception of black literature—what it is, how it must be structured to be recognized *as* black literature, its justification and use, its distinction from mere luxury. And so it didn't count. The happiness that Le Guin's treasonous artist (must that artist be white even to ask the question?) cannot summon the intellect or interest to engage is for the black writer a foolishness we can't afford to indulge.

Black fantasy, then, might be aimed at snatching luxury where, as best we can see at any rate, there is none. It is indulgent, foolish, frivolous, merely escapist, naively utopian, in some way wrong—inattentive to the real, defiant of the realist. As I've noted, thinking of fantasy as operating like a fetish is in keeping with thinking of fantasy as the poor phantom doppelganger of what's real. The fetish, even with its generative instabilities and its revelations of the structures of signification and so on, is understood on balance to be above all a misperception straying from accurate perception (i.e., an accurate perception of a problem, a wrong, an injustice), and also therefore a misstep on the pathway to the correction of the problem (which obviously has to be accurately perceived in order to be "solved"). Along these lines, I'm interested in a reconstruction of the account of fantasy in its relationship to blackness: I want to think of how fantasy engages and yet sidesteps the "real" problem that we think it poorly addresses, how it offers a solution for a problem that isn't the accurately perceived problem really but is the answer to another query altogether: This must be a query that the fantasy itself, or the fantastic itself, *brings about* by deciding on an answer to it: the question/problem addressed does not precede the fantasy-as-solution-and-answer, but the fantasy creates or fashions the question out of its sidestepped engagement with the "real," out of its fiat-like shattering of the real into pieces, as it were, that the fantasy recasts into other uses.

Viewed properly, my investigation is not of fantasy as critique of the real, though fantasy does offer such critiques. My investigation—my fantasy about fantasy?—is of fantasy as a mode of living and fantasy as the transformation of living and being.

* * *

The argument here is for fantasy as world-making. It would be more than reasonable to consider this proposition by looking at it from a sociological slant, by surveying the vast intricate and complex virtual worlds of fan communities organized around particular works of fantasy in literature, film, comic books, etc., and the networks of participants in cosplay, in video games, and the universes of ancillary text production in the myriad kinds of fan fiction and slash-fiction.

From time to time, I may cast an eye over these areas, but my interest is in thinking of my chain of overlapping coconstitutive objects (fantasy, black fantasy, queer fantasy, black queer fantasy, and beyond) chiefly as philosophical enterprises. In this, I depend on a definition of philosophy that I like, that of novelist Charles Johnson, whose novels *Faith and the Good Thing* (1974) and *Oxherding Tale* (1982) are at least in part assays of black philosophical fiction—black fiction that not only engages with canonical philosophies but concerns itself with what Johnson identifies as the central questions of philosophical traditions "East" and "West": What does freedom or happiness really mean? What does it look like to be free/happy? How does one become free/happy? For Johnson, philosophy is *a guide to living*. And black philosophical fiction would then be a mode of teaching or representing a happier or freer way of living.

Likewise, I look to black fantasy as a guide of sorts, one best understood for me by recurrence to spatial metaphors. Black-queer-beyond fantasy for me charts the road to, and/or the sites in, a habitable imaginary. This habitable imaginary is, of course, a parallel to the oft-cited "usable past." I hate the world as it is, and I'm always looking-wishing for other worlds to go to.

I like following the thought experiment of Le Guin's "The Ones Who Walk Away from Omelas" before the story gets to the beaten child: she thinks about which elements make for a happy urban life, and decides no tradition of monarchy, no slavery, no stock market, no clergy (but there is religion), no soldiers; she thinks at first that there are no drugs, but, deciding that's puritanical, invents a drug that grants languor and ecstasy and visions and great sex but that isn't habit-forming.

For my world, I start with the things I'd like to keep from this one—I like the love between beings, the sex, the beautiful varieties of clothes, the cuisines, the jokes and laughter, the entertainments, reading books, learning about things I didn't know about, and the beauty of nature and the beauty of architecture. I think the vast majority of the rest I can do without. Maybe the cliché rule in this habitation is that not only *should* you bring a knife to a gunfight, but you should bring a velvet camisole as well; and in this habitation, doing so makes perfect sense . . .

Reaching this habitable imaginary will not require exploding the whole world and starting again from scratch; nor does it require the inevitably and necessarily slow, torturous, Sisyphean struggle of eternal revolution that no one describes as convincingly (or as depressingly) for me as Fanon. It doesn't require or even encourage you *not* to follow those pathways, either. This will have to be a habitation that coexists with many others, shared and unshared, that fundamentally contradict it, others that often and perhaps most times are more demanding of my attention (and sometimes—some very few times, I'm sure—are actually more pleasurable or happier) than my habitation. The paving stones of the road there will likely have to be indulgence, foolishness, frivolousness, mere escapism, naive utopianism, just plain wrongness; these will also be how we describe its skyline as we approach, its tourist sites when we get there.

* * *

You might wonder if what I'm talking about under the term "fantasy-acts" could, at least in the realm of literature, also be described under the genre description "magical realism." No. The realism of magical realism is where I depart. In magical realism, the realistic always subordinates the magical, rendering it marginal and/or disavowed, such that the various predicates of "real" life remain at last undisturbed. In few, perhaps no, canonical magical realist text—let's choose three at random: Gabriel Garcia Marquez's *One Hundred Years of Solitude* (1982), Toni Morrison's *Song of Solomon* (1977), Salman Rushdie's *Midnight's Children* (1980)— are various fundamentals of our social reality undone: fundamentals such as that men are widely considered more important than women, white people are more powerful than black people, heterosexuality and heterosexual reproduction are more natural than / preferred to / thinkable than homosexuality and homosexual reproduction. In these texts, the laws of physics may be on occasion flouted. But not these laws. This is in no way to criticize those novels or their various political projects, as I love them all: it is to say that if this were not true, these works would qualify neither for the "realist" in magical realism nor for the canons in which they deservedly appear. And moreover, as I believe each of these authors has at least once complained, appending "magical" to "realism" is precisely a way to belittle and scorn the works' political projects.

You might also wonder if fantasy-acts could be described in the sociocultural and political realm as "resignification." No. To be sure, resignification is related to the processes I want to find and theorize as fantasy-acts. However, my object is distinguished from resignification in that resignification is a process of cultural evolution—which, precisely, fantasy-acts are far too impatient to wait for. Hence, another way to speak of this book's project is "how to find some happiness and justice in the age of mass idiocy, willful misery, and wanton injustice whose personal exemplar is 2016 Electoral College winner Donald Trump"—or, rather, the book provides not a guide to *how* but an assessment, portrait, and theorization of *"ways we can already find* some happiness and justice, etc."

You might wonder, too, if I am *advocating* for fantasy-acts *instead of* what we tend to think of as "action." Not at all. Fantasy-acts do not require secession from other kinds of acts. Though it is worth pausing to wonder about the differences between the results of fantasy-acts and the results of other kinds of action. If an action does not result, with sufficient proximity to count as an effect following a cause, in (1) someone injuring or killing someone else or depriving them of liberty or (2) someone stealing from someone else resources for living or prospering or (3) rescuing someone—or yourself—from a particular instance of being killed or maimed or deprived of liberty or stolen from or (4) dispensing resources to someone or (5) building something that can be seen, touched, and/or entered, like a domicile, then how do we measure the consequences of the action? How do we become assured of its existence as distinct from the existence of other mental constructs like fantasies? If a million people march on Washington, is the result or the activity measurable as distinct from fantasy once it becomes, as it must, a memory, write-ups in a dozen newspapers, plans for later meetings and dreams of coalition, digital photographs online and on so many smartphone hard drives?

Finally, you might wonder if this elaborate attempt to take fantasy seriously as an intellectual and political tool is like clinging to a plank of driftwood in the middle of a storm at sea: desperate, desperate, desperate. Yes. But desperation is not disqualifying. It's the other name of necessity. And the alias of invention—or perhaps invention's twin, with necessity and desperation coparenting—is radical imagination.

The ultimate project of *Keeping It Unreal*—which must reach beyond the book's end, for its achievement cannot be encompassed in this book, or any single book, alone—is to sight whether and how black fantasy can begin to undertake a description of ludicrous unreal things like black happiness, how black fantasy might retwist the twisted significations of blackness such that "black and happy" is at least not a *clearly* oxymoronic conjunction.

I don't expect to find this vision or these how-to instructions fully formed. Bloch again provides a statement of guidance. In a classless society that he is determined to maintain hope for, Bloch envisages a different sort of culture and a different function for the criticism that engages with it. This new criticism "would be, like all fruitful criticism, the mortification of the works, which means to view them as if one were viewing ruins and fragments instead of finished products, glistening works that had been given the final touch. It would be, like all fruitful rebirth, the taking seriously of that anticipatory illumination, which would no longer make the great works useful for precipitous harmony in the service of ideology; rather, it would make them useful information of justice that would arise."[26] This describes how I wish to read my fantasy-acts. Rather than looking to the various works to provide models or finished products representing or imagining new worlds and fully finished habitable imaginaries, I'll look to them instead as ruins or fragments of such representations, ruins and fragments that entrance us with their gaps—gaps where useful information is transmitted for a justice that will arise. As we'll see, the media of representation favored in this book is structurally built around, and of, gaps: the gutters between panels of comic books, the necessary incompletion of fictional worlds.

What follows in the partial fulfillment of my announced aims and speculative questions is a description of and a plea for the potential, pleasures, and the efficacy of writing, drawing, and above all of *reading*—and of reading comic books, at that. *Keeping It Unreal* entails a phenomenological account of reading superhero comics, especially—though not only—reading superhero comics with attention to the explicit and implicit presence in them of blackness and queerness and of black queerness. In this, I've chosen arguably one of the most trivial genres (superheroes) of a medium or expressive form that is least likely to be effective against antiblackness (comics). It is, however, a form that it is probably clear by now that I know well and love, and however quixotic the effort may be, I intend to carefully and attentively describe both my love for it and—which is probably the same thing—the genre's and medium's anti-antiblack uses.

* * *

Gayle Salamon's recent definition of phenomenological method is apposite: "Phenomenology is a philosophical tradition concerned with how the world gives itself to appearances, and the structures of consciousness through which we apprehend that givenness. . . . Phenomenology is also a method, committed to perceptual beginning as a way of apprehending the world and our place in it. . . . Phenomenological methods endeavor to approach our surroundings anew, shedding our sedimented interpretations so that we might apprehend the world and the things in it with greater clarity."[27]

I will always try to walk a difficult line between what is "real" and what is fantasy in producing this account: drawing our attention again and again to the two-dimensional, drawn-by-ink (or other means) effect *of* reality in comics, while at the same time also tracking this achieved-by-artifice reality-effect's play *with* and *on* perceptions of reality, such that we perceive the distinction between them as, at times and in inspiring ways, delible.

Chapter 1, "I Am Nubia," theorizes fantasy-acts through a close reading of the cover image of a single comic, issue #206 of *Wonder Woman*, published in 1973. I describe the history of my fascination with the character Nubia, the famous Wonder Woman's largely unknown and mostly unstoried black twin sister: my first encounter with her, the fantasies her image ignited, and DC Comics' relationship with its creation, which until very recently has been ambivalent at best. An analysis of Nubia provides the platform for theorizing a number of elements vital to this phenomenological account of reading superhero comics: the entangled significations attending the figuration of a black female character in superhero comics; and the queerness of comics' form, as well as the form's invitations—perhaps requirements—to read queerly; and how superhero comics show that fantasy is a form of *being*. My guides for reading in this chapter are the unlikely pair of Frantz Fanon and Ramzi Fawaz, both as theorists of comics; along with Frederic Wertham, the author of *Seduction of the Innocent* and the moving force behind the establishment of the Comics Code Authority, as prosecutor of comics; Eve Sedgwick, as queer fantasist; and Leo Bersani, as queer theorist of fantasy. Comics' requirement that readers enact "closure"—the imaginative supplement and invention that gives sense and flow to otherwise unconnected, static visual tableaux—is the key matter in chapter 1.

While in chapter 1, I engage in a reparative reading of Nubia's unprom-
ising cover image, in chapter 2, "Can the Black Superhero *Be*?," I let well-
earned paranoia take the forefront, as I identify the antiblack elements at
the core of the superhero genre. The pairing of "black" and "superhero," I
argue, is conceptually difficult, especially because of blackness's association with criminality, monstrosity, and abjection, whereas the superhero
is conceived as the innocent, all-good, usually beautiful victor. I examine
these pitfalls of conceptualizing a black superhero through analyses of
the origin stories and depictions of the characters Blade and Luke Cage.
I end the chapter with an extended consideration of the first black superhero, the Black Panther, and of what one of the Black Panther character's creators calls "the strange gripping legend of Wakanda." My analysis
of the Panther, the history of the character's creation, the cultural phenomenon of the 2017 movie adaptation of the comic, and of the Nigerian
American speculative fiction writer Nnedi Okorafor's treatment of the
Black Panther, returns the chapter to a deeper dive into a formal element
of comics briefly noted in chapter 1: comics' disarrangement of linear
temporality and "layering of time," as the comics scholar Hillary Chute
describes it. This formal fundamental of comics—something that makes
comics *queer*—enables black superhero stories and their readers to use
their paranoia to navigate the dangerous waters of antiblack and racist
modern discourse, as that discourse is reflected in the concept of the
superhero. The Black Panther, I argue, is an example of how superhero
comics may queer the history that produces blackness.

Chapter 3, "Erotic Fantasy-Acts," takes up a specter that haunts the
previous analyses and that also haunts the history of superhero comics.
This specter is the suspicion, the feeling, or the hope, and the conviction,
that superhero comics are actually queer sexual fantasies. In these suspi-
cious, or hopeful, readings, the genre's visual conventions—especially,
of course, centralized representations of the hypertrophic male body,
which become especially charged when the body is represented as
black—serve as subornation, recruitments, as it were, teaching readers,
as David Halperin puts it, "how to be gay."[28] Having identified queer
formal qualities in superhero comics and queer modes of reading/view-
ing superhero comics in the foregoing chapters, in chapter 3, I look at
queer *content* in superhero comics. And, having touched on this matter
in chapter 2, I look more closely at the intersection between representa-

tions of blackness and representations of queerness in superhero story-telling. I begin by examining an influential, if largely forgotten, essay by Gershon Legman that was published in the late 1940s. Legman was an associate of Frederic Wertham (again, the moving force behind the establishment of the Comics Code Authority). Legman was also quoted by Frantz Fanon. I consider Legman's wildly homophobic claims about the supposed queer content of Golden Age comics, claims that, I argue, are unconvincing with regard to what we actually find on the Golden Age superhero comics page, but point us usefully toward what we as readers can find in the gutters of the page, in our acts of imaginative closure. I then pivot to closely read stories that feature black male superhero or superhero-esque characters in pornographic comics—a site where we do see queer sexual content explicitly represented. I consider comic strips by two black creators, Belasco and David Barnes, both creations from the 1990s, and work by a white gay cartoonist in the twenty-first century, Patrick Fillion. I conclude chapter 3 with a meditation on how porn comics with black male superhero figures, by directly engaging the attribution of nonnormative sexuality to black bodies, find ways to represent the blackness of their protagonists not as a contradiction of the superhero concept (a problem we see wrestled with in the stories of Blade, Luke Cage, and the Black Panther) but as the *source* of their superpower. The representational strategies engaged by these porn comic strips is not of course free, however, of pitfalls in a world that so values whiteness that we are all, as Isaac Julien argues, snow queens.

1

I Am Nubia

Superhero Comics and the Paradigm of the Fantasy-Act

For me, the paradigmatic form of fantasy-acts involves reading superhero comic books: the act of fantasy is exemplified in reading/ seeing a superhero comic, with all the mental, discursive, and social processes that entangle themselves with the active reception and almost-immediate concurrent imaginative creation inherent to engaging comics. Thus fantasy-acts encompass something for which the word "reading," with its profusion of ever-branching connotations in both common and cognoscenti usages, is capacious enough and yet inadequate as a description. These entangled processes are what comics—but especially, for me, *the superhero comic*, founder of the form in *Action Comics* #1 in 1938—demand of readers, what comics summon into the kinds of existence fantasy enjoys.

Figure 1.1 shows the cover of the first comic book I remember buying using my own allowance money. I was eight years old when I saw it and had been living at that point for two years in Europe, as one of a scattered horde of so-called military brats who, variously displaced from our places of remembered origin and thereby obscurely traumatized, rode the coattails of our parents—generally our fathers—as they fought the Cold War stationed at bases across the globe. My family's little corner of the fight that I was far too young to know I was supporting lay in Fulda, West Germany. Fulda is the town that gives its name to the Fulda Gap, where, I eventually learned, it was surmised by NATO strategists that Russian tanks would roll in sinister world-ending waves in the event of the expected apocalypse.

My father was a captain in a tank battalion. I didn't know at the time that while his being a *black* captain in the US Army was not unheard of, black Army officers were also uncommon and a relatively novel phenomenon in the early 1970s. Unlike Janie Crawford in *Their Eyes Were*

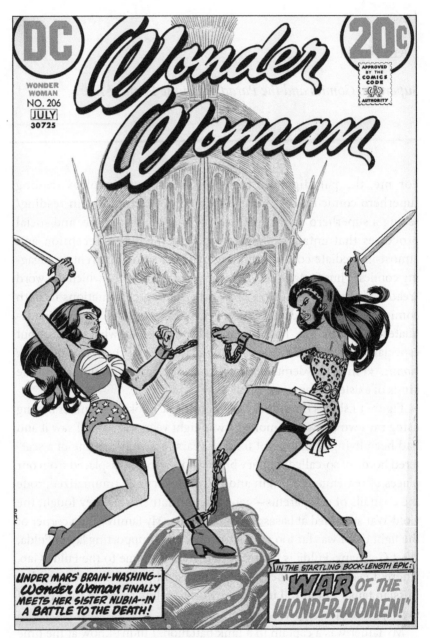

Figure 1.1. Wonder Woman and Nubia face off in 1973. (Dick Giordano, artist)

Watching God (a work languishing then in obscurity), I did know that I was black, and my two years in Germany among both white Americans and Germans—as opposed to the nearly six years previous living in the southern United States, in either all-black enclaves or on mixed-race Army bases—had powerfully impressed on me the sense of that racial status as somehow fatefully embattled. At the time of my encounter with this comic, I was, like all of us as children, routinely being pressed into the shape of a gender identity by various compelled everyday performances. And, perhaps like or unlike all of us, I was vaguely aware of some disaffection from the goals of these gender performances or some restless sense of my failure to achieve them. More unsettlingly, I was vaguely aware of my disloyalty to the cause that those compelled performances appeared to support—which *felt* like the cause of male supremacy, an idea to which no experience of mine had yet allowed me to accede, since if I had to choose the superior person with whom I would have chosen to identify, at eight it would have been my mother, not my father. I did not know—though had a discursive presence concerning sexuality obtained in my place and time approaching the power and presence of racial discourse, I would have had reason to guess—that I was gay or queer.

Thus I was on the whole unaware of the various distinctions, the little historical and geographical oddities that had given rise to the context of my encounter with the cover of *Wonder Woman* #206, only hazily, if at all, cognizant of the swirling overdeterminations of race, gender, sexuality—and certainly not of the mandates of geopolitics and economics—that shaped both the content of the cover and my placement in relation to it. I was just an eight-year-old boy who, amid the paucity of diversions available to US children on that relatively small military base, discovered the excitement of visiting a bookstore. The cover captured my eye and held my attention. As it still does now.

Issue 206 of *Wonder Woman* features "Nubia," the iconic superhero Wonder Woman's black twin sister. Following is my attempt at a phenomenological description of what it was to see and to "read" that cover. This phenomenological account thus also provides my core example of fantasy-acts.

Having had no previous exposure I'm aware of to Wonder Woman, I was entranced by the cover's image of a dark-skinned, glamorous, powerful black woman warrior. I surely *did* have previous exposure to Diana Ross and her wigs, however. Looking back at this origin story for my superhero-comics fixation, I guess my attraction to Nubia's image to be an extension of my attraction to Diana Ross and the glamor of Ross's look and stage presence (a happy synergy here being that Wonder Woman's given name is Diana). Given the aforementioned tilt toward appreciating feminine as opposed to masculine styles of personal presentation, I can also appreciate my intense attraction to Nubia's two-dimensional spectacle as an attraction to, a love for, a wish for, some amalgam of qualities, inchoate desires, and aspirations. I'll clumsily call this amalgam DianaRoss-MyOwnMother-BlackWoman-BlacknessAsWoman-feminine. Whatever it might be named, it possessed at the time a sublime and visceral coherence altogether resistant to analytic disaggregation, with a capacity to mainline into my young consciousness like a lightning bolt.

Nubia's image inaugurated and fed a hunger for a fantasy of black power and black beauty. These are conjunctions that appeared as at least partly if not wholly fantastic within what I sensed, or knew, even as a child, was an antiblack "real" world. Out of the reeking stew of things I didn't know, out of that morass of unknowings, the image brought something into conscious clarity: desire. Nubia's image created a desire, a desire that the image itself promised to satisfy. My encounter with this image, in the paradigmatic manner in which comics provide sources of fantasy for their readers of whatever age, gave me an *education* instantiating desire, before I could have named that desire, in a world that, of course, makes the satisfaction of such desires exceedingly difficult to find.

With this desire was initiated a series of creations of images related to the original but propelled by sequences, scenarios, and narrations of my own design. I imagined Nubia as the guide to adventures of power and freedom, which might simply have been childish visions of magical adulthood; but I also imagined Nubia as my superhero protector, the protector of a little queer black boy in a wide alien and alienating world determined to ignore or to squelch queerness and humiliate blackness; and Nubia as the avenger of unfair treatment dealt to me and those with whom I empathized.

To reframe and further elaborate the paradigm I'm describing, I refer back to a point I discussed in the introduction in relation to Ernst

Bloch's theory of art as the anticipatory illumination of utopian possibilities: Black fantasy *realizes the possible(s)* of blackness that reality declares *should not be*, transforming "irregular glimpses" of a radical impossible that we know *should be*. Following Bloch, then, we might see how fantasy in relationship to blackness engages and yet sidesteps the "real" problem that we think it poorly addresses, how it offers a solution for a problem that isn't the accurately perceived problem, but is the answer to another query altogether.

This must be a query that the fantasy itself, or the fantastic itself, *brings about* by deciding on an answer to it: the question or problem addressed does not precede the fantasy-as-solution-and-answer, but the fantasy creates or fashions the question out of its sidestepped engagement with the "real," out of its fiat-like shattering of the real into pieces that the fantasy recasts into other uses. Here, then, we see a comic productively directing the young me and other readers both then and later toward new desires for fantasy counterworlds that rebel against the constraints of everyday life.

These constraints were only hazily perceived, as I've described. Yet the fantasy activated by an image such as Nubia's—to be sure, as I discuss further shortly, an image rarely encountered in the comics world or even in the pop-music world where Diana Ross reigned—somehow burned through the haze of merely sensed perception to create a *picture* of what was and a *story* of what could be.[1] The fantasy for which this comic provided the template was of and for an African/Western world, an Afro-diasporic world that wasn't antiblack—neither of which existed. The image's manifest fantasy content was its immediately apparent contrast with the real world: I didn't see—apart from the singular exception of Miss Diana—such images of black women or have the feelings such images of black people might evoke, either in the world or in representations of the world; I did see this image on a superhero comic-book cover, as a drawn, two-dimensional, *unreal* fantasy representation. This contrast both clarified the real world in its racialized and racist particulars— the real world doesn't possess such images and maybe doesn't possess such people; the fantasy cover does—and illuminated the possibility that such black women, and the worlds capable of housing them, *could* exist and should. I was invited to imagine the world that makes a powerful black Wonder Woman possible; and along with this, I was invited to imagine her presence in the "real" world and the wrongs that her power and beauty might right.

Bloch describes the process in relationship to works of art (which for him probably don't include comic books but do include folktales etc.): "*A work of art is* . . . something other than a source of historical and natural historical knowledge, or even insights. It is characterized . . . above all by fantasizing, which bustles around between characters and events with a degree of license highly alien to science," Bloch notes.[2] In such works of art characterized by fantasizing, "What habitual or unblunted sense can hardly still see is illuminated" in aesthetic representation. "Aesthetically represented, this means: immanently more achieved, more thoroughly formed, more essential than in the immediate-sensory or immediate-historical occurrence," even if "undoubtedly not true in the sense that the knowledge we have acquired of the world is true."[3] Thus, "everything that appears in the artistic image is sharpened or condensed to a decisiveness that the reality of experience in fact only seldom shows."[4]

My encounter with the Nubia 1973 *Wonder Woman* cover illustrates Bloch's observations. There was no conscious question I brought to my encounter with the cover that it answered. There was no articulate understanding or conscious conception of the world as antiblack present in my mind, no awareness of a hunger for any image of blackness, even a "positive" one. There was only a responsiveness to this image (or, we might say, a preceding preparation to be alert to such an image), which ignited a cascade of excitement that was at once inspiration, wishes, desires, *hopes* that I want to theorize here as fantasy, fantasy in the mode of action.

Tracking the "reading" process of such an encounter with a superhero comic is not necessarily served by positioning fantasy as acting on the conditions of thought (i.e., acting as a theory), but rather conceiving fantasy as acting in and on the conditions of living or existence—that is, fantasy acting *as* action, acting as living, acting in the mode of existential being.

What changed, or what began, in my mode of living, my action, my existential being, in this encounter with the image of Nubia?

An understanding of how fantasy is active, of fantasy as operating by transforming being (however often immaterially), can be productively understood by discussing fantasy-sparking processes in relation to the *form* of comics.

A powerful motor of reading comics is the engagement of wishes, if by wishes we mean the imaginary conjuration of what is not actually present. Wish-summoning inheres in comics form. There is a particular kind of subjective encounter necessitated in reading comics, where, as a pioneer in theorizing the comic-book form, Scott McCloud, succinctly maps it, the reader must supply the connective action, reason, and movement that *is not* on the page but only indicated by the lines displayed on it. The reader must supply the imagination of what happens *between* panels as well as what *moves* within the stationary, nonanimated panel itself. McCloud calls this structural element in sequential-art comic-book storytelling "closure."[5] The comics reader mentally *closes*, as it were, the gap between the panels, which need not even have a temporally or spatially sequential relation between its contiguous panels. The reader contributes the action and the reason for the action, and these actions and reasons obviously must take as many different forms as there are readers of a given comic. This closure is guided, to be sure, by the cues of the lines drawn in the panels and the accompanying and sometimes explanatory text; but the connective tissue is *not there* on the page and must be supplied from the readers' own knowledge and imagination.

McCloud and all comics scholarship that follows him focus on the reader's supplement of meaning and movement directed by the sequence of image-text representations. But it's reasonable to suppose that the supplied closure—which, after all, ultimately cannot be limited by what is laid out on the page—follows or is in the nature of the readers' *wishes*. Here, then, we can also bring focus to subcreative processes, generations of meaning, that occur in response to the sequence of image-text representations but also wholly out of its published sequence: the act of fantasizing by generating fragments of story, imagined *un*drawn images, as representations of possibility at most suggested by, but not cordoned off by or foreclosed by—and even in defiance of—what is on the page and in the story.

Generations of queer readers or those inclined to read queerly can testify precisely to such forms of wish-fulfillment closure, where in the shift between the coup de grace punch that sends the villain to his just deserts and the "Later . . ." caption of the next panel in an adventure of, say, the Legion of Super-Heroes, the lasses and lads of that assemblage of youthful heroes enjoy pairings and polyamories not in the least undreamt of.[6]

If McCloud and the post-McCloud comics studies reader works *between* panels and *within* panels, we can also theorize comics reading that uses that work as a trampoline surface from which to leap—and perhaps, with the comic-book powers to transcend gravity bequeathed us within and between the representational elements of the initiating fantasy, never to return to the earth where it began. Closure, then, which must happen as a function and product of "reading" comics, is fundamentally also always the work of fantasizing and at the same time can always serve as the invitation to fantasize. Such fantasizing is always active; these fantasies always act.

The Case of the Missing Skirt

So far I've emphasized fantasy-acts as *enabling* in the paradigmatic example of my own initiation into comics reading, and I've begun to describe the form of comics as a kind of toolbox one can open for practicing a set of skills in fantasy-as-act, fantasy-as-being. But there are all kinds of problems, all manner of limits and possibly *dis*abling factors, regarding both "reading" comics and the particular example of Nubia.

For one, I have to consider the irony, the displeasure, and the discomfort of the fact that fantasy experientially reveals itself as a fantasy-act in this paradigm only where it is ignited and stoked by an encounter in a place of commerce, with a product meant to convert potential readers into buyers. Fantasy thus *acts* in this moment of origin only at the vector where my personal, internal fantasies' images and discourse (themselves reflections and refractions of external discourse) achieve consonance with a material *product* bound up in a lattice of capitalist exchange. To consider this is to recognize that the kind of fantasy-act I'm describing in the form of comics and comics reading is not without the taint of capitalist structures: indeed it is permeated by such structures; these structures are the very air such a fantasy-act would breathe if it had lungs.

Such a recognition does not, however, I would argue, wholly surrender to the pronounced suspicion, endemic to a respectable strain of comics studies scholarship, that the comic's position within a capitalist circuit ultimately determines either the content or the directions of the fantasy-acts summoned by the commercial product that the comic is. But it acknowledges how that which incites the fantasy-act is underwritten by the same profiteering-for-the-few motives and structures that the *content* of the fantasy-act in the Nubia example as I'm narrating it, aims to resist and struggles to defeat (i.e., the histories of the slave trade and enslavement that produce blackness and that give racialized meaning to modern gender).

To my mind, the fantasy-act can succeed in defeating, or at least surpassing, these circumscribing motives. Every time within this book where I trace or try to expose the act of fantasy, we will have to see this paradigm, this particular structure of unfolding, at work, and press always to perceive, even if with no greater support than will alone, the ways that what is incited exceeds the cause—especially the material cause—that incites it at the same time that it also bears the imprint, the marks on our skin of the shackles, of its origination's intended limits.

The example of Nubia is again useful in this context. Nubia was in many ways a failed superhero character. She appeared on the cover of *Wonder Woman* as part of DC Comics' bid during the Bronze Age (ca. 1970–1984) to broaden the audience of its consumers, to capitalize on the apparent success of Blaxploitation films, and to signal that the fantasy world of DC Comics, like that of its rival Marvel Comics, was engaged with "real" contemporary developments like racial integration and the emergence of the site of the black ghetto in US cultural discourse. The character Nubia, however, gained little traction, unlike other DC Comics assays in racial diversity in the 1970s, such as the now-mainstay character John Stewart, "the black Green Lantern." Nubia disappeared from *Wonder Woman* after three issues and did not afterwards become a consistently recurring secondary or even tertiary character in DC's fantasy world.

Yet Nubia's evident inability to capture the attention of her creators (Dick Giordano, the #206 cover artist; Don Heck, the interior artist; Cary Bates, the principal writer; and Robert Kanigher, the editor) and of many subsequent writers and artists of *Wonder Woman* did little to prevent the character from becoming a template figure for a range of fantasies of black power and beauty proliferating in a fan counterpublic. Typing "Nubia Wonder Woman" into an internet image-search engine nets you pages of digital fan-artist-created images of the character, as well as references to the webpage for "Nubia, The Illustrated Index." A recent book on comics by Deborah Elizabeth Whalley, *Black Women in Sequence: Re-Inking Comics, Graphic Novels, and Anime* (2016) devotes seven-plus pages to considering Nubia. Symbols and signs of "Wakanda, Forever" (about which, more later) that now adorn many a surface, article of clothing, and personal accoutrement in the wake of Ryan Coogler's phenomenally successful 2017 comic-book-superhero movie *Black Panther*, were long preceded in my consciousness, and it would appear, in many others', by an affection for the visage of Nubia. We might translate these digital images, internet publication histories, etc., into words as "I Like Nubia." Or, I want to suggest, "I Am Nubia."

(In early 2021—thus, nearly fifty years after the character's first appearance—a version of the original Nubia featured in the two-issue limited series *Future State: Immortal Wonder Woman*, in a story written by African American YA writer L. L. McKinney and drawn by Alitha Martinez. Notably, Nubia's belated return occurred in a story set in an undefined "future" rather than in the imaginary present of DC Comics' stories, though McKinney's two-part story ends with a text box promising, "ONLY THE BEGINNING." *Future State: Immortal Wonder Woman* appeared shortly before the publication of a graphic novel geared for YA comics readers and starring a teenage Nubia, entitled *Nubia: Real One*, also written by McKinney, and drawn by Robyn Smith. McKinney dedicates *Real One* to "everyone who has loved Nubia since the beginning and to all the new fans falling for her now.")[7]

* * *

But who and what is the Nubia that I and others liked, wanted to be, and were, or are?

In her character and cover image, we can suss out an example of a second set of factors disabling the potential power of fantasy-acts, especially fantasy-acts that engage, and by engaging attempt in however ephemeral a way to transform, something about the experiential conditions of *blackness*. As elating to first behold and to nurture in my imagination as it was, the cover image is of course also shot through with the discourses of antiblackness, and its use of well-worn tropes enable a demoralizing reading as much as a transformative one.

The leopard-skin skirt drew my eye as much as the depiction of Nubia's brown skin did. I thought it was glorious. It still is, but only in a way that embarrasses me in reflecting on my attachment to it.

It would seem also that the image of that skirt doesn't sit altogether well with the owners of the image, DC Comics. I discovered DC's view of this Nubia image—or rather, I arrived at my guess as to that corporate entity's stance toward the image—via the rude awakening of a denial of a request for permission to reproduce it in a scholarly context in 2015.

Some context: I've twice before published other accounts of my fascination with this comic-book image: First, I briefly discussed it in the preamble to an article I wrote about innovations in comic-book representations of race in Jaime and Gilberto Hernandez's independent comic *Love & Rockets*; this article appeared in the Fall–Winter 1994 issue of *The Americas Review* and was called "Love, Rockets, Race & Sex." In that instance, Nubia's depiction served as a generally negative contrast to what I saw (then as well as now) to be the far more productive and less stereotype-dependent representational techniques that Jaime Hernandez used to depict (and center) brown- and black-skinned characters in his portion of *Love & Rockets*. Then, twenty-four years later, I outed my interest in the Nubia figure in a longer and more careful reading—the basis for what you're reading now—in the introduction that my coeditor Ramzi Fawaz and I wrote for the June 2018 special issue of *American Literature* called "Queer about Comics."

Such is my obsession that there might have been a third iteration in between these two, deployed in an article I wrote for Leigh Raiford and Heike Raphael-Hernandez's collection *Migrating the Black Body: The African Diaspora and Visual Culture* (2017). Since the volume was necessarily replete with images drawn from various art and media, the publisher was a stickler about obtaining permission for the reproduction of every image used, having decided not to invoke "fair use" for academic purposes, as *American Literature* and *The Americas Review* had. I followed the press's policy, though I was instinctively wary of seeking DC's attention, and my concerns turned out to be warranted. In November 2015, DC's Rights and Permissions department sent me an email saying,

"While we appreciate your interest in our property, at this time we are unable to grant you the permission requested due to business and strategic reasons. Please know that we'll be happy to consider future requests of this nature."[8] *Migrating the Black Body*'s editors tried to get clarification about this refusal of permission and reported to me that the only further information they could obtain was that DC "had an internal discussion about the image and the request and the essay and they would be more than happy to give [me] . . . permissions for other images for other publications but not for this image for this essay."[9]

DC did not have access to the text of the essay in question at the time of the permissions request, only its title. In the essay's final published form, my discussion of the Nubia *Wonder Woman* cover was a preface to a longer consideration of Kyle Baker's *Nat Turner* (2008), and the parts of the essay addressing Nubia were in same vein of sketching the image's appeal and complications as I undertook in the introduction to "Queer about Comics" and have extended here. Moreover, DC had granted permission to the book publisher for Whaley's 2016 *Black Women in Sequence* reproduction of images from the very same issue of *Wonder Woman* in her chapter's discussion of Nubia—though not, significantly, for the cover image.

What was the cause of DC's unwillingness to grant permission, then? I'm guessing the leopard-skin skirt.

Perhaps this is a guess overdetermined by my own admitted fixation on this visual detail (I'm reminded, not inappropriately, of the way the brain's visual cortex in moments of trauma often selects particular visual details as the cathexis for the surrounding event, like the visage of fuzzy dice dangling from the rearview mirror as your car smashes into another). Perhaps. But in 2018, DC published an omnibus collection of a run of 1960s *Wonder Woman* issues in which the character loses her godlike powers for a time and dons fashionably "mod" clothing (or the artists' renditions thereof) to fight crime and act as a secret agent à la James Bond and Diana Rigg in the television show *The Avengers* (1965–1968). The collection's last reprinted issue is #204, the very first appearance of Nubia on the cover or in the comic-book series (figure 1.2). This is, however, Nubia in a different costume altogether, a fancifully form-fitting version of ancient Roman or perhaps medieval-knight armor that completely conceals the character's face and race.

Figure 1.2. Nubia's first appearance in *Wonder Woman* #204, in armor. (Don Heck, artist)

The last issue printed in the collection is not a part of the 1960s mod–Wonder Woman story; it's the story that brings Diana's white-suited mod-look arc to a conclusion and reintroduces Wonder Woman as the recognizable iconic superhero she'd been since her beginning in the 1940s. This reintroduction story is also not completed in the collection. In #204, Nubia arrives, is recognized by Wonder Woman's mother, Queen Hippolyta, and then departs, her origin story and her connection to Diana, Hippolyta's daughter, remaining a mystery. The reprinted omnibus collection ends there. Readers who remember, or who have access to the original issues, know that it's not until issue #206—the *Wonder Woman* issue I saw, coming in, as it were, in the middle of a story I knew nothing about—that Nubia's identity is revealed. While it would have made characterological and narrative sense to complete the story of Wonder Woman's return to superhero status with the addition of #205 and #206—and while the economic cost of doing so would presumably be negligible or easily recompensed in the book's pricing—DC chose not to do so.

Because of the skirt, I think.

Nubia's leopard-skin skirt on #206's cover, coupled there with the visual revelation of what regular readers had already observed in the interior pages of #204—that Nubia is meant to be a black character—might certainly, and justifiably, have been seen by DC's Rights and Permissions as opening the character and DC to accusations of caricature and stereotyping. The leopard-skin-skirt cover image functions, through signifying wildness, animality, and their overdetermined exemplars the "jungle" and "Africa," as though it were a kind of transnational or supranational costume of blackness. It works in all the familiar offensive ways that blackness, dark skin, jungles, wildness, animals, and Africa are routinely garbled together in the racist imaginary, tightly condensed associations that by the late date of 1973 had been sedimented like a fossil record in Western fantastic literature, and in comic strips and movies, by the endlessly clamored-for repeat appearances of that cringe-worthy loinclothed stalwart Tarzan.

Whaley describes the costume as "a tiger-print body suit adorned with a banana-leaf skirt . . . conjuring up a mix of Josephine Baker and African primitivism."[10] Whaley sees the costume differently than I do: she breaks off the yellow epaulet-like fringe as the skirt and identifies this element as banana-like (I see these lines in the drawing as evocative of the "kilt" of Roman armor) and sees a different jungle cat than I do. But the whiff of Baker and bananas, though I identify the scents differently, are evidence of the same unsavory meal being cooked.

Much turns, then, on the skirt, both in my idiosyncratic entry into comics reading and in DC's apparent desire to purge it from memory. But Nubia's leopard-skin-skirt costume appears only on this cover, where Nubia's identity has to be established with a minimum of text or story contextualization. On the cover of #204, Nubia is masked and without human features, and we might surmise that there she has no need of a leopard skin because she is visually raceless, that is, presumed white. Unmasked on #206, though, a cascade of surprises await the comic-book reader habituated to see "white" characters—a black character on the cover of a superhero comic dedicated to a white female character; a black character who looks like the white female character except she isn't white; a black female character who is either a villain or a hero matching the white female superhero in combat.

It's as though all of these surprises must be visually underlined, braced, contained, and explained by the otherwise unutilized and wholly inconsequential skirt. The skirt doubles and redoubles Nubia's blackness, by associating her with animals and with jungles and thus with Africa, with which she was already associated by dint of the representation of her skin's color. The skirt braces us for the difference of her blackness, containing whatever threat to expectation her appearance might pose by collecting her attributes into stereotypes that *explain* her presence.

Nubia never wears this costume in any comic book in which she appears. Throughout *Wonder Woman*, she appears wearing her feminine Roman-ish armor. In infrequent guest appearances over the years since 1973, either the armor or Wonder Woman's own costume is Nubia's attire, or, in one case, a blue-and-yellow strapless singlet with yellow gloves and yellow boots, giving her the color palette of Marvel's Blaxploitation hero Luke Cage, the Hero-for-Hire.

It must be noted too that these guest appearances from 1973 to 2021 are distinctly noncanonical. That is, they do not appear in stories that are deemed to actually "happen" in the continuities of the superhero comics, but rather are stories that happen in "elseworlds," in parallel universes whose characters' exploits are not usually followed; or the stories are comic-book adaptations of cartoons which are themselves adaptations of comic books. (By this definition, L. L. McKinney's *Future State* and YA Nubia are also noncanonical.) Hence, Nubia's blue-and-yellow period can be found in the 1978 thirteenth issue of *Super-Friends*, based on the popular 1970s Saturday-morning cartoon that was itself based on the long-running DC comic *The Justice League of America*. Having waited twenty-six years for another guest slot, Nubia then helps Shaggy, Scooby-Doo, and the gang in an adventure with Wonder Woman in *Scooby-Doo! Team-Up* #5. An exception to this interesting consignment of Nubia the black Wonder Woman to kids' entertainments distinct from superhero comic books—themselves often thought to be the domain of children, of course—is Grant Morrison's much more faithful rendition of Nubia, who appears in the miniseries *Final Crisis* as an alternate universe's version of Wonder Woman in a universe where all the major heroes, including Superman, are black. More recently, in 2020, Daniel Warren Johnson and Mike Spicer's *Wonder Woman: Dead Earth*, set in a postapocalyptic future, features a martial Nubia clad in bulky battle-tarnished armor.[11]

The leopard-skin skirt has no purchase on Nubia's character in the original *Wonder Woman* issues. Though Nubia as a warrior queen is attended by black male characters wearing headdresses—a detail that artist Heck (among others at the time) uses to signify "African"—Nubia is not a jungle hero like Tarzan or like Marvel's Black Panther or even like Marvel's Shanna the She-Devil, who had debuted in 1972 on the cover of *Shanna the She-Devil* #1 wearing a strapless leopard-skin singlet. (Shanna's costume is not unlike Wonder Woman's traditional garb in that it amply displays her bare—white—arms, her legs, and a hint of cleavage.)

Was *this* pernicious set of associations, then, mainlined into my consciousness along with that invigorating, fertile amalgam of DianaRoss-MyOwnMother-BlackWoman-BlacknessAsWoman-feminine? Was the latter twinned with, and thus not available to be disentangled from, the former? Perhaps the latter's anti-antiblack blackness and its imaginary Africa that Nubia caused to be dreamt of in my philosophy were actually rendered all the more powerful—or powerful, period—by the fact that Nubia's leopard-skin skirt provided part of my preparation to behold her: a stage as it were, full of familiar props in the form of myriad racial stereotypes. Perhaps, too, Nubia's glamor and superheroic aura were glamorous and powerful *because*, and achieved via the device of, the skirt's wrapping her up in the wildness and animality ascribed to dehumanized blackness. Might the skirt on which much turns have a genealogy in twentieth-century popular fantastic images such that Nubia is a kind of refiguring of the thrilling and deeply racist King Kong, standing along the pommel of a god's sword rather than atop a skyscraper, fighting the prized white woman rather than abducting her?

The answers to these questions and *perhaps*-musings must surely be yes, at least in some measure. After DC's refusal to grant permission, I pressed for further explanation in a short correspondence with cartoonist Phil Jimenez.

Jimenez had exquisitely drawn and written *Wonder Woman* for DC for more than two years in the early 2000s and brought a queer creator's sensibility to the comic that had arguably not been seen since Wonder Woman's Golden Age first years in the 1940s (or since Samuel R. Delany's brief run of scripting the series for issues 202 and 203—interestingly, just prior to Nubia's first appearance in the comic in #204). Jimenez wrote to me, "My guess is that, as they [DC] gear up for the Wonder Woman movie, they're aligning all their branding in a particular direction." The request and its denial occurred prior to the release of the 2017 Patty Jenkins movie *Wonder Woman*, which like all such cinema adaptations of comic-book franchises reboots and reinterprets the character and its past in ways that the storytellers of both movie and comic hope will freshen its appeal and expand its audience. "The original Nubia is a tricky character for them," Jimenez continued, "and I suspect they want the world to forget she exists. I have no proof of that, but this is what I suspect."[12] (Jimenez's speculation of course preceded Nubia's reappearance in 2021, during the character's half-century interregnum.)

It is the *trickiness* of that original, once-leopard-skin-clad Nubia that plucks her from the immolations to which DC's permissions department now (intentionally) and Bates, Heck, Kanigher, et al. in the past (unintentionally) would condemn her. She is not unsinged like Daniel and his companions in the biblical tale of Nebuchadnezzar's fury; but then comics readers fall short of Jehovah's angels in their powers. We do *have* powers, however: first, to read resistantly—oppositionally, as bell hooks once observed and exhorted regarding black audience reception-practices; and second, we have the powers granted us by the comics form itself, which not only permit but require us as readers to imagine our characters between and beyond panels, and enable us to clothe them in vestments of our own devising.

First, we can see that the elements we might call the jungle–King Kong problem—choosing an emblem suitable to the strength and ubiquity of the challenge, so as not to underestimate it—are *not* necessarily mainlined into consciousness as Nubia is taken up by an encounter with the comic-book reader. This we can discern from the fact that very, very few fan-art renditions of the character that an image search turns up depict Nubia wearing the leopard-skin costume. Jimenez avers that as a fan of Wonder Woman as much as a cocreator of the character, he draws Nubia for his own pleasure (the character does not appear in his *Wonder Woman* run), but, he says, "I have no drawing of her in the leopard skin because I tend to draw her in armor when I DO draw her."[13]

What is incited exceeds the cause that incites it—even the material cause, even the very image that imprints itself on the reading consciousness that puts that image in play for its own purposes.

Second, let's look again at the image (figure 1.1). As noted, on *Wonder Woman*'s cover, Nubia appears historyless, except insofar as her history is that of repeated iterations of racialized types—with all their dangers, harms, and eked-out pleasures—and of largely (but not only) malignant metonyms. The frisson of excitement and pleasure beholding Nubia in 1973, and even now, is the effect of the projections that her mute two-dimensional figure invites. As an entirely new superhero then and a rarely featured one now, her image is an example of how the comic-book form, or sequential graphic narrative form, appeals for and requires the participatory imagination of the reader/viewer.

We receive even in this image alone, without passing beyond the cover to read the story, a concatenation of effects and affects that spark, in "tricky" unpredictable ways, a flurry of possibilities. Nubia and Wonder Woman are flanked by the presence of an enormous sword and a Roman-helmeted villain in ghost form looming behind. This is Mars, the god of war, chosen by Wonder Woman's creators back in the 1940s as one of her archenemies, the antithesis to the gospel of love that she was supposed to carry from Paradise Island and bequeath to the world. Mars would be recognizable to regular readers, but even for a new reader, as I was in 1973, he clearly sets the stage of the cover's battle in some way indicative of *power*. The ghostly image links the characters to familiar imagery of the classical ancient world and to classical evocations of mythic heroism: in such a way that the combined Barthian *studium* and *punctum*, as it were, of the image possibly achieves what Kobena Mercer says (provisionally) of some of Robert Mapplethorpe's photographs of black men, where men "who in all probability" come from the disenfranchised, disempowered late-capitalist underclass are "in the blink of an eye" "elevated onto the pedestal of the transcendental Western aesthetic ideal."[14] Thus both characters, by virtue of proximity and by the three-part composition of the page, which functions in classic image production to stabilize and unify a picture, are associated with and prospectively endowed with divinity. Part of Nubia's power may be the leopard-skin skirt, but part of it too is her position within the penumbra of godhood.

The participation of the reader in completing the story usually is invited to occur between separate panels of images, in the "gutters." Scott McCloud identifies six different kinds of panel-to-panel transitions that insist on the reader's imaginative contribution of completion or story elements: moment-to-moment transitions, action-to-action, subject-to-subject, scene-to-scene, aspect-to-aspect, and non sequitur transitions (i.e., no apparent sequential relation). Nubia's comic-book cover image is not strictly speaking an instance of this kind of structure of graphic storytelling, since Nubia here is iconic, presented in the recognizable postures of the adored superhero (or the combative villain), rather than placed in a sequence. Yet the function of the gutter is taken up within the "panel" itself by Nubia's clear mirroring of Wonder Woman in all but skin color and costume, a repetition with a difference that asks to us to wonder at the sibling relationship announced in the caption between the two characters and to ponder at once the possibilities and the limits of their equality. It is possible to see that in fact there *are* transitions from McCloud's taxonomy in operation: an implied action-to-action transition, because Wonder Woman and Nubia have their swords raised and appear to be charging at each other; a subject-to-subject transition, because the characters are divided by the sword and because they are presented as radically differentiated mirror images of each other; and perhaps even a non sequitur transition, precisely because of the image's invitation to see the characters as so radically different, a difference underlined and intensified by the unnecessary presence of the leopard-skin skirt, which acts like a multiplier of racialized difference and an elaborate stage hook begging us to pull stereotypes into the frame.

Superheroes Teach You "How to Be Queer"

The cover image's comic-book *formal queerness*, though, throws open and makes at least ephemerally manifest what racialized modes of beholding foreclose and defer. The repetition within the cover image, its mirroring and reversal of mirroring, is also an education about the proximities of the supposed gulf between races (the image makes Nubia's difference from Diana only one of coloring process and costume). And this repetition is a microcosm of the seriality of comics representation, where the stories and images, as they extend and repeat with alterations from issue to issue in the hands of different artists, writers, inkers, and colorists—both professional and fan—allow for no stable fixity of image, form, or meaning.

Hence, we can find in reading this image and the palimpsest of many readings that layer it from 1973 onward a paradigm of comic-book fandom—a young boy buys a comic book and falls in love with superheroes—and an illustration of how that paradigm, by usual accounts masculinist, covertly raced along the lines of white supremacy (i.e., baseline human = white), and imbued with a nostalgia conducive to any number of wicked conservative politics, is far queerer than it may appear.

The story I've recounted is that of a black boy's introduction to superhero comics happening via identification and disidentification (in the José Muñoz sense) with an image of a female character presented as "black," and in a context where this image is a novelty within the pantheon of superheroic images, since few black-appearing characters graced comic-book covers (significant exceptions being Marvel's Luke Cage in 1972 and John Stewart on a *Green Lantern* cover in 1971). In this light, the marginal appearance in a marginal dismissed-as-childish genre of representation rendered that marginal world of comics a world for my own differences—of blackness in an antiblack world, of gender-performance-attachment in a misogynist world that punishes boys for "girly" behavior as it constantly punishes cisgendered girls as "inferior."

Phil Jimenez describes an illuminatingly parallel process of attachment to Wonder Woman in his introduction to the omnibus collection of his *Wonder Woman* issues:

> Growing up, I never occurred to me that my hero couldn't be a woman.
>
> While so many I knew loved and idolized a certain kind of hero—stern-faced, muscle-bound alpha dudes . . . who threw trucks over their heads and showed no fear while pounding villains into submission and rescuing their damsels, . . . my fictional heroes were different. Being a closeted gay kid, I never imagined I could be like those men. I was too beta, too queer. . . . I certainly fantasized about being one of their glamorous damsels—or glamorous, certainly, and theirs.
>
> My fictional heroes were not people like me, though they might have qualities I shared. They were people I wanted to be *more like*. And they were almost always women, because my heroes exemplified all the positive attributes I saw in my mother, even if I had no vocabulary to articulate it at the time.[15]

Thus this particular story of comics fandom—and the paradigm it offers for the fantasy-act—is a story of queer intimacy linking character, reader(s), genre, and form.

* * *

Jimenez's account doubling mine brings us to another aspect of a phenomenological account of "reading" the superhero comic, and of such reading as the paradigm of fantasy-acts. Jimenez more so than I strikes the notes of *identification* through fantasy engagements with superheroes: people he knew *idolized* the likes of Batman and Superman; he knew he could not be *like* those heroes, but there were others, including Wonder Woman, whom he did wish to be *like*. This description partakes of the now commonplace understanding of superhero comics as providing models for the impressionable young people who read them, as offering examples for emulation.

It's useful to pause and dilate on the question of superhero comics and identification, and to try to glean from debates and insights regarding that supposed link further ways to understand my immediate claim in this chapter for reading superhero comics as a fantasy-act par excellence. As I hope I've already demonstrated, each "reading" even of a single page or cover of a comic book may, and probably must, occasion a layered engagement. Comics as providing a source of identification, then, we should see as one of the possible layers of such engagement.

In 1954, Frederic Wertham, a psychiatrist who taught at Johns Hopkins, published a book called *Seduction of the Innocent*. Henceforward no history of comic books in the United States is complete without a frowning mention of his name. *Seduction* took aim at representations in popular culture that Wertham deemed deleterious to young minds. Among his warnings about comic books was a claim that the relationship between Batman and Robin was homosexual and that, therefore, reading comics with Batman in them was a not-so-subtle endorsement for young boys to enter into homosexual relations. Likewise, Wonder Woman was Batman's lesbian counterpart, a character who used violence to express sadistic hatred for men—and surely no good could come of that, for either girl or boy readers.[16] Wertham's book sparked a great deal of controversy, capitalizing on concerns about the content of comics that was already fermenting among US adults in the postwar world, and it helped bring about Senate hearings on the contribution of comic books to juvenile delinquency.

Thus comics' use of and participation in fantasies that help fashion their readers' prospective self-conception and behavior have long been recognized as a fundamental aspect of reading comics. Comics, and superheroes in particular, as the source and the vectors of identification were usually seen as an evil or a social peril, as Wertham insisted.

While Wertham's judgment of the outcomes of comics reading has been and should be challenged, I would suggest that his divining of the *process* of comics reading is not without merit. Frantz Fanon devoted two pages of his 1952 *Black Skin, White Masks* to a discussion of how "weekly comics for the young" play a principal role in the inculcation of white supremacy and racialized self-perception in their readers. Fanon, in one of several moments of crescendo in *Black Skin* where he is ferreting out the source of black Caribbean citizens' often-unconscious but fundamental attachment to notions of white superiority, says the following:

> We are entitled . . . to ask how *total identification* with the white man can still be the case in the twentieth century? Very often the black man

[of the French Caribbean] . . . has never come into contact with Whites. Has some former experience been repressed in his unconscious? Has the young black child seen his father beaten or lynched by the white man? Has there been a real traumatism? To all these questions our answer is *no*. . . .

If we want an honest answer, we have to call on the notion of *collective catharsis*. In every society, in every community, there exists, must exist, a channel, an outlet whereby the energy accumulated in the form of aggressiveness can be released. This is the purpose of games in children's institutions, . . . and *more generally, of the weekly comics for the young*. . . . The Tarzan stories, the tales of young explorers, the adventures of Mickey Mouse, and *all the illustrated comics* aim at releasing a collective aggressiveness. They are written by white men for white children. And this is the crux of the matter. In the Antilles—and there's no reason to believe the situation is any different in the other colonies—these same magazines are devoured by the local youth. And the Wolf, the Devil, the Wicked Genie, Evil, and the Savage are always represented by Blacks or Indians; and *since one always identifies with the good guys, the little black child, just like the little white child, becomes an explorer, an adventurer, and a missionary "who is in danger of being eaten by the wicked Negroes."*

. . . The identification process means that the black child subjectively adopts a white man's attitude. He invests the hero, who is white, with all his aggressiveness—which at this age closely resembles self-sacrifice: a self-sacrifice loaded with sadism.[17]

Fanon, unlike Wertham, is not often brought to the fore in theorizations about comics. But I do read him as a theorist of comics. For Fanon, comics are a primary mode wherein racial identity is disseminated, and apart from these two pages I've quoted, *Black Skin*'s pathbreaking examination of how blackness and whiteness take meaning and establish a racist foundation for the modern world notes the *activity* of comics twice more in its slightly over two hundred pages. "Look at children's comic books," he notes in passing in one such instance, in the middle of a larger discussion of how values of white supremacy imbue education in the French language; "all the Blacks are mouthing the ritual 'Yes, boss.'"[18]

We should take note that Wertham and Fanon expressed their concerns during a period when comics reading was far more universal than it now is. Carol Tilley reports that in 1953, the year between the publication of Fanon's and Wertham's books, the consumption of comic books in the United States reached 100 million issues per month.[19] By contrast, in the first six months of 2019, comics sales (of single issues, not graphic novels or bound collections) averaged about 6.42 million per month.[20] Nevertheless, analyses such as Wertham's and Fanon's—buttressed by the Kefauver hearings in the US Senate and given ultimate quasi-legal expression in the subsequent establishment of the Comics Code Authority—gained wide currency and set terms for discussion that are still resonant. And while the numbers of actual comics issues sold and presumably read have declined by some 94 percent, the narrower readership of the contemporary moment is considerably supplemented, if not supplanted, by the large audiences that thrill to comics images and narratives in cinema, television dramas, and animation.

There are significant implications in taking up Fanon regarding *black readership* of comics—particularly significant for my own reading of the image of Nubia and my attachment to it. I examine these black dimensions of comics reading in my case and others later in the chapter. For the moment, I want to direct attention to the points of convergence for Fanon and Wertham. I cite Wertham and Fanon not in order to begin mounting a defense of comics against the charge of harmfulness or even to use what they wrote as a defense against the charge of comics' puerile insignificance. Rather, I cite them as pointing to comics "reading" as a fantasy-act and to the formidable *strength* of fantasy-acts' processes of imaginative engagement.

Both Fanon and Wertham track an interface between the text-images of comics and the readers that involves *identification*. The explicit proposition is that the reader *identifies with* (for Wertham, the covertly queer) Batman and Wonder Woman and (for Fanon, the overtly white-as-dominant-race) Tarzan et al. This is a proposition that Jimenez also takes as fundamentally true for his narration of both his own comics reading and that of other comics readers he knew.

Fanon's and Wertham's analyses of the possibilities inherent to comic-book reading—arrived at in part by the not entirely accurate then, and certainly inaccurate now, assumption that it is mainly children and adolescents who read comic books—are, to my mind, entirely Freudian in structure. The two analysts of the reading of comics I've cited here are, of course, trained in Freudian analysis, so this is to be expected—of them. The marvel is that this Freudian structure obtains in analyses and assumptions well beyond psychiatric practice, such as those undergirding the US Senate's hearings about the dangers posed by comic books and their contribution to juvenile delinquency. That is, such analysis sees the Oedipus "complex" unfolding at the site of repetitive comics reading. The superhero figure stands in for the Father, whom the little boy—it is usually, of course, a *boy*, with secondary consideration of the girl (much like assumptions about superhero comics readership)—must aim to be "like," while navigating the treacherous shoals of a possibly gender-busting identification with his mother, to whom he is necessarily and dangerously, i.e., potentially erotically, attached. In the Wertham comics-reading analysis, this is most clearly seen: the dangers of failing to submit to paternal authority via identification, and failing to cede pater's claim to the mother are dispersed among the elements of the superhero story or, more troublingly for Wertham, inherent in the superhero himself, who is a *bad* model, a perverse Father.

I note this Freudian structure to underline the constitutive confusions between identification and desire. This confusion has been examined in nearly every account of identity and identification across a wide variety of contexts in feminist work and queer studies. Personally I like the following formulation by Jonathan Dollimore, here pressing to its logical limits the prescriptions of Oedipal identification in the specific case of the male (to whom psychoanalysis's centering of the Oedipal drama is of course a love ode): "The necessary identifications of male bonding—'I desire to be like you'—produce an intensity of admiration some of which just cannot help but transform into deviant desire for, rather than honourable imitation of, 'man's' most significant other (i.e., man). And it occurs so easily—almost passively—requiring little more than a relinquishing of the *effort* of emulation, the erasure of '*to be like*' and the surrender to what remains: '*I desire . . . you*'; thus: 'I desire (to be like) you.'"[21]

Identification, then, is not simple, nor simply (or completely) achieved. Was I Nubia, or was Nubia the object of an obscure, fitfully clarifying desire? Probably both. Yet there are dimensions of this encounter that aren't described by either proposition, and it is these to which I wish to draw attention next. We might view reading comics as performing a subtler function than either Wertham or Fanon envisage, as being less clearly a site of imaginary mimesis wherein reader and comic-book figure are matched one-to-one.

One way we can highlight the assumed identification orientation of superhero comics as *not* staging a one-to-one, reader-to-superhero imaginative encounter is to come back to the primary term at play here, "fantasy." Fantasy plays a key role in establishing the subject qua subject, which assumes its social position through identification. "To be like" another person and to be like a figure are both born of fantastical investments.

Consider a definition of "phantasy" in Jean LaPlanche and Jean-Bertrand Pontalis's *The Language of Psycho-Analysis* (1973). The spelling "*ph*antasy" is preferred in psychoanalytic theory outside the United States because its derivation from the German *Phantasie* encompasses a broader sense of both the content and the creative activity of imagination, rather than the reduction to whimsy and triviality that often occurs with the English word "fantasy." Both sets of meanings have relevance here: the work of closure seems well described as the creative activity of imagination, while whimsy describes well enough a comics story or reader's investment in, for example, talking ducks. LaPlanche and Pontalis describe "Phantasy (or Fantasy)" thus: "Imaginary scene in which the subject is a protagonist, representing the fulfillment of a wish (in the last analysis, an unconscious wish) in a manner that is distorted to a greater or lesser degree by defensive processes"; and "Phantasy has a number of different modes: conscious phantasies or daydreams . . . , unconscious phantasies . . . , and primal phantasies."[22] Further, LaPlanche and Pontalis note, "It is not an *object* that the subject imagines and aims at" in phantasy, "but rather a *sequence* in which the subject has his own part to play and in which permutations of roles and attributions are possible. . . . The primary function of phantasy [is as] the *mise-en-scène* of desire."[23]

This formulation of fantasy's function as the mise-en-scène of desire means not only that fantasies provide the stage settings and roles for the playing out of desire's fulfillment but that they establish—they create, psychically—the structure that sets desires in motion, that makes desire possible or recognizable as desire. These desires themselves actualize a subject-object relation even if their objects are not clear or singular: what is significant is an apparent separation between the perceiving and receptive consciousness and some thing or things which that consciousness perceives in relation to what must then thereby become its own "self." Part of the way you build a self—an always imaginary, fantasy-driven process—is to organize the self around qualities and attributes that you at once perceive yourself lacking and that you project onto figures that are disguised as external and alien (thereby defining you via negation) but that are also, or in truth, idealized portions or versions of yourself.

Thus it is possible to view fantasy (and comics as a form centralizing fantasy) as providing the templates or the content of imaginative mental play—again, played out individually and collectively. But we also can intimate that fantasy (and comics) provides an education *in* desire: where desire is one of the primary modes (if not *the* mode) of establishing a sense of self. This is a self that, in psychoanalytic theories as in other theoretical accounts, is in any case by its nature in large part chimerical and might well be described as a fantasy.

It is very worth noting that the extension of Dollimore's logical sleight of hand to the contexts of superhero idolization warningly described by Wertham and Fanon casts light on a process that has already, in some cases (mine, Jimenez's), shrugged aside the mandate for identification with one's *proper* gender. The comics readers whom Jimenez knew may, he implies, have been questing after the alpha-male-dom that is the supposed (and violently enforced) goal of their cisgender embodiment's maturation—even while their questing via reading superhero comics was misleading them into homosexuality, Wertham argues. But Jimenez and I—without, it must be said, any apparent stopover in the domain of Batman required—were already both desiring and desiring to be like a female figure who reminded us both of our mothers. The education in desire and provision of objects of desire, as well as subject aspirations from which to desire, were queer. Were they always already queer? Was the very *form* of superhero-comics reading an invitation, a solicitation to "reading" comics queerly and thus to being educated in queerness and risking *becoming* queer? Was it, as such, a recruitment, as Wertham feared? I'm proposing that it was, though Wertham missed the terms of the recruitment's address.

* * *

The queerness of comics, and their formal invitation to—or openness toward—reading/viewing queerly, is something we learn from Ramzi Fawaz's *The New Mutants: Superheroes and the Radical Imagination of American Comics* (2016). Two arguments Fawaz undertakes in *New Mutants* are salient for gauging the ways that superhero comics potentially queer their readers and thus partake of, and also demonstrate the substance of, fantasy-acts. One is that superhero comics, in their dance with the psyches and imaginations of readers, constantly invite *identification* with definitionally nonnormative figures. The second is that the elastic form of comics—their centering of fantasy content via a relatively simple representational technology whereby whatever is drawn is provisionally invested in by the reader as true; and their simultaneous attentiveness to linear temporality and insouciant discarding of linear temporality—ensconces readers in queer reading practices that are also always queer ways of thinking.

For me, the corollary of both observations is that the slippery identification that is possible and likely with queer figures in superhero comics, and utilizing the queer thinking necessary to navigate the form, beckons, risks, queer becoming and being.

Fawaz analyzes superhero comics' constant celebration of difference or freakishness—especially following the explosion of new comics characters at Marvel in the 1960s—as a ready-made metaphor for any number of otherwise-degraded departures from societal norms. The fantasy aspects of the medium of comics have lent themselves to the depiction of a vast array of nonnormative expressions of gender and sexuality—from the most metaphoric (in hyperbolic camp visuality or the metamorphosing of human bodies into forms that put into question traditional gender norms etc.) to the most literal (the actual depiction of queer bodies and erotic attachments). Postwar Marvel Comics, especially its flagship commercial success *The Fantastic Four*, which began in 1961, "reinvent[ed] . . . the superhero as a distinctly 'queer' figure," Fawaz says.

> Postwar superheroes' mutated bodies and alternative kinships thwarted the direction of heterosexual desire and life outcomes and cultivated an affective orientation toward otherness and difference that made so-called deviant forms of bodily expression, erotic attachment, and affiliation both

desirable and ethical. The postwar superhero comic's embrace of indefinitely unfolding narratives with no predetermined outcome, its unraveling of the traditionally gendered physiology of the white, male superhero, and its centralizing of cross-cultural encounter and mutually transgressive engagement popularized a mode of storytelling that was largely uninterested in traditional heterosexual reproduction, family forms, or gender norms. . . . Instead of solidifying a "straight" future organized by the nuclear family and the promise of heterosexual reproduction, postwar superhero comics framed the proliferation of difference, its ceaseless alteration of the social world, and the pursuit of ever more complex forms of affiliation and collective action *across* all manner of cultural and geographic divides.[24]

In identifying the queer reading practices demanded by comics, Fawaz follows a plethora of comics studies scholarship that describes and theorizes comics' unique form: due to comics' serial production—generally appearing as ongoing stories paced by intervals, whether daily, weekly, monthly, quarterly, or yearly—action and occurrence are elongated and elaborated, as well as condensed and abbreviated. Time moves backward as well as forward, and any sequence may be read in or out of order, whether in linear narrative or in jarring non sequitur, perceived at a page-length glance or panel by panel. In ongoing comics series—which superhero comics provide the primary and paradigmatic example for—where a succession of different creative teams of artists and writers tell stories that begin in 1938 or 1961 or 1977 and continue today, whatever was seen to "happen" in the stories before is revised, rewritten, redone, undone.

In a separate essay, Fawaz writes,

Put simply, comics teach us to read lots of different things (words, images, aesthetic styles, characters, panels, colors, textures, formats and page-layouts) in lots of different sequences, patterns, and juxtapositions on a single page, between and across pages in a single text, and often enough, across numerous texts in a serialized chain of installments. In this sense, comics demands . . . that we . . . read and interpret everything—including but not limited to cultural objects that fall under the label of "the literary"—along far more axes or angles of approach than we could have ever imagined. Comics are formally multiplicitous to a sometimes nauseating degree, and they demand we read and interpret multiply. And unlike say, a novel, which has a generally well-defined format as a long-form fictional narrative in bound print form, comics appear in numerous formats, including daily comic strips, single panel cartoons, single issue or serial comic books, zines, graphic novels, digital comics, and a vast range of sequentially organized visual art, that demand a multiplicitous account of content, form, *and* format simultaneously.[25]

Being a Fantasist, Doing Fantasy

In *The New Mutants*, Fawaz quotes from Eve Kosofsky Sedgwick's 1993 field-foundational essay "Queer and Now" to help establish his understanding of superhero comics as queer. Sedgwick writes,

> What's striking is the number and *difference* of the dimensions that "sexual identity" is supposed to organize into a seamless and univocal whole.
> And if it doesn't?
> That's one of the things that "queer" can refer to: the open mesh of possibilities, gaps, overlaps, dissonances and resonances, lapses and excesses of meaning when the constituent elements of anyone's gender, of anyone's sexuality aren't made (or *can't be* made) to signify monolithically. The experimental linguistic, epistemological, representational, political adventures attaching to the very many of us who may at times be moved to describe ourselves as (among many other possibilities) pushy femmes, radical faeries, fantasists, drags, clones, leatherfolk, ladies in tuxedoes, feminist women or feminist men, masturbators, bulldaggers, divas, Snap! queens, butch bottoms, storytellers, transsexuals, aunties, wannabes, lesbian-identified men or lesbians who sleep with men, or . . . people able to relish, learn from, or identify with such.[26]

Fawaz's reproduction of this Sedgwick passage in *The New Mutants* serves to provide a definition of queerness that dovetails with the content, form, and reading practices of superhero comics. Following Fawaz back to Sedgwick, I wish to underline his insights but am also intrigued by Sedgwick's inclusion of the *fantasist*—that little-seen, unicorn-like creature—in her list of queer possibilities.

I understand Sedgwick's wildly asymmetrical list as a conscious refusal—and playful mockery—of sexological taxonomies. Sedgwick eschews the monolithic signification of sexual identities or demarcated types. Sexology proposes that such supposed types can be understood in parallel relation to one another and diverge from each other largely in their unvarying orientation toward different objects of desire—the way that, for example, as Sedgwick puts it, "'gay' and 'lesbian' . . . present themselves (however delusively) as objective, empirical categories governed by empirical rules of evidence (however contested)." By contrast, Sedgwick's antisexological queer nontaxonomy "seems to hinge much more radically and explicitly on a person's undertaking particular, performative acts of experimental self-perception and filiation."[27]

The inclusion of "fantasist" among this list of social stylings, sexual practices, political positions, and gender queerings is perhaps more anomalous than any other—even more than the comparatively prosaic, if equally incongruous, "storyteller." A *fantasist* is usually not grouped with either sexual or gender performances or with the many kinds of politics generally signified by–*ists*, and, as I've noted in the introduction to this book, it is in any case an infrequently used description in common parlance.

I'm interested in what Sedgwick might have been suggesting by the inclusion of "fantasist" in her queer nonsexological list: a fantasist as a queer positionality; a fantasist as one who engages in, believes in, affiliates by the coordinates of, fantasy, where fantasy might therefore evoke a meaning akin to, and might in part be described by, the performative in the J. L. Austin sense, in that much-cited definition of the performative utterance: "Utterances can be found . . . such that: A. They do not 'describe' or 'report' or constate anything at all, are not 'true or false,' and B. The uttering of the sentence is, or is a part of, the doing of an action, which again would not *normally* be described as, or as 'just,' saying something."[28] To use this definition either as an analogical understanding of fantasy or even *as* a definition of fantasy—such that "fantasy" and "performative utterance" are nearly synonyms—is of course to emphasize fantasy as not wholly immaterial, as *doing* something, as an *act*, which indeed is what Sedgwick implies.

Drawing from Sedgwick and Austin (which is to say, drawing from performance studies protocols), the fantasy-act in its dimension of *act-*

ing thus appears to be not unlike theatrical acting—an acting *as if*. Or, put differently, an acting within the bounds of a supposition and under- standing shared by *actors* and those with whom or before whom they act that interpreting what one sees and hears as "real" is interdicted. Following the way that the distinction of performative utterance from utterance is that the performative utterance accomplishes that which it represents in language, I choose to emphasize here crossing in the other direction, where the mimesis of an accomplishment—as, say, repre- sented in the two-dimensional images on a page—is an act that *happens*, like acting, but is not held to have repercussions (concrete, legal, politi- cal) in the social or in physical experience and its duration: this non- consequential action—nonconsequential, that is, vis-à-vis what presents itself as consensus real experience—I am now going to describe as, in the moment(s) of the act's commission, a kind of *being*.

To invoke "being" necessarily is to invoke a raft of ontological theory—and such theories' baggage. There is a powerful and persuasive argument, which draws from Fanon (and thus draws from Sartre and thus from Hegel, etc., etc.) that blackness always figures as an antitheti- cal term conferring the properties of "being" on what it is not, that is, whiteness, and that hence blackness's claim to "being" is constantly if not definitionally under erasure and must at the very least always be consid- ered skeptically. This argument is a part of Afro-pessimist thought. My desire is to bracket this argument until chapter 2, gambling that however persuasive it is, my encounter with Nubia is not fully accounted for, and thus that encounter is not wholly blotted from significance, by the argu- ment's power.

That said, I turn here to give meaning to "being" by consulting one of queer theory's founders, Leo Bersani. In the past Bersani's theorizations, as I myself have argued (but not I alone), have sometimes poorly thought through the interplay of race—or more particularly blackness—with sexuality, and race and blackness with subjectivity. It is not unreason- able to suggest that Bersani's occasional blindness to the possible impact on his otherwise-lucid writing of better accounts of the way blackness makes meaning in the modern world is in fact a perfect illustration of how the terms of modern universality—"being" as one such in philo- sophical ontological inquiry—function by, and indeed cannot function without, displacing, subordinating, or erasing blackness and black people's experience. How, you might ask, can Bersani have something useful to contribute to an account of blackness in relation to fantasy when he rarely if ever seems to account for blackness in his thinking?

Yet, even acknowledging the undertow I may struggle against taking Bersani as a guide, here again I draw attention to my conviction that what is incited exceeds the initial incitement. And I make explicit here the idiosyncratic "method" I'm using in this book of reading down the road paved by what I love—and, as in the past I've loved a lot of what Bersani has to say about sex and masculinity, I also love and find very useful what he has to say about fantasy.

Bersani's 2006 essay "Psychoanalysis and the Aesthetic Subject" comes upon the notion of "being" in reaching a set of bracing conclusions about psychic fantasy as it interrelates with textual and visual art. He writes, "Psychic fantasy is a type of unrealized or derealized human and world *being*, the figure, not for a taking place, but rather for all taking place—for all relationality—in its pure inherence."[29] For Bersani, fantasy is the figure not for an act that will only be significant when it is real or material but rather for the very process of the relation between the real and unreal, between the inner and outer, a process (or *the* process) that is inherent *to* the world as the world and that constitutes the world: or at least the world as human beings move in it and are of it.

Bersani works this out in the following ways that I think are illuminating for thinking fantasy-acts in the context of superhero comics (though I imagine that context couldn't be further from Bersani's mind):

Bersani—as a psychoanalytic critic will do, it seems—considers fantasy as something undertaken by the individual psyche and as something that helps give rise to the subject, the "I." According to Freud via Melanie Klein, as Bersani traces the development of this thought, the "external" world—that which cannot in a sustained way be understood by the aborning subject to be itself—is readily identified with threats. All objects thus are essentially bad objects. "It is the bad object that gives birth to the object as object. . . . From the very beginning, the object as conceived by psychoanalysis is inherently a . . . fundamentally foreign object that I must struggle to appropriate."[30] Thus the response to the external world is appropriative, with a tendency—perhaps a drive?—to project oneself in the world as the world or to meet the world with suspicion and hostility in a relation of antagonism. Such appropriative relations between the subject that knows itself by knowing itself not to be these hostile objects and the (always bad) objects is the dance of desire: "the human power not exactly to satisfy desire but to see desire everywhere, to be thrilled by the universal representation of that which it lacks"[31]—that is, "identification, projection, introjection."[32]

This, Bersani observes—in a place where I think he *does* take note of the impact of race on his account—"could perhaps have only have been theorized in a civilization that has privileged an appropriative relation of the self to the world, one that assumes a secure and fundamentally antagonistic distinction between subject and object."[33] (Later in the essay, Bersani notes, "Whiteness . . . [which is what figures the essentially arrested state of] an indefinitely prolonged possibility of possibility . . . is the gravest threat to ontological intransitivity," or the persistence of being.[34] I refer to this observation about whiteness—which I read as offering a definition of it—in chapter 3.)

Seeing the self-against-the-world, the-world-as-(appropriative)-projections-of-the-self, is, however, Bersani says, a failure or blind spot of psychoanalytic theorizing: psychoanalysis's continual sighting of this dynamic effectively limits the reach of "psychoanalytically inspired approaches to art" (examples we can supply: Wertham and Fanon) and skews what such approaches can detect. The resighting and theorization of this limited dynamic reproduces the antagonisms it diagnoses and fails to map "the subject in ways that open us to the solidarity of being both among human subjects and between the human and the nonhuman."[35]

In this failure, Bersani thinks that psychoanalysis and psychoanalytic approaches to art miss the implications of what he deems to be one of psychoanalytic theory's most profound discoveries: "psychoanalysis invites us to think a register of *being* radically different from a subjectivity grounded in psychology ([psychoanalysis] . . . calls that other *mode of being* the unconscious)."[36] "Can the work of art," Bersani asks, "contrary to psychoanalytic assumptions, deploy signs of the subject in the world that are not signs of interpretation or of an object-destroying *jouissance*"—that is, interpretative fantastical psychic and artistic acts constituting the world via aggressive fusion, aggressive illusory suppressions of otherness—"signs of what I call correspondence of forms within a universal solidarity of being?"[37]

Analyzing textual works but linking his conclusions back to what he can discern via a different kind of psychoanalytically inspired approach to visual art as well, Bersani finds that art can and does deploy such signs of the correspondence of forms. From these readings, Bersani proposes that "interiority . . . , far from refashioning the world into the structure of a psychic obsession, is actually produced *by* the world. The narrator's subjectivity is an effect of external reality."[38]

This is, we may surmise, essentially a Lacanian point: "Lacan relocates the subject . . . in the world, not as projections, but rather as that which has been detached, cut off from the subject, as result of our entrance into language as signification."[39] If language—"outside," preexisting each of us—constitutes the subject, then it is also the source of that which we experience as "inside" us. Interiority is nonsubjective—a point we have already rehearsed in the introduction, with a reference to Zen Buddhist thought.

Hence, the individual psychic unconscious does not precede the external world; rather, it "is perhaps an essentially unthinkable, intrinsically unrealizable reserve of human being—a dimension of virtuality rather than of psychic depth—from which we connect to the world, not as subject to object, but as a continuation of a specific syntax of being."[40] And thus, "The world configurations that constitute and individuate a subject wait to be received by the subject; . . . the subject is in the world before being born into it. The unconscious is not the region of the mind most hidden from the world; it resists being known because it so vastly exceeds what might know it, because it is not of the same order as what might know it."[41]

Here I take Bersani to be saying that the unconscious is of another *order* than the conscious deployments of subject-constitutive language/ signification that might endeavor (and fail) to "know" it; the unconscious is the discursive activity and meaning-making in its totality and in its hidden unguessable histories that precede our entry into the world as part of the world. It is, for humans, the substance, and in part the source, of the ontological itself. To make further sense of this, I refer back to one of the earlier statements of Bersani's that I quoted: the unconscious as "a *register of being* different from a subjectivity grounded in psychology."[42]

Bersani suggests that film and painting, the visual arts, provide "documents of a universe of inaccurate replications, of the perpetual and imperfect recurrences of forms, volumes, colors, and gestures, . . . evidence of the subject's presence everywhere, not as an invasive projection or incorporation designed to eliminate otherness, but rather as an ontological truth about both the absolute distinctness and the innumerable similitudes that at once guarantee the objective reality of the world and the connectedness between the world and the subject. We are born into various families of singularity that connect us to all the forms that have, as it were, always anticipated our coming, our presence."[43] I take Bersani to be saying that as users and producers and products of the agency of our slippery processes of signification—as selves crafted by such signification—we are variations on an "identityless miasma" to which the forms of the visual arts are one privileged expressive form of response, though they do not in any way contain or capture it. "Deep within our brain there is the unimaginable imagination of an identityless miasma, of something before articulated being, which the human can only 'think' as before the realization of any being whatsoever."[44]

Given this definition of the unconscious—its fundamentally nonsubjective quality, its being produced by, and hooked into, as it were, the world of phenomena from which it flows and with which it is in constant play—"fantasy" cannot be properly understood as the self-contained whimsy of the individual, separate psyche. "There is a perspective on fantasy that would imprison it within subjectivity," a product of "limited individuality." But if the unconscious from which fantasy draws, or that fantasy rides, is not the product of such a contained and separate individual, nor even of that individual subject's relations to objects in the world, but is rather a much wider engagement with being—of which both the cultural and the existential are but facets—then that common perspective on fantasy as directed against lack in the "real," the analysis of fantasy as an attempt to obliterate the threat of differences inherent to subject-object relations, is misdirected. "It is as if the world stimulated the activity of desiring fantasy, not by lacking objects of desire, but by their very proliferation."[45] Describing an example in a fictive text, Bersani says, "He is not, exactly, in psychoanalytic terms, a subject without an unconscious, but one whose unconscious can only come to him from the outside."[46]

Thus, *"Fantasy is not the symptom of an adaptive failure. . . . It is the sign of an extremely attentive, highly individuated response to external reality. . . .* Fantasy is thus on the threshold between an invisible (and necessarily hypothetical) inner world and the world present to our senses."[47]

Bersani's statement quoted earlier that "psychic fantasy is a type of unrealized or derealized human and world *being*" we can take to mean that fantasy is a mode of being insofar as it is, rather than a maladaptation to reality, a response to reality's call. "Derealized" being refers to the fact that fantasy and memory are indistinguishable in an ontological and perhaps neurological sense: events "in the past" are no longer "real" but "derealized," existing only in the sense of memories existing, and thus memory is a "derealized" form of being and in this sense similar to fantasy. "Memory is an illusion of consciousness, as there is no past to remember; instead, there are innumerable inscriptions of the world that define us by mapping particular positionings in the world and that simply persist, immanently."[48] "To remember events is to recognize ourselves in their imaginary presence," he writes. "The past is what has passed from the phenomenological to the virtuality of the imaginary."[49]

Fantasy, then, is a derealized and unrealized mode of being, a mode of being in excess of individualized subjectivity, insofar as fantasies are responses to the call of the world: fantasies are variations of the elements stimulated by the world (which is itself both the discrete external phenomena and the signifying actions/processes that roughly correspond with and mediate those phenomena), and thus participations in, and examples of, the relations of correspondence that make up "the world."

Bersani's inclusion in his description of fantasy as *unrealized* being brings us to the crux of a paradox that lies in calculating what in the introduction, borrowing from Fanon, I referred to as the "weight" of the fantasy-act. In the introduction, I proposed that coining "fantasy-acts" allows that *fantasy is without the weight or carry or power of "reality," but* it also reminds us that *fantasy has some accountable weight or carry or power, so that we have to call fantasy an existent or an act of some kind.* I asked, What can we say is the "weight" of these fantasy-acts?

Bersani avers, "If fantasy is a major site of our connectedness to the world, *it is not an act that touches or changes the world.* It represents the terms in which the world inheres in the fantasizing subject, terms that can change as our position in the world changes."[50] And "the world is not overwhelmed by fantasy."[51]

If I'm following Bersani, these statements would seem to obviate my claim to fantasy as a fantasy-*act*. But for Bersani, there is not an absolute cordoning off of fantasy in relation to activity in and of the world. Fantasy is one of the "diverse representations of the interface between the moving subject and a world whose relational map is itself continuously modified by the moves of all the units—including the human units—that constitute it." Fantasies as one of these kinds of diverse representations thus are modifying the world insofar as fantasies participate in and contribute to the "moves"—which are not only physical—that make up the world. It is true that "all these figures do not have the finality of acts that materially modify the world."[52] Moreover, "There is neither a subject-object dualism nor a fusion of subject and object; there is rather a kind of looping movement between the two. The world finds itself in the subject and the subject finds itself in the world. What the world finds in the subject (in addition to physical correspondences) is a certain activity of consciousness, which partially reinvents the world as it repeats it."[53] "Desiring fantasies both determine and are determined by their replications in the world."[54] Bersani thus assigns some weight—if necessarily inconsistent and even vanishingly calculable as it constantly "moves" and changes—to the activity of fantasy.

Bersani links fantasy to the "unrealized"—which elsewhere he describes as "the possibility of the act that *may* of course precede the act" but which, being thus contingent, must in its own moment remain most accurately described as *un*realized, as possibility only.[55] *And* simultaneously Bersani links fantasy to the "derealized," that is, that which *has happened* but that is now only memory and past.

Thus described are an ephemeral not-yet and already-done, both *types of being* for Bersani, concurring and potentially contradictory elements. My description of this concurrence and contradiction tries to assign relative weights to these differing and crisscrossing elements: fantasy-acts describe a process that is a significant form of *being* in that they partake of that same "derealized" kind of being that the past and memory are, but fantasy-acts are also always dubious in the extent to which they involve consequential or "real" action, such that we might describe them as a minor form of *doing*. This draws us back to the useful paradoxes gleaned from likening fantasy-acts to Sedgwick and Austin on fantasists and performative utterances.

Thus we can track through Sedgwick, Austin, Bersani, and Fawaz how the queer "identification," which is also an education in desire, the "reading" practices and content of superhero comics that are routinely and perhaps necessarily queer, hinge into queer becoming and queer *being*. Here the queer being that fantasy-acts entail refers to that which carries weight not unlike memories of the past (which are all that the past "is"), a weight not unlike what "has happened" but is not presently happening, while simultaneously referring to "as if" possible acts that have little or no finality and effect little or no material modification on the world but nonetheless *do* participate in its modification: thus, a minor form of *doing*.

This, then, is also how we can see comics as a privileged *form* for fantasy-acts.

Another way to understand this is via a typically pithy formulation of Toni Morrison's:

> The resources available to us for benign access to each other, for vaulting the mere blue air that separates us, are few but powerful: language, image, and experience, which may involve both, one, or neither of the first two. Language (saying, listening, reading) can encourage, even mandate, surrender, the breach of distances among us, whether they are continental or on the same pillow, whether they are distances of culture or the distinctions and indistinctions of age or gender, whether they are the consequences of social invention or biology. Image increasingly rules the realm of shaping, sometimes becoming, often contaminating, knowledge. Provoking language or eclipsing it, an image can determine not only what we know and feel but also what we believe is worth knowing about what we feel.
>
> These two godlings, language and image, feed and form experience.[56]

Morrison is not—so far as I've read, she almost never is—talking about comics. But through her, we can see comics form's inextricable marriage of language and image as the conduit to, the provision of, "experience," which we might see in light of our discussion as something that overlaps with doing *and* being.

Might we also think the obverse proposition, less apparent to the experience of reading a comic but perhaps revealed by analyses such as those described earlier of the process of reading comics? Such a proposition might read, *The content of fantasy-acts in the modern world of readers is shaped by comics. Fantasy-acts are a form of expression that privileges comics.* These are assays of a relationship between comics and fantasy-acts that sees them not only as connected or analogous but as deeply informing one another, as coconstitutive. Comics are the fantastic stories or fantastically (i.e., nonrealist) structured stories of their creators, which in the hands and minds of comics readers also become templates for readers' fantasies, individually experienced and collectively (yet combatively and unharmoniously) worked on and elaborated, in the letters pages of comics, in online forums, in the sharing of fan art, in comics conventions, and so on. Such a description seems to echo in structure Bersani's line quoted earlier: "diverse representations of the interface between the moving subject and a world whose relational map is itself continuously modified by the moves of all the units—including the human units—that constitute it."

Was I Nubia, or was Nubia the object of an obscure, fitfully clarifying desire? The proposition here is that reading/viewing comics, even or especially superhero comics, does not only or simply provide *models* for behavior or educations in how to see yourself in relation to the world— the primary activities of young minds, so we like to think, as though we have magically shed these activities or prioritized them downward by age eighteen—but that reading/viewing comics and fantasy-acts, or what for purposes here I might denote by comics/fantasy-acts, is *a mode of being you*, whether child or adult or, as we almost all are, an amalgam of the two.

To return to Wertham and Fanon, but having stretched and turned inside out their assumptions, we might say that the greatest fantasy, perhaps the ur-fantasy, is to transform oneself into another, fantastically better self. Reading many kinds of comics, but especially the core genre of superheroes, fits this wish beautifully.

This being that is transformed by fantasy, this not-you-but-You, will probably be wealthier—think Bruce Wayne (Batman), Tony Stark (Iron Man), T'Challa (Black Panther), and Richie Rich; and anyway, do Thor or Hawkman ever worry about money? Probably this You will be considered universally beautiful, will be ultra-intelligent and ultra-invulnerable to all the hurts and emotional wounds of life we suffer as social beings, may be able to teleport vast distances, read minds, create, destroy, and resurrect loved ones with a snap of the fingers.

The ego-fluffing grandeur-delusion trajectory of such fantasies is clear enough. One persistent criticism of the male superheroic figure is its availability to the kinds of masculinist and white-supremacist iconography and narration that underpin fascism. The splash-page images of powerfully muscular figures drawn as male and white attired in versions of the US (or Canadian or British) flag would seem to confirm this reading. Indeed a recent story line in the superhero comic series *Captain America* mined such implications for dramatic effect, transforming the earliest and arguably paragon character of the comics company that would become Marvel Comics into the sleeper agent of a fascist organization bent on Fourth Reich–like world domination. I explore the resonance of superheroes with fascism in chapter 3. For now, I note that this *Captain America* story arc was not popular among many fans and generated considerable controversy online (though, truth be told, most story arcs have that effect). Captain America was after all created to fight fascism in the fantasy world of comics and could be seen on the cover of the March 1941 first issue pummeling Hitler himself with a vicious right hook to the face. Might there be an echo that traveled from this image to the memes-plus-images that are popular in the Antifa movement, of punching Nazis in the face? Might not this then be an example of the "looping movement" as Bersani describes it, where "the world finds itself in the subject and the subject finds itself in the world . . . , the subject . . . partially reinvents the world as it repeats it"?[57] A similar if less directly politicized description can be made of 1939's Superman; it is now fairly commonly agreed among comics historians that Superman's escape from a world on the brink of destruction to adopt the United States as home and, eventually, fight for "the American Way," was the fantasy reimagining of the character's creators, Joe Shuster and Jerry Siegel, of Jews' harried flight from Hitler's Europe.

Nevertheless, these fantasies are not only projections of what psychoanalytic theory describes as the ego's constitutive defenses against vulnerability: it is not only the singular self that is transformed in the forge of such fantasies: the *acts* of such fantasies cannot be and are not confined solely to identification but work their threads into wider nets of meaning in the manner I have used Bersani, Sedgwick, Austin, and Fawaz to describe.

My Nubia, and perhaps others' Nubia, reshaped my world into one where a black woman was a goddess, a destroyer by means of her great powers of hand and body, and by means of her very "existence," a challenger of racial-gender injustice, a terrible and beautiful Diana Ross with Olympian powers, a mother, both my own mother and better than my own mother and a mother *for me* as well *as me*. She *was*, I was "like" her and "liked" her and was her, "experienced" "being" her, and she did do it, it did "happen"—on the stage of the superhero comic image and text.

2

Can the Black Superhero *Be*?

Blackness vs. the Superhero

I can change the order of things to suit my desperations.
—Essex Hemphill, "The Edge"

One of comics' cognate representational forms—also defining late modernity, though preceding comics in their post–*Action Comics* form—is film. Much has been written about the entangled and mutually destructive (not of each other but of everything else) relationship between film and race. A few slivers chipped off that massive nightmarish iceberg provide a useful way to begin to understand how the pairing of blackness and the superhero—carefully twined together in chapter 1—presents a formidable challenge to the acts of being and doing that I'm ascribing to fantasy-acts.

On blackness in film, my go-to theorist for this initial consideration will be again, and again perhaps surprisingly, Fanon. Here in three among several instances in 1952's *Black Skin, White Masks*, we find Fanon in a descriptive and reportorial rather than incisively analytic mood: "Whether he likes it or not, the black man has to wear the livery the white man has fabricated for him. Look at children's comic books"—this, as you may recall, is the same moment we encountered in chapter 1. Fanon goes on, "In films the situation is even more acute. Most of the American films dubbed in French reproduce the grinning stereotype *Y a bon Banania*. In one of these recent films, *Steel Sharks*, there is a black guy on a submarine. . . . He is a true nigger, walking behind the quartermaster, trembling at the latter's slightest fit of anger, and is killed in the end."[1]

Later Fanon describes the acute predicament of watching movies while black: "I can't go to the movies without encountering myself. I wait for myself. Just before the film starts, I wait for myself. Those in front of me look at me, spy on me, wait for me. A black bellhop is going to appear. My aching heart makes my head spin."[2]

Elsewhere Fanon expands on this description after observing that "a host of information and a series of propositions slowly and stealthily work their way into an individual through books, newspapers, school texts, advertisements, movies, and radio and shape his community's vision of the world." Here he drops a footnote: "We recommend the following experiment for those who are not convinced. Attend the showing of a Tarzan film in the Antilles and in Europe," Fanon suggests. "In the Antilles the young black man identifies himself de facto with Tarzan versus the Blacks. In a movie house in Europe things are not so clear-cut, for the white moviegoers automatically place him among the savages on the screen. This experiment is conclusive. The black man senses he cannot get away with being black."[3]

These observations should bring us back to one of the problems posed when looking at Nubia in her leopard-skin skirt.

Contrast Fanon's account of moviegoing with that of his contemporary Gore Vidal, another perhaps-unexpected guide here, but like Fanon someone whose writing style is married to a politics that I admire and from which I learn. Vidal here writes circa 1992 and thus forty years after Fanon, recalling his own more rhapsodic moviegoing but mostly describing films from the same period, the 1930s through 1940s. Vidal's account is not explicitly or even implicitly *about* race in the movies, and yet, read in light of Fanon's testimony, what he has to say is almost unintelligible to the neighborly interstellar visitor from Alpha Centauri without an understanding of race in relation to the movies:

> As I now move, graciously, I hope, toward the door marked Exit, it occurs to me that the only thing I ever really liked to do was go to the movies. Naturally, Sex and Art took precedence over the cinema. Unfortunately, neither ever proved to be as dependable as the filtering of present light through that moving strip of celluloid which projects past images and voices onto a screen. Thus, in a seemingly simple process, screening history.
>
> As a writer and political activist, I have accumulated a number of cloudy trophies in my melancholy luggage. Some real, some imagined. Some acquired from life, such as it is; some from movies, such as they are.

Sometimes, in time, where we are as well as were, it is not easy to tell the two apart. . . . For instance, I often believe that I served at least one term as governor of Alaska; yet written histories do not confirm this belief. No matter. Those were happy days, and who cares if they were real or not?[4]

Vidal's dreamlike association between watching movies and memories of an otherwise unrecorded gubernatorial sojourn in Alaska link up in the Harvard lectures that this quotation is drawn from, which braid together memories of movies, memories of personal life, and references to world and national history. Vidal's first novel, *Williwaw* (1946), is set in Alaska, and the writing of the novel, Vidal muses, depended in a curious way on watching movies. Convalescing in an army hospital in Alaska after "having been frozen in the Bering Sea," Vidal concludes,

I had, by then, started a novel, about a ship in a storm in the Bering Sea. After the hospital, I was transferred to the Gulf of Mexico. I was unable to finish this novel until I went to see *Isle of the Dead* [1945], with Boris Karloff. As Boris Karloff first haunted my imagination in *The Mummy* [1932], so Boris Karloff, as a Greek officer on an island in a time of plague, broke, as it were, the ice and I completed my first novel right then and there. . . . I have no idea what was in the movie that did the trick.[5]

The kind of haunting evoked by his encounter with moving images on celluloid is of course markedly different from the haunting of similar images for Fanon and his imaginary-cum-clinically-observed-patient Black Everyman. For Vidal, the fantasy evoked is of decidedly white American male imaginary *possession* of political territory—"my *un*screenable Alaska," Vidal calls it.[6] Fanon and his black moviegoer, meanwhile, suffer vertiginous anxiety attacks and are all but hounded out of the cinema. Notice that *identification* with the hero or the villain, that somewhat misleading vector of engagement with comics discussed in chapter 1, is not required for Vidal's fantasy of plenitude as it mingles with and becomes indistinguishable from memory. It is the very milieu of the film-as-story, the agreed-upon assumptions that facilitate the suspension of disbelief necessary to imaginatively enjoy via observing the film, everything about the movie and movies themselves, that guarantee the possibility, indeed the enticement, of an intermingling between past recorded image and present imaginations of the past.

This seamless transfer of information across the boundaries of real and imaginary, the active production of fantasy as world, world as fantasy, requires the payment of a particular ticket (to evoke James Baldwin): entry is difficult, and perhaps even barred, without white skin and, probably, without male embodiment. Both "white" and "male" here should be understood as socially designated, with very little *give* accorded to those persons who are not socially designated white/male but who might nevertheless think, dream, and imagine both themselves and the world in accordance with one or both those designations. Fanon's Black Everyman *was* Tarzan in the Antillean theater, but cannot escape becoming savage or bellhop in the theater in Paris.

Yet I've been trying to think about and describe the ways that the very faculty beckoned into collusion by movies—imagination—is in comics not rigidly determined either by the one-to-one correspondences of identification or by the social position and embodiment of the comics reader. And we know, too, how nimble movie viewers' imaginations can be in response to such proffers of the terms of entry and identification, and that one need never look at a movie star onscreen and experience a complete disjunction between him or her and one's own self-conceptions. See, in this regard, almost anything written in the 1980s and 1990s in then-young cultural studies texts, but especially those of the black British cultural studies school. See Baldwin's attachment to Joan Crawford in *The Devil Finds Work* (1976). See José Muñoz's *Disidentifications* (1990).

I noted in the introduction how I could simultaneously both imagine having the privileges of whiteness and yet fail to fully invest in such an imaginative proposition. Another way of describing this contradiction—a way that parallels and neatly traces the contradictory elements—is the impasse I'm staging here between Vidal and Fanon at the movies. In both cases, the activity of fantasy is at once ignited and impeded. What I have begun to suggest in considering superhero-comics reading as a key paradigm of fantasy-acts is that superhero comics in both content and form also meet this impasse, and surpass it.

As a comics reader, my attention is not as limited as Fanon's Black Everyman by the director's construction of the camera's frame in the

Figure 2.1. Whitewash Jones hits the familiar minstrel comedy notes in the popular sidekick comic series *The Young Allies* 1, no. 1 (Summer 1941). (Joe Simon, editor; Jack Kirby, artist)

movie theater. Yes, I reading a comic *might* "wait" cringingly for a too-familiar racist rendition of my own image to appear, I *might* see myself therein, I might perform seeing or viewing along the lines of a constant restless quest for identification and self-reflection compelled by my embattled sense of self among similar brethren in an antiblack world. Reading comics in the 1940s, as Fanon observed, there are images laboring to achieve precisely this end. See here the dreadful Whitewash Jones, pickaninny sidekick to the team of Captain America's and the Human Torch's sidekicks, *Young Allies*, in the summer of 1941 (figure 2.1).

But in my reading of comics, I don't *have* to perform seeing and viewing according to these racist mandates, because the multiplicity of images splayed across the page's grid (or other arrangement of panels), even if they repeat themselves with slight differences, don't compel the monological focus inherent to the camera's frame. This multiplicity offers more, even, than the comparatively capacious proscenium span of the theater's stage in a playhouse. The multiplicity of images invites, or at the very least the images permit, a dispersal of attention across a number of points, and in various combinations and sequences. Hence the quest for identification, if I have (foolishly) embarked on it, may be productively frustrated, rerouted to other quests or brought again and again to a failure to achieve identification.

What is offered by the comics page—something obscured in chapter 1 with our focus on the iconic singular image, however multilayered, of Nubia on the cover—is a kind of manipulability that lies not only in the hands of the author and artist (the analogue to the film director), but in the mind of the reader/viewer. According to W. J. T. Mitchell, the comics page is less like the movie screen and more like the computer screen in its availability to, and requirement of, "viewer" action. We may be (mis)led, Mitchell opines, to consider comics via the medium's "inevitable rootedness in the extremely old media of drawing and writing; or its technical pedigree in the very modern invention of the printing press and the rise of newspapers and magazines; or its contemporary articulation as a kind of bookish and materialist alternative to the dominance of virtuality and screen-based media."[7] But we should rather see comics as "transmediatic," "moving across all boundaries of performance, representation, reproduction, and inscription to find new audiences, new subjects, and new forms of expression. . . . Comics is transmediatic because it is translatable and transitional, mutating before our eyes into unexpected new forms."[8] In this way, we can see comics formally "as *a media platform that, like the computer, can host every form of mediation.* The main difference between these two platforms is that computers provide a mechanical-electronic platform via a screen interface whereas comics offer *a manual-neurological platform via the page interface.*"[9]

Whereas, then, as we see via Vidal, cinema—long understood as bringing into being a "male gaze"—also performs the inculcation of a white male gaze, which roves like Sauron's Eye in search of differences to assimilate and territories to conquer, the comics transmedium offers a perspective that invites relationships to representation that do not assume and cannot compel conquering, assimilative responses that obliterate the threat posed by difference. "But what is the perspective of comics?" Mitchell asks. "Is it the point of view of comics artists? Or is it something impersonal, built into the very structure of comics as a medium? How can an impersonal system have a perspective? Is there a comic view of the world?"[10] These are questions only answerable with/via the participation of readers. Comics' "perspective" is not unlike the perspective of a computer—not just its screen, but what we do that registers on the screen. Thus "closure" provides the answers to Mitchell's questions, but this means that the answers are as various as the kinds of closure, the kinds and qualities of participatory imagination, the kinds and qualities of fantasy-acts, that many readers provide to the comic singularly and in the uneven collectivities of fan communities, conventions, online message boards, printed letters pages, and so on.

I have circled back to comics-reading closure because it is central to the idea of fantasy-acts, and because it is with closure(s) that we put the sword to the Gordian knot tying together my imaginative adventure of having the privileges of whiteness and yet failing to fully invest in such an imaginative proposition. Put another way, this is where my inquiry crosses paths with a number of other currently urgent inquiries in African Americanist, Afro-diasporic, and Afro-pessimist thought, which we can see from such disparate and overlapping projects as Saidiya Hartman's and Tavia Nyong'o's discussions of critical fabulation and "Afro-fabulations," and Christina Sharpe's *In the Wake: On Blackness and Being* (2016): which is whether it is possible to have fantasies of freedom and power in the hold of the slave ship—if such ontological captivity is where we always remain, post-1492—and if so, what kinds of fantasies and to what, if any, avail.

Thus prepared, let's now consider at greater length the questions I bracketed in chapter 1 that raised the strong possibility that a superhero cannot "be" a superhero and "be" signified as black at the same time. Let's consider what "black" and "white" mean, and could mean, in the two-dimensional paper and digital world of superhero comics and in the multidimensional imaginations of their readers.

Black Superhero, Black Name

The white privilege in watching movies that gives rise to Gore Vidal's fantasy of being a governor of Alaska is the same as, or linked to, the fantasy that forms the superhero in the character of Superman, in 1938. That the Superman character might be read as *Jewish* and therefore only aspirationally or provisionally white—he is the alien other who awaits the crown granted him by assimilation—supports rather than undercuts this proposition.[11] Superman's history recapitulates the history of whiteness for American immigrants, as ontogeny recapitulates phylogeny. Thus the paradigmatic comic-book superhero is in important ways *conceptually* white: if a superhero isn't white, then the hero is an exception, a different case, since part of what defines the hero is his whiteness. Viewed conceptually, the superhero figure is historically "white" and cannot be understood except in relation to fantasies inspired and underwritten by social positions of whiteness.

It is worth noting, however, that since the comic-book superhero is a figure summoned into its fictional existence via the process of drawing and writing, its whiteness is also always the production via the ink, color, or digital process indicating the character's "white" "skin" tones. This is a production that is both simple (because its practice has sedimented into a convention of the craft) and laborious (because the practice of coloring a character "white" requires work and finagling, just as giving Bruce Wayne and Superman black hair required playing with blues and blacks up through the Bronze Age). We can therefore perceive this production of *the effect* of whiteness as both conscious and unconscious in comic-book superhero creation and representation.[12]

Jeffrey A. Brown's *Black Superheroes, Milestone Comics, and Their Fans* (2001) provides a field-initializing analysis of how the black superhero, in the fantasy universe where Whitewash Jones blazed the path, at first—if not always—threatens to burst apart as incoherent, as a potentially fantasy-busting derangement of the reader's willingness to suspend disbelief. Brown's focus is on the male superhero, because the superhero is also conceptually *male*, not unlike the way the "perspective" of Vidal's (and Fanon's) movies embedded the male gaze. Nubia's departures from the norms of superhero representation—the departures that make her rich as a source for readerly imagination, both mine and many others'— are, again, transgressions of expected race *and* gender representation (a twinning of transgression that almost necessarily summons to mind other nonnormativities, including those of sexuality, thus giving rise to queer readings of various kinds, as I'll discuss shortly). This is notwithstanding Wonder Woman's iconic industry-standard status; Wonder Woman was always an outlier and, for many reasons, a queer figure.[13]

Jeffrey Brown argues that comic-book male superheroes' extreme hypermasculinity (armor-plated musculature, varying degrees of invulnerability, etc.) presents various kinds of potential anxieties for superhero comics' mostly male readership, not least the inevitable negative comparison between the hero's drawn physique and the reader's own. However, these anxieties are generally well managed within the conventions of the genre. Brown is working from the assumption, shared, as we saw, by Wertham and Fanon, that *identification* is the source and the end product of superhero-comics fandom or of reading superhero comics. Thus, Brown implies, the superhero characters' represented effect of gender presentation—I parse this phrasing in order to again remind us that the characters are an achievement of drawing and writing, rather than beings of flesh—may impede the ease with which a putatively juvenile reader can "identify" with the male superhero, but nevertheless the channel for identification is sufficiently clear to be traversed and for the match to be made.

But Brown suggests that race—or rather, not adhering to or achieving the standard represented effect of whiteness—poses a less surmountable obstacle. The management of the anxieties about the possibilities of identification and idolization does not work well when the superhero is a black male, a figure already overdetermined in Western cultures as an exemplar of extreme, out-of-control physicality. "If comic book superheroes represent an acceptable, albeit obviously extreme, model of hypermasculinity," Brown notes, "then the combination of the two—a black male superhero—runs the risk of being read as an overabundance, a potentially threatening cluster of masculine signifiers."[14]

The evidence for the operation of this risk and threat lies not only in the relative paucity of numbers of black superheroes, male or female; that is a sin that can be laid at the door of the overwhelmingly white male creators of the superhero comics. The evidence lies chiefly in the fact that superhero comics featuring black male superheroes as their primary characters have historically underperformed commercially, even with the lower sales expectations that obtain for post–Golden Age comics. Black male superheroes in their own comics generally don't sell very well relative to the majority of white superhero titles, and no title centrally featuring a black superhero has yet had the ongoing commercial presence of Superman, Batman, Captain America, Spider-Man, etc.

The phenomenal ticket-sales and pop-culture-zeitgeist success of the 2017 *Black Panther* movie—which coincided with the 2016 restart of the fifth iteration of *Black Panther* comics, written by MacArthur Genius

Award winner Ta-Nahesi Coates—may ultimately make the Panther the exception to this rule. But *Black Panther* series (including its first iteration, *Jungle Action*) have begun with a flourish and then been canceled for lack of sufficient sales four times previous, which means that, so far, the Panther has been the strongest evidence for this rule rather than its outlier. It's true that many, perhaps indeed the majority, of superhero titles are also canceled when the hero isn't represented as black or a person of color. It's also true that superhero titles featuring white *women* superheroes have traditionally suffered this fate, too, with Ms. Marvel / Captain Marvel having had almost as many cancellations and restarts as the Panther. Yet it is the case that none of the enduring single-hero titles that hail from the Golden Age of the 1930s and '40s, like Superman, Batman, and Captain America, or that hail from the Silver Age of the 1950s and '60s, like the Flash, Spider-Man, the Fantastic Four, Thor, and the Hulk, are represented as black or as a person of color.

The black superhero is always therefore an oddity, perpetually a lame duck anticipating his constitutionally mandated removal from protagonist status.

The names of black superhero characters once they arrived in the 1960s and '70s exemplify the underlining and emphasis on the *difference* of blackness in the comic-book world. The fact that comic strips are a visual medium means that the creators' drawings and color will prompt a reader to *see* that such a character is black—though as noted earlier with respect to the representation of whiteness in comics, this involves a not-uncomplicated series of illustrative choices for the artists and colorists. Note, for example, the peculiar cross-hatchings denoting shadow or melanin that Charles Schulz chose to place around the edges of the face of Franklin, the only black character among his round-headed cartoon philosophers in *Peanuts*.[15]

But the visual rendering of blackness was not enough of a representational gesture for the comic-book creators who crafted the early black superheroes. These creators often took the tack of also choosing a character name denoting blackness, as though offering instructions to the colorist who would enter the production process well after the drawing and writing were completed: *Black* Panther, *Black* Lightning, *Black* Goliath. We have already seen that the 1970s black version of Wonder Woman was called Nubia—and that even as that character has only fitfully reappeared since 1973, almost never with her Wonder Woman powers intact, she nevertheless retains and is identifiable by that name. This insistent tack is revealing in the way that someone's saying, "He's a male stripper," is revealing—the redundancy shows that the speaker assumes that strippers are by definition women; as the early naming of black superheroes reveals that superheroes are by definition white.

The conventions of representation that provide the ground for superhero-comic-book literacy, then, retain as a lingering effect the unacknowledged white-supremacist assumptions at work in the establishment of the genre in the late 1930s and '40s, when pioneer figures Superman and Captain Marvel burst onto the pop-culture scene. The black male superhero disturbs or fails to comply with assumptions established in the genre's infancy; he is not entirely legible within those conventions. Due to the "overabundance" of signifiers coalescing around a black superhero figure, readers are not quite able to see, or are resistant to seeing, black superheroes and taking them on board as they do with Spider-Man and Superman.

Brown's argument thus applies the well-established analysis whereby we understand the black male *figure* as exemplifying, indeed exaggerating as a thrilling spectacle, the contradictions and instabilities that inhere in the pairing of masculinity and power, of male bodies and the Phallus, in our patriarchal and misogynist cultures. The black male figure is generally described in cultural analysis as operating according to a kind of erection/castration paradox (to put the matter in vulgar Freudian terms). The figure is thus contradictory, at once hypermasculine and feminine. The powerful allure-and-threat of the black male figure's insistent phallic preening is also an index of its bearer's degraded social status, its position as object prone before an observing subject, which fears, desires, and aspires to control it. The two, degraded status and potential power, are inextricable from each other.

Here, then, in the realm of the consumption of black male superheroes, which is the consumption of images and narratives of fantasy, the black male figure, because he is at once ultramasculine and without masculine power, is both a spectacle (because he is different and cannot but shout his difference to all before whom he appears) and not fully visible (because he is different and the filters dictating what can be recognized do not recognize the peculiar data of his presence).

Black Superhero: Bad-Ass and Criminal

We can pose this problem that the black male figure as superhero presents at a slightly different angle, as well, which illuminates further the pressures besetting black male superheroes and throwing up hurdles to the successful elaboration of such a fantasy. Filmmaker Reginald Hudlin, the cocreator of commercially successful films centrally featuring African Americans, such as *House Party* (1990) and *Boomerang* (1992), took over a retooled *Black Panther* title in 2005. In an afterword Hudlin wrote for a collection of his first six issues, he describes the guiding principle of his vision of *Black Panther* and what he believed would probably ensure the title's success. Hudlin says he was determined to align the Black Panther with what he saw to be most appealing about black male cultural icons in the "post-integration, post-Reagan" hip-hop era: black male cultural icons were bad-asses, Hudlin observes, and Black Panther needed to be bad-ass, too. Hudlin writes that what Spike Lee, P. Diddy, "Malcolm X, Miles Davis and Muhammad Ali, all have in common, is the knowledge that the act of being a black man in white America is an inherent act of rebellion. They are WILLING to be bad@$$es. . . . That's what hip hop is all about. Being a bad@$$. Everyone wants to be a bad@$$. That's why white kids have always loved black music. . . . Black music is the music of bad@$$es." And "The *harder* the Panther is, the more appealing he is to both black AND white audiences."[16]

It's tempting to quibble with Hudlin's reading of the history of black music pre-hip-hop and undercut his general cultural observation. We might counter by tracing a genealogy of his point of view back to like-minded comments made by the mid-1960s LeRoi Jones. Jones (before becoming Baraka) wrote when there was a prevailing tradition of images of black males that were rather more castrated than erect, and far from bad-ass—which Jones's essays, poems, and plays often strove with all his rhetorical might to overcome. Nevertheless, Hudlin's reasoning and choice of how to depict a venerable superhero character that he was tasked with making popular highlights for us the narrow gamut that the black male figure runs, and demonstrates another of the various traps which that narrow range lays for conceiving black superheroes. Hudlin assumes and tries to work productively with the spectacularity of the figure of the black body, the fact that its visibility is produced as an indica-

CAN THE BLACK SUPERHERO *BE*? | 101

tion of difference that signifies hyperembodiment (with its implication of being inversely possessed of intellectual capacities) and/or "perverse" sexuality, elements that Hudlin could mine in creating the fantasy image of a *bad-ass* capable of dispatching any number of foes and villains— and, à la the Blaxploitation hero, attracting more than his fair share of adoring women.

But though a superhero beats up villains, a superhero in its basic conception isn't necessarily a bad-ass, while a *villain* or an *antihero* very often can be one. The claim of the black male figure to bad-ass-ness owes a debt to histories of rebellion, as Hudlin notes, but it is also owed to the nigh-systematic production of the black male figure as exemplifying a difference so alien that it justifies, even seems to compel, surveillance, policing, imprisoning, and assassinating. The paradox at this angle simply reconfigures its basic terms: the black male is an "inherent" rebel in "white America," which is thus to wield a kind of power, but the fact that he cannot but appear so on the stage of an America rendered white by his presence is the very achievement, indeed perhaps the foundational achievement, of white-supremacist conventions of representation and perception. The black male bad-ass is also thus a *criminal*.

It's difficult to overstate, and difficult too to fully encompass, the extent to which the equation of blackness and criminality tangles the knot of signification presented by the black superhero—female as well as male. The black hero runs counter to that strain of superheroic ethos that's all about the celebration and mythologizing of policing. The great majority of Superman's and Batman's early adventures involved hunting down bank robbers and murderers and other criminals, such that in many ways they were, and yet remain eighty-odd years on, costumed superpolice.

We begin to see, then, how the superhero is constitutively white insofar as whiteness is defined by, and is the offer of, innocence. To be or to have innocence is to be free of guilt, and to be free of guilt is to be constitutionally insulated from the consequences of harmful actions. To be innocent or guilt-free is never to have engaged in harmful actions (which is why it can be ascribed to the constitutionally irresponsible: children), or to have such harmful actions purged ("redeemed" or "forgiven," notions obviously highly charged by Christian mythology in Western and Western-dominated cultures). The latter, the purging of accountability for consequence, is most efficiently accomplished via the allocation of overweening responsibility to a *guilty* party, whose presence and repeated condemnation thus secures the other party's claim to innocence. The fusion of innocence versus guilt with whiteness versus blackness has of course been accomplished in history with all the vicious obsessive determination that our political, economic, educational, and cultural institutions could have brought to bear on that project—so evidently vital to the making of modernity—and continues to be feverishly, bloodily reiterated, primarily though not only via police violence, in the present.

To illuminate the machinations of innocence, guilt, and racial marking, I refer us to philosopher J. Reid Miller's *Stain Removal: Ethics and Race* (2016). Miller challenges the enshrined conviction that ethics is a field of inquiry without necessary purchase on the racialized character of lived realities and thus ideally without antiblack bias. Miller exposes how a racially "neutral" ethical valuation can never be honestly proposed: imported into, and constitutive of, ethical categories themselves, is a foregoing valuation, a valuation that is newly inherited with each birth into the social world, as *race*. Miller carefully examines the biblical story of the curse of Ham, the son of Noah, mythological progenitor of post-Adam humankind, sifting through commentaries and teachings on the story that Miller argues establish it as a foundational text in the development of Western epistemes. The myth of Ham, as we know, has been deployed both to "explain" the otherwise apparently inexplicable presence of "black" people on the Earth and to justify their enslavement.

Of central import for Miller in the story of the curse of Ham is the fundamentally formative role played by inheritable guilt in giving meaning to the category of the human. Criminality founds the human. And the inheritable nature of criminality founds the notion of race. Miller shows that in the story of Ham, one *is* criminal not because of an act, but rather as a function of status over which one has no control, which is the nature of inheritance and legacy. Key here is that the law precedes the crime; the law makes the act a crime by designating the actor a criminal. Examining fundamental prohibitions that "Thou shalt not kill" and the incest taboo, Miller writes,

> "Murder" and "incest" . . . are . . . conceivable as such only as what the law has already thematized as perceptive possibilities. If, therefore, the

law does not merely judge these acts as crimes but simultaneously and actively "founds" them, this could occur only via the identification of phenomena as criminal within an existing economy of value. Moreover, even if a crime or its anterior prototypes *could* generate directly a law it still could not found *the* law: that which remains . . . a vast yet shallow procedural technology whose manipulability—that by which one could think and act "outside" or against the law—confirms it [the law] as an inessential apparatus rather than a worldly expression of value.[17]

Ham's crime, for which he was punished by the curse of servitude and degraded status relative to his brothers, apparently involves the obscure offense of seeing his father naked, but otherwise is never satisfactorily detailed in the biblical texts or in their commentaries. What is important in the story is that Ham is given the position of bearing a guilt, however mysterious in origin or dimension, that is henceforward inherent to his being and that then is borne as an inherent "stain" by those on whom Ham's *role* is imposed down through the ages. That it is the mythical Ham and his mythical lineage of descendants who bear the "stain" of criminality, without which there can be no ethics, is arbitrary; it could have been someone else, some other lineage, some other race. But it is this very arbitrariness that entrenches the power that orders human relations according to hierarchies and according to chosen "values," that is, the fundament of ethics.

Thus,

> The crime of Ham does not receive from the law a name upon its commission. . . . The transgression does not violate a rule, formula, or principle but rather strikes at the very source or possibility of rulemaking, threatening the assemblage of the law-producing machine. . . . Ham . . . represents . . . [a] means by which power is not so much redirected as it is enchanted in its effects. In a drunken display of indiscretion, the law, like Noah, lies exposed; but this revelation in which there is nothing to reveal is necessary for its acquisition of a "body." The stain of value . . . generates discovery of the "body of law" in its naked or pure state of "natural law"—a nakedness covered and defended by its progeny who must invoke routinely that *unstained purity* as the law's original and authoritative subjectively constituting force.[18]

Miller's readings of the many versions of the Ham myth strongly suggest that the structural possibility of subjectivity is subjectivity's antagonistic pairing with criminality. This criminality is apportioned to Ham's lineage (the black) as the mode of confirming its opposite's "blessings"—though even the blessed are never free from the precarity of being swept into criminality, because criminality is what determines and safeguards the privileges of blessing by serving as their limit. In Miller's reading, all subjects of the West's imperially created globe stand or take shape as subjects *in relation to criminality*, but Ham's lineage is definitely "cursed" with the burden of taking shape as almost coterminous with criminality, rather than in distinction to it.

In this light, we can hazard that the superhero figure captures our collective imaginations in part by partaking of and playing out in bright colors and grand Kabuki gestures the drama of the Subject and his defining criminal, of Noah and his blessed sons defined by Ham and his cursed descendants. The superhero as figure performs *as a fantasy-act* the pleasures in fantasy and the offer via fantastic aspiration (insofar as identification is the pivot of the reader's engagement with the superhero) of *innocence*—"unstained purity," which, naturally, needs its guilty opposite in order to be innocent. The superhero is violent, yes, and he is engaged in fantastically consequential acts of beating others up, but those others, the villains, are the guilty—whose very names and modes of appearance and structural position in comic-book narratives indicate that their raison d'être is to harm the innocent.

The hero in turn *becomes* the innocent by receiving the villain's harms *or* by violently punishing the villain—not only for his actions but, in a way that passes through the reader's consciousness without comment or question because it is so unexceptional, for *being* the villain. The villain is a kind. The villain, when the map of his story is held up against the map of Western ethics as Miller sees it, is playing the role of the criminal race. This structure of story, repeated weekly in countless variations decade upon decade, can—or must—in this light be seen as a vigorous performance of the fantasy of whiteness: thus the superhero is constituting or effecting whiteness in the realm of fantasy: the superhero is doing (in a minor way) and *being* (in a major way) whiteness as a fantasy-act.

Black Superhero: Monster

The black male figure is of course often criminal or menacing, especially if he is presented as "strong" or "powerful." His power is not infrequently in his criminality and his threat, which is what Hudlin implies.

The Marvel horror-comic superhero character Blade provides an example of how all these matters get knotted up in the practice of conceptualizing and presenting a black superhero. The vampire-hunting part-vampire Blade was the lead character in a three-movie film franchise starring Wesley Snipes (*Blade*, 1998; *Blade II*, 2002; *Blade: Trinity*, 2004). Blade is an example therefore of the Hudlin bad-ass black male hero, and was a precursor in film to the zeitgeist cultural apotheosis of Black Panther. Blade's spike of popularity in the late '90s and early 2000s did not appear to translate into lasting strength of presence in the imaginations of superhero-comic-book readers, however. As of yet, the character has enjoyed no title of his own that was not either a miniseries or canceled for lack of sufficient sales, though Blade frequently guest-stars in other popular series such as *Deadpool*, and as of this writing, he has been a recurring cast member in *The Avengers* and a lead in the new team series *Strikeforce*.

Blade was originally a supporting character—and nemesis—of Dracula in the 1970s Marvel horror-comics series *Tomb of Dracula*, written by Marv Wolfman and drawn by the great Gene Colan (figures 2.2 and 2.3). In this first incarnation, the character was a more or less normal human being rather than a superhero—appropriately enough, since *Tomb of Dracula* was not a superhero series, even if superheroes occasionally guest-starred in it. Blade's visual signature—the elements by which he was distinguished from other figures on the pages of the comics, not a few of whom carried wooden stakes just like he did—was brown-colored skin tones and a short afro, and a set of clothing choices that appeared to do the work of racial marking in that they were faintly redolent of Blaxploitation film icons Shaft and Superfly: these included a short, sometimes-green, sometimes-brown peacoat (supposedly leather, though it never looked it) and green goggles (evidently to help him see at night when hunting vampires).

Blade's raison d'être was a vengeance mission: a vampire had killed his mother, and he was determined to eradicate the species from the Earth.

Figure 2.2. Blade's first appearance in *Tomb of Dracula* #10 (1973). (Gene Colan, artist)

Figure 2.3. Gene Colan's Blade, in *Tomb of Dracula* #45 (June 1976). (Marv Wolfman, writer)

In pursuit of his revenge, Blade struggled with a doppelganger who was, in fact, a vampire that had been mysteriously created via mysterious nineteenth-century German superchemistry at the behest of Deacon Frost, the same vampire who murdered Blade's mother. For a few issues of *Tomb of Dracula*, this doppelganger killed the original Blade and managed to somehow absorb Blade's memories and knowledge. But this challenge to Blade's identity and mortality was soon rectified by the timely magical assistance of the Son of Satan—a half demon with father issues and hence a superhero in his own right. When *Tomb of Dracula* came to its end after about seventy issues, Blade and his green goggles and vampire-hunting heroics sank into comics limbo with it.

In the movie franchise and in the comic-book appearances inspired by the films' success from the late 1990s onward, Blade became what the comic character had fought not to be, a vampire-human hybrid—thus, in two senses of the word, revamped. This new, more existentially troubled Blade became retroactively the result of Deacon Frost biting Blade's mother while Blade was in utero. The filmmakers and Snipes chose a number of visual and behavioral alterations in order to impress upon viewers Blade's more highly charged and now superheroic status—as well as his otherness, his *difference*, which was, as it turned out, the primary source of his power and superheroism, more so than vengeance and the pursuit of justice. Blade's look was transformed: the brown/green leather peacoat and goggles became sexy tight leather pants and a flowing cape-like black leather duster coat; the original Blade's '70s afro became what appeared at the time as a 1980s-style fade (the fade not yet having had the renaissance it currently enjoys), with a widow's peak ever more severe with each subsequent movie. Blade's persona, previously voluble and unconvincingly hip during the talky thrashings he would administer to the evil undead, became Hudlinesque bad-ass, his face always stony or clenched in inexpressive-to-angry expression and his speech laconic and replete with growls and grunts. Plus the revamped Blade sported the big muscles of a bona fide superhero (the old one's leather jacket was too loose to discern much by way of physiognomy), he bristled with exotic weaponry, and he had big fangs.

Figure 2.4, from the cover of one of the short-lived series inspired by the movies, is an apt rendering of Snipes et al.'s redo of the character. There and in figures 2.5, 2.6, and 2.7 from the comic, we can observe

Figure 2.4. *Blade* cover image from a 1998 short-lived series. (*Blade* #2, November 1998; Bart Sears, artist)

Figure 2.5. Cover image from another short-lived *Blade* series. (*Blade* #1, vol. 1, December 1999; Bart Sears, artist)

Figure 2.6. Splash page image from *Blade* #5 (vol. 2), September 2002 (Steve Pugh, artist; Christopher Hinz, writer)

Figure 2.7. Back cover image for *Blade: Sins of the Father* (2007). (Marko Djurdjevic, artist)

the way that Blade's superhero image steps into that narrow range of bad-ass appeal allowed to the black male figure. The authors of Blade's look clearly mine the black male figure's tendency to signify threatening difference itself—and thus frequently to appear in various discourses as alien, nonhuman, or animal—into a constitutive aspect of Blade's superhero power. The contrast with the appearance of the Superman paradigm is evident. Blade's post-film-franchise revamped look emphasizes his being other than human, while Superman, who is also not human, passes for human, albeit human of a white paragon sort.

The emphasis on Blade's vampire nature in his *look* can be said to tap into the menagerie of grotesque images commonly used to elicit audience discomfort in the horror genre. In this respect, Blade takes up an aspect that the *other* paradigmatic superhero, Batman, was originally meant to exemplify (though in Batman's case, with only occasional success throughout the character's long history)—that of being frightening, presumably to his enemies but also, in the thrilling way of horror, to his readers. But this representational tactic is given a particular twist in Blade, in that it is the black male body—always already borderline monstrous—that is the bad-ass hero, a hero who is visually as or even more terrifying and more potentially productive of nightmares and horror than the vampires he hunts.

In the movies, especially the first entry, most of the villains, including Deacon Frost, played by the slim, seraglio-eyed Stephen Dorff, are dressed chicly in nightclub attire and bright colors and look more or less like the attractive young white people usually cast as victims in a slasher flick. (Deacon Frost in the comics was a white-bearded old man, depicted wearing a kind of shapeless robe that completed his vaguely biblical look.) Snipes, whose good looks and smoldering onscreen sexiness made him more than adequate to play romantic and heroic leads on several occasions, is in the film's reconceptualization of the comic-book character a different genre of black male body, one that is the site of discomfort with an erotic frisson, and perhaps of horror (with its usual erotic frisson).

The comic-book images repeat and actually push this representational tactic farther, as though making up for the lack of audible growls in Snipes's onscreen performance with elaborate visual disfigurements. Thus the post-'70s *popular* Blade is both the monster of whom the audience is horrified and the hero who slays the monster. His figuration at once capitulates to and exploits the familiar erection/castration paradox.

Blade is an extreme, but he is not alone in the universe of comic-book black superhero depictions in being *other* and inhuman in his appearance and in tending to be depicted as less than Superman-handsome. Note figures 2.8 and 2.9—cover renderings of the first black superhero, Black Panther, at his most cat-like, and you'll recognize that the hero with whom he's most closely visually identified, Batman, boasts greater contrast in costume colors and a partially visible, and therefore humanizing, face.

Along parallel lines, but with more subtle references to monstrosity, we see in figure 2.10 a 1973 cover of *Luke Cage, Hero for Hire*. Cage is the often-parodied but also beloved paradigmatic 1970s black hero, crafted by creators who doubtless spent instructive time watching Blaxploitation films. Not unlike Blade in his original version, his attire was a costumey noncostume, minus the typical cape, domino mask, or cowl. Cage wore a canary-yellow shirt, blue pants, yellow boots, an iron chain as a belt, and an iron headband to accent his short afro. (A well-crafted and generally well-received Netflix dramatic series—reported to be the fourth-most-watched show on the streaming service in its 2016 first season—adapted the character into live-action film capture. Among many other knowing nods to the various credibility-busting aspects of the 1970s comic-book series, the series lampooned the comic's yellow-and-blue attire when Cage, played by the beautiful Mike Colter, was forced to don an absurd yellow shirt in one episode.) In figure 2.10, Luke Cage looks more like the monstrous Hulk than the heroic Superman, complete with clenched, menacing facial expression, quite unlike Superman's typical splash-page serenity.

Underlining the general stress marking Cage's appearance is the fact that his signature yellow shirt is being bullet-flayed from his body, so that the achieved color effect of his "black" skin is exposed. Indeed the ripping of Cage's clothes (mostly his shirt, but sometimes his pants were shredded as well) and the exposure of the muscular dark-skinned body beneath was arguably *itself* Cage's "costume" for the bulk of his early appearances. Certainly it was a signature visual trope of Luke Cage the superhero—like Batman backgrounded by shadows or perching on a

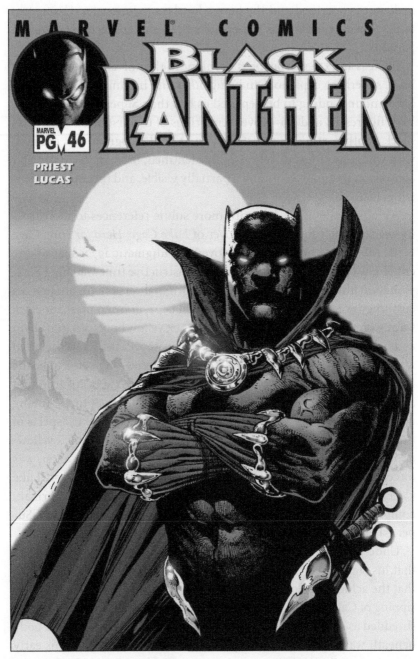

Figure 2.8. The Black Panther by Jorge Lucas on the cover of *Black Panther* #46 (vol. 3), September 2002.

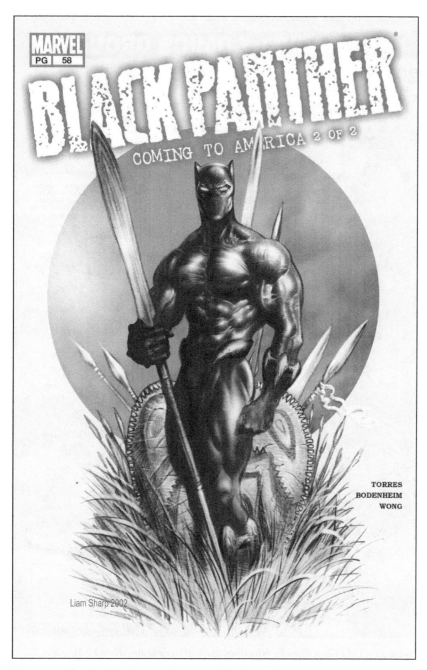

Figure 2.9. The Black Panther on the cover of *Black Panther* #58 (vol. 3), June 2003. (Liam Sharp, artist).

Figure 2.10. *Luke Cage, Hero for Hire* loses his shirt once again. (*Hero for Hire* #16, December 1973; Billy Graham, artist)

rooftop. Of the first twenty-five issues of *Luke Cage, Hero for Hire* (re-named after issue 16 as *Luke Cage, Power Man*), which appear between the issue dates of June 1972 and June 1975, I count thirteen covers depicting Cage's shirt and other clothing being ripped from his body. Within the pages of the first twenty-five issues, only twelve do *not* show Cage's shirt being ripped away (though the thirteen where Cage's clothes are being ripped off inside the comic are not necessarily always the same comics as those where Cage's shirt is ripped on the cover).

The ostensible logic justifying the repetition of Cage's clothes being ripped was that his superpower is his diamond-hard skin. To acquire this power, Cage agreed to be subjected to a scientist's dangerous experimental treatment, because he hoped doing so would earn him parole from prison, where Cage languished on trumped-up charges. (In order to receive his power-granting treatment, Cage had to be naked—of course—and this was depicted with shadows artfully covering the figure's crotch. This scene was pivotal in issue 1 and repeated whenever Cage's origin was recounted; I have not counted issue 1 or any of its replays as one of the issues in which Cage's clothes are flayed.)

This superpower, essentially a take on Superman's fabled invulnerability, allowed Cage to be seen with bullets bouncing off his chest just as they always bounced off Superman's. Unlike Superman, however, Cage's clothes lacked the resistance to bullets that is evidently a property of Kryptonian flying togs. In a bid for the "realism" that Superman's adventures fighting-in-costume lacked, when Cage was shot or knifed or ray-blasted, as he *always* was, Cage's clothes could not and did not survive. This was, however, a dictate of realism that had been bypassed in the depiction of the iconic Marvel Comics heroes the Fantastic Four, whose clothing morphed with the changes of their bodies (stretching, invisibility, bursting into flame) and kept their modesty intact. This representational convention maintained the Fantastic Four's depictions within the strictures of the Comics Code Authority, presumably, but was explained in the comics stories to be the result of the scientific genius of clothing made with "unstable molecules." (In a typical Marvel Comics crossover, Cage meets the Fantastic Four and their resident scientific genius, Mr. Fantastic, in issue 9 when Cage battles the Fantastic Four's archnemesis, Dr. Doom. He borrows a rocket to fly to track down Doom, but neither asks for nor is offered a canary-yellow shirt made with unstable molecules.)

The availability of the figure of the black body to "pornotroping," as Hortense Spillers elegantly terms it, is obvious here.[19] But let's place aside—for the moment—the meanings and possibilities for imaginative flight that coalesce around superhero-comic storytelling that repeatedly relies on unclothing a black male superheroic body in comics read by a great many if not a majority of consumers who were white, male, and young.

It is noteworthy that the defining visual insignia of this superhero character is to recur to the slashing of his shirt. As though this repeated shirt-slashing and body-baring were a stand-in for the violence directed against black male bodies in practices of lynching and routinized punishments of slavery, imprinted in the American cultural consciousness. As though the violence of ripping his clothing apart were a kind of counterweight necessary to render more appealing or more *believable* the concept of a black man possessed of superheroic power, the other side of a coin needed to make the currency of the image recognizable for the exchange of fantasy inherent to the commercial life of the comics industry. As though the writers and artists gauge that we readers need, or perhaps simply crave, an *underlining*, a reassuring or bracing reminder, of the black superhero's blackness: that is, if we can't get what it's deemed we need in the character's name—"Luke Cage," "Hero for Hire," and "Power Man" lacking the signal "Black" that is so conveniently appended to the Panther, the Lightning, the Goliath, and lacking the inherent blackness of "Nubia" or the telltale minstrel flavor of "Whitewash Jones"—then the character's costume must be ripped away to reveal the color of the fantasized "skin" underneath: this, in a universe of disbelief-suspensions and shared imaginative conceits where a superhero's costume is the very thing that *shows* us they are a superhero if they happen not to be doing something clearly superheroic in a given panel (like flying, or punching through a wall).

At every turn, what we see is that an *adjustment* in expectation, a reframing and rethinking gesture, must be made in the text or the image or both where the black superhero has the temerity to appear. The superhero is white; when or if they aren't, new visual vocabularies or nomenclatorial legerdemain must be put into play. Or so the creators of the superheroes have apparently gambled.

Black Superhero: Power to the People?

The adjustment needed in the minds of the creators of the white (male) paradigm superhero, of their later followers, and of their imagined readers and buyers—at least as evinced by their creations—is not only visual and textual. A *conceptual* adjustment is also needed. Luke Cage's problem (and Black Panther's and Blade's) might well be that as a black figure he's confined by the history that produces blackness, a history that a range of shorthand cultural references renders into a history of defeat and loss and suffering.[20] In this vein, we might surmise that part of what prepared the warm reception for Superman in the imaginations of millions of readers is that he arose alongside the World War II triumph of US military and economic dominance and the post–World War II United States' arrogant international exportation of US cultural products: thus the triumphs of superheroes in the fight against evil on the comic-book page were, and still are, secured in the readers' imaginations by the perceived political, economic, and military triumph of the nationality (and people or race) of which the hero is a *super* representative. Given such a context, it's difficult, then, to pose even an edgy antihero character like Blade, even in the postintegration, post-Reagan hip-hop era, in which Hudlin detects a tendency to worship the black male bad-ass. This is because by simple dint of the character's blackness, he is tethered to a history in which triumph has by and large not been secured in reality or in the readers' imaginations. (Again, he is a bad-ass insofar as he is an inherent dissenter from an order from which he is a dissenter because he does not control it.) Blade is a *super* representative of a historically subordinated or defeated group or, at least, a group that is so perceived: How can comic-book creators, fantasy purveyors, and we who consume their creations as templates for our own fantasies imagine a powerful black hero who is triumphant, given such a history? And if he is truly powerful, why does he not use his power to transform the history he lives through to effect justice for his people?

Three ways to solve the problem:

One way is for such a hero not to be noble in his intentions, that is, for him to be shady, quasi-criminal—as Luke Cage originally was. The way the character's creators, Archie Goodwin (the writer of *Hero for*

Hire) and George Tuska (the artist), both white men, conceived Cage's origin story, Cage was put in prison for a crime he didn't actually commit. (The inker for most of the first twelve issues was Billy Graham, who was black; Graham was the sole credited artist for issues 13, 14, and 15.) The story that Goodwin and Tuska invented was that Cage's compadre Willis Stryker planted narcotics in Cage's home to punish Cage for stealing the affections of a woman they both desired, Reva. But prior to this Stryker and Cage had become bosom buddies—"closer than brothers," Cage testifies in issue 1 (see figure 2.11)—by surviving the "streets" and "slums" of Harlem together. Their mutual survival involved engaging in petty crime: the panel art shows Cage and Stryker counting the money of a purse they've stolen, knocking out a white man with a stick, and grabbing a fistful of bills from a cash register. It is during the time that Cage forges his brotherhood with Stryker that Cage becomes a proficient and feared fistfighter, earning "street gang leader" status due to his pugilist skills.

The differences are striking between these images and those of baby Superman lifting a tractor on a farm, or of the mild-mannered Clark Kent in his glasses choirboy-ing it up in the offices of the *Daily Planet*, or of the images of wealthy Bruce Wayne and his parents accosted by a similar kind of criminal (a mugger) that Cage is depicted to be. The story of Luke Cage's origin, the story, that is, that introduces him to readers and that justifies his powers and his position as a superhero, is a story of criminality, however petty. The story of how Luke Cage becomes a hero is a story that partakes of and cements one of the most widely believed dictums of white-supremacist meaning-making—*blacks commit more crime; blacks are criminals*. In precisely this way, Cage is a *super* representative of his race. What makes him a *black* superhero, then, is his criminality. Luke Cage's criminality is the past of his origin, the kernel and seed of his elaboration and unfolding: it is through this gate—a bloodstained one, à la Frederick Douglass?—that Luke Cage enters into the sphere of imaginary superhero fantasy. Cage's origin is in criminal associations.

It's true that the trajectory of Cage's development is that he breaks free from criminal activity in his journey toward heroism, after a purgatorial sojourn in prison. But it must be said that even the break from criminality is sidetracked by the character's creators' "realist" innovation

Figure 2.11. Luke's criminal past remembered in *Luke Cage, Hero for Hire* #1 (June 1972): 9. (Archie Goodwin, writer; George Tuska, artist)

of having Cage hang out a shingle as a "hero for hire," rather than offer his services gratis to a needful public. This innovation was actually a retread, the same tack having been tried and quickly discarded within the space of a single issue by spider-bitten Peter Parker, who gives up trying to make money with his powers once he learns via tragic loss that with great power comes great responsibility. Cage, however, holds onto the idea of mercenary heroism much longer, as though, in order to answer the questions raised by the very concept of a black superhero, he has to remain connected to his "hustler" past for a time, fully as much as he has to be stripped of his clothing for a time. (After issue 25, Cage's episodes of having his clothes flayed from his body decrease.) Thus the condition for Cage's becoming a hero—where "condition" refers both to a state or mode of being, and to a prerequisite or stipulation without which the performance of a thing cannot proceed—is his criminality. Following J. Reid Miller's observations of the concept of the guilty category as preceding and founding the law that apportions guilt to acts and persons in that category, we would expect nothing different.

Black Superhero: Victim of History

A second possibility for conceptually appending "black" to "superhero" is that the black superhero can be a *victim* en route to the acquisition of his powers, so that his history recapitulates that of the people whom he represents. In this way, the operation of that history remains undisturbed, offering no challenge to our imaginations of what blackness signifies and thus neatly cordoning off avenues of imagination along which we might travel toward blackness with hitherto-undreamt meanings—or, for that matter, toward conceptualizing the superhero in ways we haven't before. Blade exemplifies this tack. Like Superman, he is an orphan, whose lost parentage is the source of his superheroic difference: Superman is the son of aliens from Krypton, Blade the offspring of a vampire. Both are made heroes by leveraging what is imagined to be a biological difference in order to fight against evil. Essentially like Superman but to a much lesser extent, Blade is super strong and fast and is always able to heal from injuries (i.e., he is invulnerable). Yet this triumphant and powerful and even, in fantasy or ideological terms, paradigmatically (white) *American* position—escaped or exiled from the Old World, willfully remade stronger and better in the New—is for Blade the result of a *curse*: a vampire bit his mother and/or murdered his father, depending on the version of his origin. The curse is of course an apt, if never fully adequate, abbreviation of the position of blackness and black people in that quintessential American mythology of rebirth: this part of our common ancestry, the large portion that "arrived" in order to be made black, did not escape and was not precisely exiled—rather, they were condemned to be made anew. If the black hero is a victim (as Cage is, too, in addition to being a criminal), then the white-supremacist order requires no imaginative restructuring.

Here in comics as elsewhere, the historical and culturally sedimented truth of white-supremacist domination over black people becomes a stumbling block to the imagination of black characters possessed of power and to the imagination of blackness articulated to power. What this speaks to is that in addition to what Brown observes as the surfeit of signification that attends the black male image in superhero comics, there is also the conceptual problem of *imagining* a *black* hero in comics when white supremacy is or has been the actual order.

Contrasting this second tack with the first, it appears that it is not only the *ontological* attributes of blackness—that is, to *be* black is to *be* criminal—that must be kneaded to fit the shape of a superhero concept that otherwise resists or cannot accommodate such attributes. The stories that white creators of black superhero characters have told provide the trace of yet another level of conceptual wrestling: what is confronted in this second tack is the presence of a *history*, a social history, which the putative blackness of the superhero summons inexorably to the comic-book page.

In this light—revising my observation earlier—an ontological attribute of blackness *is* history. As Fanon describes in that fateful moment on the train when his Black Everyman persona is assailed by the cry, "Look, a Negro!": "I couldn't take it any longer, for I already knew there were legends, stories, history, and especially . . . *historicity*," Fanon declares.[21] Historicity attends the interpellation of the black man. In our context, this observation suggests that a story told and/or imaged in superhero comics where blackness or black(ened) bodies appear(s) must be a story importing into it a certain referentiality, a pointing *toward* meaning and story beyond the simple appearance of the black character (inevitably a supporting character, of secondary importance): the black image and body is *different* from the norm (it is queer) and thus compels explanation or storytelling devices that situate its nonnormative presence—hence, it conjures the presence of history. Or we might, following Fanon, say that the appearance of blackness carries the weight, otherwise unacknowledged, a subsurface undertow, of the histories that produce whiteness and blackness but that the effectuation of whiteness necessitates remain concealed and ignored: whiteness is masked as "normal" and hence requires no explanation; but whiteness does require blackness, somewhere and somehow, or else it will not be white, and part of blackness's function in securing whiteness is to carry the burden of signifying the historicity without which neither racial category has any meaning at all.

References to or evocations of history have no necessary purchase when the hero is colored "white." Indeed, a foundational premise of the (white) superhero is that the fantasy in which we as readers participate leaps beyond the limits of any particular historical condition. A man can only leap tall buildings in a single bound in an imagination unfettered by—or (to return us to Jerry Siegel and Joe Shuster and the origins of Superman) an imagination actively seeking relief from the fetters of—all the histories told and untold when humans have not flown. If the (white) superhero belongs anywhere in *time*, then it is to a posthuman future—or to another planet, where the extraterrestrial is the figure for the speculation of histories alternate to our own.

Regarding the latter, it would seem that the representational tactic of mining the ore of *alternate history* is richly promising, if we're trying to break through impasses of imagination when creating a black superhero or taking a black superhero up as the template for our own fantasy-acts. Surely one way to hurdle these problems is not to concede to the history that produces blackness as the victimized handmaiden of white supremacy but—since this is fantasy—to refuse the link between blackness and its particular history. Imagine a history that played out counter to our own. There is, after all, filmmaker Quentin Tarantino's *Inglourious Basterds* (2009) solution: You're creating fantasies, so why not make the story you tell have a history that diverges from the one we know? In Tarantino's film, Hitler, Goebbels, Goering, and the whole of the Nazi command were machine-gunned and burned to death in the makeshift crematorium of a theater fire in Paris in 1944 at the hands of an avenging Jewish woman and her black male friend (and perhaps lover) and employee.[22]

In the introduction to *Black Skin, White Masks*, Fanon writes, with a flourish, "Man's misfortune, Nietzsche said, was that he was once a child. . . . As painful as it is for us to have to say this: there is but one destiny for the black man. And it is white."[23] In that statement and in much of the argument of his first book, Fanon not only replaces a supposedly raceless but actually white/European normative account of child development within a patriarchal family with the history of racial formation. I understand him also to be describing the way that we are always, as I've written before, abject to the histories that precede and make us, imprisoned within a network and a frame and perhaps above all a language of "rules" and "the way it is" and "reality" that are not our creations or choices, but the sediment of preceding events and their calcification in practices and discourses that support and decree the continual repetition of those practices.

What is lovely to me about fantasy-acts is that it is possible to propose, to conceive, and to begin to flesh out a different rule and a different "way it is," which can *be* because the fantasy society occurs someplace and somewhen else, and its *history* is different. Instructive as to the project of this kind of motivated fantasy-act is another ringing statement of Fanon's "By Way of Conclusion" in *Black Skin*: "The problem considered here is located in temporality. Disalienation will be for those Whites and Blacks who have refused to let themselves be locked in the substantialized 'tower of the past.' For many other black men disalienation will come from refusing to consider their reality as definitive."[24]

Comics in its form, and not only in its superhero genre variety, provides a powerful tool for refusing to consider an unjust reality as definitive, precisely because it presents its information, stories, and effects in and on readers' minds by rendering temporality, and the problems entangled in the chains of linear temporality, as malleable. Hillary Chute, borrowing from cartoonists and comics-theorizing luminaries Art Spiegelman and Scott McCloud, observes, "Comics . . . most fundamentally, 'choreograph and shape time.' . . . *In the vocabulary of the comics, the other key element aside from the gutter is the panel, also known as the frame. Comics shapes time by arranging it in space on the page in panels, which are, essentially, boxes of time.*" Chute continues, "The conventions of comics would seem to dictate that each panel is a moment, . . . [but] time in comics . . . is *weirder than that.* The *weirdness* of time in comics is part of the medium's force as a storytelling form. . . . Comics has the ability to powerfully *layer* moments of time."[25]

Chute's observation here is primarily about the challenge in comics' representational *form* and representational tactics to temporality as we live it (i.e., the past is gone and irretrievable except via inexact and incomplete methods of reconstruction; only the present exists, etc.). Chute also guides us to an understanding of how we can—and do—*read* comics in ways that play with and refuse ordinary linear temporality.

When we try to find umbrella terms for the study of comics, we tend to privilege the sequential relation of comics' image-and-text boxes, as in Deborah Whaley's book title *Black Women in Sequence* (2015). But Chute, Spiegelman, and McCloud all suggest that sequentiality as it's generally understood may not actually account for or define comics. Here W. J. T. Mitchell describes a commonplace of comics reading: taking in the whole page at once, skipping ahead to the end, returning to savor and reread the earlier pages (the past of the story). Analyzing a thank-you note given to him in the form of a comics page by cartoonist Nathaniel McClennen, Mitchell notes, "So far my analysis of Nate's comic has emphasized its multiple temporalities and alternative pathways through sequences of images and words. But there is another way of looking at this work that is *specific, if not unique, to comics*, and that is

the possibility of seeing the whole thing as a unified, synchronic structure,
. . . a unified, yet internally differentiated body, playing upon temporal
sequence and spatial synchronicity."[26]

Following Chute's method of looking to the testimony of comics creators themselves, I find a passage in New Zealander Dylan Horrocks's
comic book *Hicksville* (2010) especially helpful for describing what's
useful about comics in working with what Fanon identifies as "the problem . . . located in temporality." *Hicksville* layers multiple stories: in the
main narrative, the reporter Leonard Batts travels to remote Hicksville
to make biographical inquiries about the hometown origins of a famous
comic-book creator named Dick Burger; this is laid alongside several
ministories in which favorite classic comic strips like *Peanuts*, *Tin-tin*,
and superhero comics are lovingly parodied, and in which Batts seems
to interact with Burger's creations in "real" life.

In one of the ministories, a character called "the New Zealander"
mimics Batts's investigative journey as he travels to "Cornucopia"—a
land bounteous in imagination, it appears—to interview "their greatest cartoonist, Emil Kópen." The New Zealander asks the sage comics
creator Kópen, "How is a comic strip like a map?"[27] Kópen, naturally,
speaks Cornucopt, helpfully translated for us into English with the help
of a third character, a woman who translates between the New Zealander and Kópen. In Cornucopt, the New Zealander learns, the word
for comics translates as "text-picture."

The conceit buttressing this exchange is that the world-famous cartoonist Kópen has previously referred to himself, somewhat mysteriously, as a cartographer. Nevertheless, the New Zealander's question
strikes an odd note, appearing to assume connections that no casual
reader of comics would be likely to make. Indeed, it is the kind of question asked by a more-than-casual reader, one who brings to the question
a set of conclusions about the centrality of sequence to comics form
and a clarity he thinks is commonplace about the metaphoric relation
of comics' formal sequentiality to the kinds of directions provided by
a map—enfolding within the choice of metaphor a conviction that the
relationship between a map and places in the world is one of transparent
accuracy.

I read this conversation as a dramatic staging of a philosophical and
formal question—or about philosophy of form? about the forms philoso-

phy can take?—which has to do with asking how a comic strip relates to that very "reality" that Fanon urges us to refuse. The philosophical and formal question is how a comic strip relates, then, to something that so profoundly *is* that it's the contours of the Earth we stand on; and this is thus a question about the relationship between the fantastic and the real.

The sage Emil Kópen replies to the New Zealander's question,

> They [comic strips and maps] are the same thing; using *all* of language—not only words or pictures. . . . Maps are of two kinds. Some seek to represent the location of *things* in space. That is the first kind—the geography of space. But others represent the location of things in time—or perhaps their *progression through* time. These maps tell stories, which is to say they are the geography of time. . . . I have begun to feel that stories, too, are basically concerned with spatial relationships. The proximity of bodies. Time is simply what interferes with that, yes? . . . The things we crave are either near us or far. Whereas time is about *process*. I have lived many years and I have learned not to trust process. *Creation, destruction.* These are not the real story. When we dwell on such things, we inevitably lapse into cliché. The true drama is in these relationships of space.[28]

The translator, perhaps speaking for the New Zealander, perhaps raising her own objections, interjects, "But a flame, even a touch, are processes, not things." Kópen answers, "But behind such processes, there is a stillness; and in that quiet exist spatial relationships which transcend time."[29]

This is a reckoning of comics form—which we must understand as therefore an account of *reading/seeing* comics, of the reader's active engagement with the formal properties of the comics and their contents—that may perhaps verge on the megalomaniacal or the messianic, appearing to claim for comics what only our guesses of divine or transuniversal perspective could boast. Nevertheless, combining Horrocks-via-Kópen with Spiegelman, McCloud, and Chute, we can surmise that the most conventional of comics storytelling devices need not lead to the most conventional representations of blackness: if comics form does not conform to linear temporality, if comics transcend time, if comics may delve beneath process to find stillness, then as a form, comics offer, and should indeed entice and encourage, opportunities to knock that devil history off his horned feet.

Comics' spatialization and thus transcendence as well as layering of time, comics' disarrangement of even the linearity of the sequence on which its structure relies, the queer temporal indeterminacy of the way comics tell stories and the way comics compel reading, all are useful tools for fantasy-acts. Comics can make historiography itself cartographic—what the reader and the comics creator both are enabled to do is to leap not just buildings but epochs, to scramble cause and effect across time. Rendering historiography in the mode of cartography can be aimed at Fanonian "disalienation," can bring forth keys for unlocking the iron-bound "tower of the past." And at the same time as one can come to comics with such goals in mind, the very reading of them can provide a demonstrative example, a "map," that unspools in the readers' minds the possibility of refusing reality.

As we know, such moves are entirely precedented in African American and African Americanist letters.

See Ashraf Rushdy's observations of how neo-slave narratives (the novels by African American authors that thematize slavery from the 1970s to the 1990s) repeatedly return to the trauma-curing tactic of reimagining traumatic events in a manner that empowers the traumatized:[30] For example, in Gayl Jones's *Corregidora* (1975), the protagonist Ursa's inheritance of the intractably traumatizing legacy of her foremothers' rape and forced incest at the hands of a Brazilian slave master—Ursa's own great-grandfather—imprisons Ursa in a kind of stuttering replay of her foremothers' lives. This cycle breaks when Ursa begins to reimagine the stories of her foremothers' assaults with a recognition of how pleasure as well as pain inhere in those experiences, and in her reimagination, she assumes a position to choose which (pleasure or pain) she desires. And in David Bradley's *The Chaneysville Incident* (1981), a folktale of fugitive enslaved black people who were reported to have killed themselves to avoid being recaptured is transformed from a story of despair and futile defiance to—from a West African cosmological point of view, adopted by the novel's narrator—a story of joyful reunion with beloved ancestors and a figurative return to Africa, once the narrator, a historian, reimagines the folktale as his own version of "real" history.

See also Saidiya Hartman's pathbreaking essay "Venus in Two Acts" (2008). Hartman calls for historians of enslavement to confront the violent erasure in the historiography of the slave trade and slavery of en-slaved black women's consciousnesses and being (such erasure being a foundational act of the trade, the practice, and the historiography that ac-counts for it) via the adoption of "critical fabulation," a practice that turns a gimlet eye to the authoritative claims of orthodox historical method:

> Is it possible to exceed or negotiate the constitutive limits of the ar-chive? By advancing a series of speculative arguments and exploiting the capacities of the subjunctive (a grammatical mood that expresses doubts, wishes, and possibilities), in fashioning a narrative, which is based upon archival research, and by that I mean a critical reading of the archive that mimes the figurative dimensions of history, I intended both to tell an impossible story and to amplify the impossibility of its telling, . . . laboring to paint as full a picture of the lives of the captives as possible. . . .
>
> The method guiding this writing practice is best described as criti-cal fabulation. "Fabula" denotes the basic elements of story, the building blocks of the narrative. A fabula, according to Mieke Bal, is "a series of logically and chronologically related events that are caused and experi-enced by actors. An event is a transition from one state to another. Actors are agents that perform actions. (They are not necessarily human.) To act is to cause or experience an event." . . .
>
> By playing with and rearranging the basic elements of the story, by re-presenting the sequence of events in divergent stories and from contested points of view, I have attempted to jeopardize the status of the event, to displace the received or authorized account, and to imagine what might have happened or might have been said or might have been done.[31]

These, however, are precedents for *us*. The creators of Luke Cage, of Blade, of the Black Panther, and of Nubia conceived their characters without the benefit of such examples—though it is probably not unfair to suppose they would have been unaware of this trend in African American letters even had it preceded them or been contemporaneous. Creators of black superheroes for Marvel and DC *might* have taken up the challenge to thoroughly or convincingly imagine black triumph via an alternate history in order to conceptualize their black superheroes. But often they didn't.

In this sense, the limitations I've been stumbling over trying to articulate "black" to "superhero" may be limitations enforced by chosen representational tactics, rather than due to the inherent properties of the superhero figure. Were these representational tactics inscribed within the figure of the black superhero in Marvel and DC comics because Luke Cage's, Blade's, and Nubia's creators were white and unconsciously or consciously inured to white privilege, with commitments unconscious or conscious to white supremacy such that they could not or would not dare imagine a black character unfettered by the subordinate status that white-supremacy requires, despite the powerful tools offered by comics form?

Doubtless, yes. An important example from comics history would tend to support drawing this conclusion, at least insofar as we can discern in this history comics creators being concerned not to challenge the white-supremacist assumptions and white privilege of their assumed readers.

In 1973—many of the seeds of my own personal fantasy-acts of anti-racist or anti-antiblack revisions and additions to the superhero figure were planted by superhero stories published during those early-1970s years—Marvel Comics debuted the character Killraven in *Amazing Adventures*. The second Marvel title of its name, *Amazing Adventures'* 1970s run had previously featured characters who played supporting roles in *Fantastic Four* (Black Bolt and the Inhumans) and *X-Men* (the Beast). In issue 18, Marvel offered readers a spin-off of a version of H. G. Wells's sci-fi classic *War of the Worlds*. "BASED ON CONCEPTS CREATED IN THE PROPHETIC NOVEL BY *h.g. wells!*" the cover proclaims.

The claim for Wells's late-1890s scientific romance, detailing an imperialist Martian invasion of England, as *prophetic*—whether viewed from 1973 or now—is obscure, unless the creators of the comic, in their attempt to make *Amazing Adventures* stand out on the newsstand where it competed with dozens of other titles, were taking too seriously the soon-to-be-full-fledged series's conceit and judged themselves as well as Wells to have precognitive powers. *Amazing Adventures, featuring War of the Worlds*, took place in the future—a future dated 2018 AD—in which Killraven, a white male freedom fighter wielding a sword in one hand and a futuristic laser gun in the other, fought the good fight against Martian colonizers who'd successfully enslaved the human race, after having failed their first attempt at conquest "more than a century ago" (i.e., when Wells's anti-imperialist fantasy was first serialized).

Killraven's visual signature was striking. He had long hippie-ish red hair and, unlike nearly every other male superhero at the time, wore very little clothing, at least in his first appearance: in figure 2.12, Killraven's knee-high boots and star-blazoned singlet with thin shoulder straps, laced with a bit of corset stringing that rendered ineffectively modest the singlet's deep skin-baring plunge from shoulder to the nether regions between navel and doll-smooth crotch, was the kind of costume more often given to heroes with "woman" or "girl" as part of their names.

This combination made Killraven a potentially volatile mash of butch masculine androgyny that hinted of the then-young gay liberation movement and of disco. Or more than hinted. As comics creator genius Grant Morrison, in his almost equally genius guise as superhero-comics historian, writes of similar costume developments during the 1970s in DC's *Legion of Super-Heroes*, "The modest Girl Scouts of the Legion of Super-Heroes were being made over by the artwork and costume design skills of artist Dave Cockrum into Studio 54 disco bunnies with bell-bottoms and bunches, belly cutaways, plunging necklines, and high-heeled, thigh-high Paco Rabanne space platforms. It was an equal opportunity era and the Legion's substantial gay following was catered to with new costumes for characters like Element Lad, Cosmic Boy, and Colossal Boy that emphasized lurid cutaway panels and acres of rock-hard exposed muscle."[32] Morrison's observations are of a period following Killraven's debut, and thus what Morrison describes of the Legion's costumes should be seen as following Killraven's influence. By my reading, Cosmic Boy's costume was first stripped down to its bare essentials in *Superboy* #215, with a cover date of March 1976, three years after Killraven first appeared (figure 2.13).

Thus, set in a future "prophesied" by H. G. Wells, and premised on a fanciful rewriting of the past in which Wells's fiction became a report of historical events (much as Orson Welles's celebrated radio-broadcast revision of the novel in 1938 was apparently taken to be a live news broadcast by many audience members), Killraven's *Amazing Adventures* fully partakes of comics' flexible play with temporality. We can see *Amazing Adventures* incorporating in its visual representational choices the

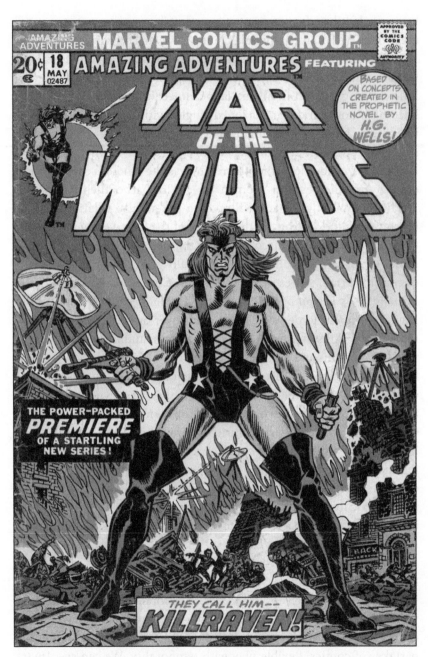

Figure 2.12. Killraven bares nearly all in *Amazing Adventures featuring War of the Worlds* #18 (May 1973). (Neal Adams, artist)

Figure 2.13. Cosmic Boy of the Legion of Super-Heroes follows Killraven in *Superboy starring the Legion of Super-Heroes* #215 (March 1976). (Mike Grell, artist; Jim Shooter, writer)

imagination of a future characterized by departures from early-1970s norms of gendered clothing—at least for its men—and, implied by these choices, a concomitant guess that such attire might reflect more "liberated" gender and sexual social arrangements in the future. These guesses responded to the post–Stonewall Rebellion, early-1970s present of the comics' creation, allowing Morrison to recall an identifiable "substantial gay following" for the Legion of Super-Heroes, a following that could be known to comics creators by the middle of the decade, when such a following of any number would probably have been difficult to identify, much less cater to, ten or twenty years prior.

Alterations in gender and sexual relations are often confluent with alterations in race relations. This is because the boundaries between so-called races, the concept of race itself, with all its delirium-inducing totems of "blood" and "lineage" and "purity" and so forth, cannot hold without constant policing of sexual relations: in particular, the coherence of a racial concept requires that women must be forced or cajoled into "choosing" to sexually reproduce with men bearing a similar phenotype to their own; otherwise, the phenotypes "mix," and the race loses its "purity," which is to say its identifiability.[33]

Accordingly, the Killraven comic's visual flirtation with queerness manifested most tangibly in a story element in which an interracial black-man/white-woman romance blossoms. (In light of the mutually constitutive entanglements between gender/sex and race I've just briefly mapped, the trajectory of this examination of Killraven comics suggests that interracial sexual and/or romantic relationships are themselves—in a world where a keystone of normativity is the reproduction of race—inherently queer.)

Don McGregor took over scripting *Amazing Adventures featuring War of the Worlds* in its fourth issue, when, as he describes in the preface to a collected edition of Killraven's comics appearances, the comic was assumed to be doomed. McGregor was a rising star and fan favorite among Marvel's writers because of his work on *Jungle Action*, a title that featured the Black Panther—about which more shortly. In the process of trying to save *War of the Worlds* from cancellation, McGregor decided to make Killraven's supporting characters, his band of "Freemen" fighting against the Martians, more individualized, with their own dramatic arcs. Among the most prominent of these changes was his decision to romantically pair the comic's one black male supporting character, M'Shulla, with a white female character, Carmilla Frost, giving rise to what would become famed (or infamous) as the first interracial kiss in mainstream comics.

(Quick side note on names here: McGregor didn't create the character M'Shulla, as the character was first named in issue 19, written by Marvel stalwart Gerry Conway. McGregor writes that he "suspect[s]" the name M'Shulla "came from the Parkway in the Bronx."[34] The Mosholu Parkway in the Bronx is a name or word from the Algonquin language. If McGregor is correct, Conway took a Native American name and gave it a faux-African tinge with an orthographic transformation, and the resultant sound of the name was suspiciously close to one of the few other black male characters one could find among Marvel's comics in 1973: T'Challa, the Black Panther. And is it possible that McGregor's selection of the character Carmilla *Frost*'s surname forewarned—or seeded the unconscious requirement—that her *whiteness* would be emphasized by her pairing with a character that visually and by nomenclature exemplified blackness?)

McGregor's creative decisions to pair the two secondary characters—Morrison describes the writer as "radical" and says that his "work burned with the holy fire of a just and loving wrath" and excited a "passionate" fan base[35]—were met with skepticism and racist resistance by his coworkers and his editors. "I know it's difficult for some people to know where this country was at in 1973–74," McGregor writes. "There were certainly no interracial couples in comics. There were certainly no gay couples in comics." (Again, note the rhetorical braiding here of alterations in the codes governing sexual and gender relations and those governing race relations.) In the short essay "Panther's Chronicles," McGregor's account of how he came to write the first series featuring the Black Panther, he succinctly details,

> It was a different time, the early '70s, and what many people take for granted now in storytelling media—and especially what can or can't be in comics—then was *verboten*. Writing about race, or sexual preferences other than heterosexual were virtually nil. In the world of comics these and other topics were considered a taboo.
>
> Many of the rules in comics are unwritten, but get inside the conclave, and they are there, some insidiously, some absurd, some shrewd. But the rules are there, and it didn't take long for me to begin to realize they shaped what I could do as a storyteller.[36]

Elsewhere in his recollection of his writing of Killraven stories, McGregor similarly notes,

> As I look back on it, I realize I was so naïve. I believed in the Bullpen [Marvel Comics' name for its collection of writers, artists, inkers, etc.]. I'd read about in the comics growing up. It was a creative environment, but the Hallowed Halls could be a minefield. I didn't realize that there . . . were people who would be prejudiced and *did not want any color but white in the books*, and certainly no intermingling between people of different races. . . .
>
> . . . If you pay attention, you'll note early on that there are scenes in *Amazing Adventures* where M'Shulla and Carmilla have a moment together, just the two of them. . . . Then, someone complained to an editor that if I were doing a "salt and pepper" relationship in "Killraven," he wanted off the book.[37]

This unnamed coworker and cocreator's racist threat ultimately resulted in McGregor appealing to the executive editor, the man whose name and work were strongly stamped on Marvel Comics' creations by the 1970s, and even more so now: Stan Lee. "I felt if I appealed to Stan's desire for Marvel to innovate, I could get his approval. Rumor had it that DC might do an interracial kiss in one of their romance comics," McGregor recalls, "so I told Stan, 'Wouldn't it be a shame if DC has an interracial couple before Marvel?' Well, Stan clearly didn't want that. . . . What a shame it would be if DC did it first when our fans loved Marvel being the more progressive company." Lee, though famed for his liberal (if often stridently anticommunist) screeds both in his "Stan's Soapbox" column that appeared in several titles and within the comics stories themselves, evidently was not at ease with being a racial trailblazer, at least not in this instance. "Stan asked, 'But does she have to [be] white, Don? Can't she be green?'" McGregor remembers. "Stan was concerned that some Southern states would hold the comic up at a PTA meeting, protesting what their kids were seeing."[38]

The cautionary picture that McGregor reports Stan Lee conjuring—the almost bizarre and certainly nonsensical idea of "a Southern state" sufficiently personified to wave around a comic at a PTA meeting (in that same state? in some other state?)—is interesting, suggesting the ways that a popular entertainment form dismissed as mere fantasy was nevertheless understood (and feared) by the industry's arguably most powerful editor—no doubt in light of the Comics Code Authority's many restrictions on what could be depicted.

In addition, Lee's rhetorical question pertains to what had been established at Marvel as a fairly common representational and editorial tactic. Along with Jack Kirby, Lee had created the X-Men, superheroes born with their powers and therefore mutants. For reasons never wholly logically coherent, mutants, despite being costumed just like other superheroes were and being engaged in the very same crime-busting superheroic acts of salvation of the nonsuperhero public, were shunned objects of prejudice because they were mutants, that is, because they were a different "race" or perhaps a different "sexuality." Thus stories written about the prejudice faced by the mutant X-Men—all of whom, originally, were depicted as racially white—could always be read, and were intended to be read, as partly about the prejudice faced by black people or other "minorities."

In this established Marvel tradition, it no doubt made sense to Stan Lee in 1973–1974 to deflect any unwelcome censorious attention that might be drawn to an interracial relationship in his comics by representing a metaphorical or fanciful interracial depiction—like a black man and a green woman. Indeed Lee's initial editorial decision was to allow the interracial kiss to occur (and thus beat DC to the punch) but to literally *color* the panel depicting the kiss in such a way as to obscure what was being represented. "Finally, it was decided . . . that the panel where M'Shulla and Carmilla kiss would be done in knockout colors," McGregor writes. "Essentially, that term means both characters would be done in one color, both of them purple, or something like that. This way, I guess, the thought was no one could hold the page up in high dudgeon and rant about race purity or whatever the hell it is they do."[39]

Ultimately McGregor along with his artist P. Craig Russell and colorist Petra Goldberg performed an end run around this decision, and the panel was not produced in knockout colors when issue 31 reached the stands, but was colored "naturally," with the races of the two characters conventionally denoted (figure 2.14).

I recount McGregor's recollection at length because it reveals the extent to which the everyday operation of comics creation under editorial direction has historically been undertaken with the assumption— not uncommon to arts and entertainment production across various media—that comics, immersed in fantasy as they are, should never dream dreams without white supremacy.

We are, after all, talking about two-dimensional figures drawn in pencil and ink and mass-reproduced on cheap newsprint paper (at the time), colored in by a pixelating process that at best imitated but could never represent with full accuracy even a narrow range of actual human skin tones. Somehow these two-dimensional drawings appeared to be a threat to "race purity" in the eyes of at least one of the comic's creators (evidently not the writer, penciller, or colorist; perhaps the inker, the letterer . . . ?)—so threatening, in fact, that this colleague of McGregor's threatened to quit work on the comic. And it was thought the drawings would *certainly* appear to be a threat to the politically powerful southern

Figure 2.14. *Killraven* characters M'Shulla and Carmilla's dangerous lip-lock in a story titled "The Day the Monuments Shattered": the first interracial kiss in superhero comics. (*Amazing Adventures* #31, July 1975)

reader-slash-PTA-provocateur imagined by one of the industry's premier editors.

Since M'Shulla and Carmilla are not "real" and cannot actually reproduce sexually, they logically cannot pose any threat of any kind in reality to (an always-already insupportable anyway) "race purity." (To suppose that these figures *could* do so is of course to demonstrate the feeble hold of racial purity on reality.) They only do so by presenting images to young minds who, it is somehow presumed, will immediately or proximately upon closing the book rush out to imitate what they have seen. They do so only—but, as I've been arguing with respect to fantasy-acts all along, significantly—by challenging the *imagination* of racial purity.

This challenge to the imagination of racial purity amounts to a negative act as much as a positive one—that is, McGregor et al.'s innovation was as much *not* following the unwritten but pervasive rule that super-hero comics should not depict "any color but white in the books," as it was affirmatively representing the hitherto-unseen spectacle of imagi-nary people with imaginary races imaginarily pressing their imaginary lips to each other.

The kind of behind-the-scenes battles between politically liberal cre-ative decisions and publication pressures that McGregor describes in-dicates that we shouldn't ascribe a monolithic white-supremacist view or stubborn lack of awareness of racial injustice to white comics cre-ators. As we have seen, the concept of the superhero appears to be teth-ered to its being imagined as an exemplar of the imaginary qualities of whiteness—that strange and incoherent, and so necessarily fanciful and fantastic, combination of innocence and invulnerability, absolute good and absolute power. But, as we'll see shortly, the concept is subject to being reworked and reshaped so that the superhero does not have to be fundamentally white. The reshaping of the concept—wholly possible, we would think, because it is an imaginative enterprise and thus ca-pable of overcoming, as Ernst Bloch elegantly phrases it, "the resistance of the empirical"[40]—is actively resisted in McGregor's account. White-supremacist conventions of superhero representation and the practices that adhere to those conventions are owed to avowed white-supremacist allegiances on the part of individual comics creators (the inker/letterer who "wants off" any book figuring "salt and pepper" relationships) and/ or to relatively spineless accommodations of those announcing such al-legiances (the editor who wonders if we might avoid the whole problem by making the white character green), and to the continual repetition of these avowals and their accommodation from 1938 onward.

These are failures, willful or weak-minded, of *political* imagination: wherein we see that where blackness is figured in superhero comics, the fantasy is of political matters. To fantasize blackness in superhero com-ics is not to fantasize something wholly unreal but to fantasize possibili-ties of the disarrangement of temporal and social realities.

Wakanda Forever: The Sovereign Maroon

Thus the third way to conceptually link "black" to "superhero" is to take seriously that if blackness is a fact, as an early English translation of Fanon averred, it is a *political* fact, and to address blackness or to represent it in the fantasy worlds of superhero comics demands explicitly political invention. Representing blackness in the fantasy worlds of superhero comics demands a reimagination of the sine qua non of politics in modernity: the nation.

This is the third tactic in my accounting but historically the first. The first black superhero in Marvel or DC comics—the first black superhero character of mainstream comics—was created by the selfsame Stan Lee who later cringed at the thought of an interracial embrace between two-dimensional figures. Working in collaboration with the great, boundlessly generative artist Jack Kirby—it remains a point of heated contention as to which of the two, Kirby or Lee, contributed the greater part to the fecund list of the pair's many cocreations—Lee and Kirby hurdled the limits that seem to have plagued the imagination of a black superhero, by rendering the figure inherently political, in 1966—even if politics was something that, as we'll see shortly, Lee wanted to avoid (though Kirby didn't).

In this third way, we imagine an alternate history of blackness that exists alongside "real" history, tucked into its folds, hidden away. This tack draws for its use on a common trope of superhero comics and of comic-strip adventure stories, to which superheroes are heir: the hidden land that follows its own histories, its own customs, and shelters its own versions of humanity: Atlantis, home of Namor the Sub-Mariner in Marvel Comics and, in DC, of Aquaman, and of the water-breathing Atlanteans; Paradise Island, home of Wonder Woman and the immortal Amazons; Asgard, home of Thor and the Asgardian gods. In the case of the black superhero, this, then, is the way of *the sovereign maroon*. And thus we come at last to the Black Panther. But arguably more significant than the Black Panther himself, we come to the hidden nation of Wakanda.

In 2000, Stan Lee's introductory essay for a deluxe reprinting of early *Fantastic Four* issues, including July 1966's issue 52, in which the Black Panther first appears, has an interestingly laconic recollection of the creation of the Black Panther. "Another favorite [story from *Fantastic Four*] of mine is 'The Way It Began . . . !' featuring the mysterious and charismatic Black Panther, the first African super hero in comics," Lee writes. Lee is referring to issue 53, in which the origin of the black superpowered character, who attacked the Fantastic Four in the previous issue and appeared to be villainous, is revealed, and the Panther's essential superheroic goodness is affirmed. "I've always strongly believed [the Black Panther] . . . has all the qualities necessary to become one of the most popular, best-selling heroes in all of comicdom. When you combine his unique and glamorous panther power with the strange gripping legend of the Wakanda nation and add the fact that T'Challa is guardian of the world's only priceless store of vibranium, you've got a combo that's hard to beat."[41]

Lee's pithy assessment of the Black Panther's potential—but as of 2000, not-yet-realized—*commercial* appeal becomes the title for the introduction to the reprint collection as a whole, which bears the title "A Combo That's Hard to Beat." The title of the introduction suggests that the Black Panther's story is the most enduring signal creation of the run of issues 51–60 that this collection covers. But even so, Lee has no more to say about the Black Panther and considerably less to say about him in this introduction than about how much he enjoyed writing the Thing, the Human Torch, and Mr. Fantastic (Sue Storm, the Invisible Girl, is unsurprisingly of little note in Lee's catalogue of character favorites in this introductory essay). The political import of the character is given no shrift in Lee's account. The nearly undeniable fact that the Black Panther as superhero character evinces a kind of sideways, glancing confrontation with the race politics of the United States circa 1966, a time of no small ferment on that front, and the likely fact that the historical moment was influential in the process of the character's creation, do not rise to the forefront of Lee's recollection.

By contrast, this context and its political implications are acknowledged, and stand near or at center stage, in the account of Lee's collaborator, artist Jack Kirby. Kirby was certainly the creator responsible for the Black Panther's costume and overall look, but quite possibly also the moving force behind the introduction of the character, period.[42] In a 1986 interview, Kirby recalls that circa 1966 he "got to hemming and hawing": "'You know, there's never been a black man in comics.' And I brought in a picture [that he, Kirby, had drawn] of the costumed guy which was later modified. . . . The Black Panther came in, and of course we got a new audience! We got the audience we should've gotten in the first place." Years earlier, and closer in time to the events in question, Kirby told an audience at the San Diego Golden State Comic Con (forerunner to the present-day cultural event the San Diego Comic-Con) in August 1970, "There was no pressure [to add a black character]. I thought it was time to do it. I found that there was a lack in myself. I found that I, myself, had not been doing it, and I felt it was my responsibility to do it, and I did it, because I'd want it done for me."[43] (Kirby, it should be noted, was the artist who first drew Whitewash Jones, twenty-five years before he drew and cocreated the Black Panther.)

Kirby's 1970 statement foregrounds his sense of *personal* political and artistic responsibility and deflects or holds at a distance any connection or response to larger political events—"There was no pressure," he asserts, which seems to be prompted by an audience member's or interlocutor's question asked with the dubious (and perhaps sinister) assumption that Marvel Comics could conceivably be under "pressure" from the civil rights and Black Power movements to create a black superhero for the movements' political gain.

It was this very suspicion or accusation that we may guess dogged Stan Lee's chary 2000 introduction, which is uncharacteristically lacking in Lee's usual self-congratulation. Indeed, we find Lee in his own 1970 interview suggesting that the Black Panther had faltered in the popularity contest of superheroes due to his being overidentified with race and blackness in the United States—not so much because of the character "being" black but because of the character's name.

Marvel Comics introduced the Black Panther character months prior to the announcement of the organization of the Black Panther Party in Oakland, California, in October 1966 (though *Fantastic Four* #52's cover date is July 1966, it would have appeared on newsstands weeks earlier than that date). There was, however, evidently no connection between the superhero and the selection of the name for the new political movement; rather, the overlap was a case of coeval invention.[44] It was an unhappy coincidence, to hear Lee tell it, as he is reported saying in a 1970 interview, "I made up the name Black Panther before I was conscious that there is a militant group called the Black Panthers," Lee says. "And I didn't want to make it seem that we were espousing any particular political cause. And because of that we're not able to push the Panther as much, although we're still using him."[45]

Lee's feeling of having had his character's fortunes hijacked by political fates beyond his control is obliquely confirmed in a report by

Roy Thomas, who was assistant editor to Lee at Marvel in 1966 and late that year began a long and popular stint writing *The Avengers*, a superteam that soon included the Black Panther. As his contribution to an anthology that adapted Michael Chabon's Pulitzer Prize–winning literary-fiction superhero the Escapist (the character is an homage to Lee and Kirby's—and Siegel and Shuster's—Golden Age superheroes) for bona fide comics, Thomas concocted an imaginary publication history of comics featuring the Escapist. Inventing a Silver Age publication existence for Chabon's superhero and mixing this account with real history, Thomas notes that in an iteration of the Escapist supposedly published by "Conquaire Comics," "'the publishing arm of Conquaire Grooming Products, manufacturer of hair-care and skin-care products for African-Americans,'" the Escapist, though always otherwise white like any Golden Age superhero, was drawn as black. "Conquaire dubbed its version [of Escapist comics] *The Black Power of the Escapist*," Thomas writes, as the puns accumulate. "'Black Power' was a phrase just coming into vogue," he adds with a hint of wry amusement, "as was 'Black Panther,' a name Lee and Kirby used . . . just as the recently founded African-American organization of that name began to gain notoriety and cause considerable consternation up at Marvel."[46]

Thus Lee's consciously brave, even pious declaration in 2000 that he "always strongly *believed*" the Black Panther "has all the *necessary* qualities" to be a best-seller and front-rank superhero along the lines of Spider-Man is a concession to the view—a view that Lee evidently imagines to be settled at least as of 2000—that, possessed of necessary qualities though the character may be, the Black Panther *has not* been a best-seller or front-rank superhero. And this failure would be, must be, because he is black and, worse, affiliated by name to an evidently notorious political movement for black people's human rights.

Lee's 2000 statement also appears to slightly cloak his character's blackness behind the perhaps less threatening, racially neutral-*ish* pseudonationality of "African." The Black Panther was "the first African super hero," Lee notes—not wholly inaccurately, at least with respect to US-based major comics companies. But certainly this is an incomplete and tellingly fudging epithet to bestow on the Panther, since really he is the first *black* "African" and thus the first black, period, superhero. Lee's relatively restrained, even shell-mouthed, introduction of the Black Panther reads as though as late as 2000—thirty-six years after what appears therefore in retrospect to have been something of a commercial gamble Lee undertook with Kirby in *Fantastic Four*, but seventeen years prior to the phenomenal commercial and cultural-zeitgeist success of Ryan Coogler's *Black Panther* movie—Lee still felt compelled to kowtow to the "unwritten rules" against "writing about race" that Don McGregor cites.

Little wonder, then, that McGregor has no memory that Lee offered him encouragement when McGregor set out to write a Black Panther–centered comic set in the imaginary black African nation of Wakanda. McGregor recalls, "An all-black cast in a comic book, from a major company, at that time? Wasn't happening. . . . Believe me, no one in the editorial hallowed halls was applauding this approach. In fact, I can't recall a single, encouraging word from editorial during the entire run of the series [*Jungle Action*]."[47]

In fact, the hallowed halls of Marvel editorial, where Lee at the time held the highest seat, were clearly troubled by the violation of those unwritten rules. "Along the way, issue after issue, editorial wanted to know where the white people were," McGregor remembers. "Always, 'Where are the white people?' And my response was, 'This is a hidden, technologically advanced African nation. Where are the white people supposed to come from?!' . . . They wanted the Avengers in there. They wanted white people helping black people out."[48]

They wanted, in other words, for the stories in McGregor's Black Panther series to follow the formula established by the kinds of stories that preceded Black Panther's arrival in issue 6 of *Jungle Action*. McGregor writes of his early months at Marvel, "One of my jobs was to read all the [Marvel] reprint titles. One of the titles was *Jungle Action*, a collection of jungle genre comics from the 1950s, mostly detailing white men and women saving Africans or being threatened by them."[49]

Yet Lee had already violated the Mr. Livingston–colonialist–fantasy rules meant to frame the depiction of black Africans in inventing Wakanda. Lee and Kirby's creation Wakanda was like Atlantis and Asgard and Paradise Island, a world unto itself, with magical properties and full of magical, impossible people (water breathers; immortal women warriors; Norse gods) with wildly advanced and inconceivable "technology" (like the telepathic radios and Purple Healing Ray of the original Wonder Woman and the insane weapons of Kirby's Asgard, like "the Odinian Force-Arrow"). But unlike them, Wakanda's conceit placed it within a terrestrial political entity as its home—the at once mythic and concrete "Africa."

Moreover, the magical properties of Wakanda's people were, precisely, that they did not adhere to the colonialist assumptions by which they were supposed to have been imagined; they were magical Negroes who, given that they were conceived to be hidden, supersecret, and possessed of impossibly advanced technological marvels, were not magical by dint of being Negro in any other way than being placed in Africa and being colored black; their magic lay in their *having to be*, in order to *be* at all, apart from, secessionist with respect to the history of Africa and of blackness itself. This, in truth, was theirs, and the Black Panther's, superpower.

This is all to underline that the Black Panther, and the legendary invention Wakanda of which he is representative and that is in story terms an extension of him and his raison d'être, is a superhero by virtue of confrontation with the *concept* of the superhero as inherently racialized and therefore presumably white, a concept calcified by the continual practice of "unwritten rules" and conventions of superhero-comic representation. As McGregor recalls thinking about how he would write the Black Panther series in *Jungle Action* that he had been assigned, "I . . . realized that Wakanda was a *concept*, but that detailing how the country *worked* had never been explored."[50]

McGregor felt it was his task in taking on *Jungle Action* to elaborate on assumptions underlying the character that had never been pursued—if Wakanda was hidden, supersecret, technologically "advanced," a comic depicting it would not be full of white people, and stories told in such a comic would not center white characters, and white characters would neither save nor necessarily be threatened by the black Wakandans. Lee, by contrast, did not think these implications through in a sustained act of conscious world-building, judging from his abbreviated, race-eschewing, sorry-not-sorry endorsement of his own Black Panther creation.

We may judge the lack of thinking-through, too, from Kirby's visual rendering of Wakanda in its first appearance: unlike the wild inventiveness of monumental sci-fi Asgardian architecture that Kirby so beautifully rendered as a routine matter in *Mighty Thor* comics, or similar flights of visual fancy in depictions of the land of the Inhumans, who like the Panther were supporting characters in *Fantastic Four*, Wakanda in its 1966 version is a land of huts and grassy jungle with men and some women dressed in loincloths, headdresses, and draperies that hint of dashiki, all set with conscious incongruity alongside fantastical machinery and outlandish weapons.

It seems, then, that Kirby and Lee came to their character and his country via intuitive leap, which in recollection Lee refers to, at once blandly and tellingly, as "the *strange gripping legend* of the Wakanda nation."[51] It is *strange*, yes, because the conjunction of blackness (even hiding behind a spurious Africanity) with power, let alone superpower, is odd, out of kilter with the assumptions underwriting, framing, and determining the antiblackness and white-aspiration of modern civilization's cultures—Wakanda is odd, not-like, and threatening. It's *gripping* for the same reasons, since what is strange and threatening grips the imagination; but it is also gripping in that the adhesiveness of such imagination, the swirling undertow to which it makes the imaginer present, is a grappling with the strangeness, the essential unrealness, of racial categories and their power to form and deform. It is a *legend* because such a challenge to the assumption of blackness as always-necessarily-already the lesser of whiteness can only be a *story*, an imaginarium plucked from an otherworld temporally and spatially distant, as in the past where legends lie or in the future where legends will be. And it is a *nation*—much more than Wonder Woman's Paradise Island is a nation or Thor's Asgard is a nation—because these appeals to and effects of strangeness, of threatening and thrilling grip, and of the legendary are all twists of *political* import, creations of political imagination: Wakanda is an alternate, perhaps an *involute*, of the known political history that produced and produces blackness as well as "Africa."

I use the adjective and noun "involute" here to describe the Black Panther's and Wakanda's relation to the histories of blackness as well as of comic-book superheroes and propose that it might be equally descriptive of how I guess Stan Lee and Jack Kirby's invention of Wakanda to have proceeded: intuitively, propositionally, heuristically. For Lee and Kirby, I guess their creative process to follow a trajectory that begins, *if* the superhero is black, *then* there are a number of "qualities" that he must possess, a number of touchstones to which he must refer and from which he must at the same time depart, and the result *might* look *like* this but *unlike* that: a succession of deductions, syllogisms, and suppositions that we cannot precisely chart or follow but that have a conclusion we can, via the act of fantasy, bring into being. The black superhero will have to be black, but black in a different way, and a superhero in a different way.

For me, my intuitive, memory-ransacking search for a word that describes the Black Panther's relation to history brings me to "involute," where that word carries its meaning of margins rolled inward, and of whorls obscuring the axis around which they wind, and of long, curving grammatical construction. Here, then, to make the black superhero, to conjoin black with what is imagined (but largely due to imaginative failure or cowardice) as constitutively white, we travel via curl and curve backward from the margins of the latter-day productions of the meaning of blackness and the moment-ago-modern production of the comic-book superhero toward the origin points, the central axes of these terms' meanings, not to return to what was and what was meant then or now, but to retell the story of origin using hitherto-undreamt rearrangements of its constituent elements, such that what was meant before becomes obscured in favor of what is desired after.

This describes the Black Panther's involute relation to the superhero. The original idea, its casual, repeatedly practiced and therefore seemingly naturalized dependence on white positionality is not destroyed, not shattered, not upended, *not gone*. But so long as we sustain our imagination of the Black Panther and Wakanda, both what it means to imagine being black and what it means to imagine a superhero mutually transform each other in such a way that the original, consensus-enforced, *real* meanings of both become obscured by the diaphanous dress of our repeated, individual and collective, divergent and coordinated, whorled action of fantasy. And since what it means to imagine being black or to imagine blackness can never be completely cleaved from, and must be understood as on a continuum with and messily contiguous to, the *being* of blackness, here again with the Black Panther we can perceive an instance when fantasy *acts*, when if it is a minor form of doing, it is nevertheless a powerful or at the very least not-negligible form of being. To imagine the Black Panther, to participate in the imaginary worlds of Black Panther stories, to invent such stories—to take up imaginary residence in Wakanda—is to make, to do, to be black: but a different black, an involute black, perhaps some inchoate version of that black existing in the habitable imaginary where, as I proposed in the introduction, one brings both a knife and a velvet camisole to a gunfight—since in Wakanda, after all, a knife made of vibranium or a camisole laced with it might stand up surprisingly well against hostile bullets.

The act that is fantasy in the case of the Black Panther and Wakanda has implications that curve backward toward the center from which they emanate, à la the action of involution—that is, the fantasy-act participation in the worlds of the Black Panther and Wakanda has *effects* in the political life of blackness at this latter-day point in the production of blackness's meaning.

We can divine these effects with a closer look at a present-day version of Black Panther comics featuring his sister Shuri—a character of late provenance, first appearing in the fourth distinct *Black Panther* series written by Reginald Hudlin starting in 2005—and with a look at Coogler's 2017 movie version of the comic.

My discussion of Coogler's wildly successful movie adaptation, I must caution, pays attention to the film itself only insofar as the film illuminates aspects of audiences' or readers' fantasy-acts in relation to the comic-book character. I am therefore most interested for present purposes in engaging how the Black Panther superhero-comic character has become a cultural phenomenon.

Nevertheless it is significant, perhaps even of the highest significance, that *Black Panther* could not claim its cultural status (about which more shortly) existing solely in its medium of origin. The character's position as a known quality depends on the popular reach of the movie form and the story's dissemination as a blockbuster film. Its content and narrative are nested within an array of other commercially successful (and not-so-successful) movies of the so-called Marvel Universe franchise, much as every *Black Panther* series is tied by many threads to comics that precede and are contemporaneous with it published by Marvel Comics.

There is the typical prosaic chicken-and-egg mystery here—typical, that is, to the phenomenon of adaptations across form and media—as to which medium provides the motor of the character's and story's great present popularity (which Stan Lee in 2000 lamented it might never achieve). This mystery has manifested—from my perspective, devolved—in a recent contretemps in which those towers of film art

Martin Scorsese and Francis Ford Coppola rail that "Marvel Universe" movies are "not cinema." Marvel Universe movies are not cinema, it's said, because the stories they tell have baked-in audiences, and the movies are thus oriented toward "fan service"; and so the "risk" that Scorsese et al. see to be inherent to "real" cinema, where "art" and the grand unifying vision of a director are at stake, is lacking.[52]

In fact, the extent of comic books' popularity among various entertainment media is, as noted earlier, actually considerably less than it once was during the industry's one-hundred-million-copies-sold-per-month heyday. It is less than clear that if the corporatized top-down moviemaking that Scorsese decries—I'm sure with very good reason—were truly devoted solely to servicing its ready-made fandom, that such servicing would actually be a winning formula. Hollywood's various forays into superhero-comic adaptations even from as late as 1989's *Batman* (directed by someone with a claim to standing somewhere in the skyline of cinema artistes, Tim Burton) have had at best mixed results: one can scarcely claim baked-in success of commercial or critical variety, for example, for Ben Affleck's 2003 *Daredevil* or Jennifer Garner's 2005 *Elektra*, early versions of linked-story Marvel Universe franchise cinematic assays. In this light, if "risk" is what makes for cinema, only selective attention and truncated historical memory will support the claim that "Marvel Universe" films altogether lack it.

In any case, Scorsese and Coppola can hardly imagine that *Black Panther* at least did not have some aim, like the "art" they rightly see themselves making, of beautifully or innovatively representing through its form a vision of meaning or significance that reaches beyond the content of its story, its visuals, and its performances; or that with its nearly all-black cast, it lacked *risk*—especially since all-black casting is the kind of risk that neither Scorsese nor Coppola have ever taken. As Kirby recognized and as Lee wished to dissimulate, there is risk and there is meaning—political meaning, and therefore always also potentially artistic challenge—in rendering a *black superhero*, for all the many reasons this chapter has detailed.

Black director Ryan Coogler's *Black Panther* mined this meaning as the film rose to and surmounted the challenges to its commercial success, surpassing a gross of $1 billion globally. The *New York Times Magazine* proclaimed the film a cultural watershed in a February 2018 feature story titled "Why 'Black Panther' Is a Defining Moment for Black America." The *Times*, the so-called journal of record, ran no less than forty-four stories with references to the movie in their headlines in 2018 and 2019. Hence, the movie, its character and story, and most especially its fantasy setting of Wakanda have become a cultural phenomenon, an achievement that cannot be adequately explained by the movie's placement within the Marvel Universe franchise, or by its particular film genre of superhero movie—with the dubious claims of each to ephemeral ready-made audiences—or even to the popular reach of movie entertainment and art.

I make the claim that this achievement finds its high level because it brings "black" and "superhero"—where "black" is a name for a diaspora and not just a population within a country or even its world-striding cultural products—into dazzling contiguity despite the wide array of forces that have in the past made the terms mutually repellent.

I'll begin with a scan of some of the responses to *Black Panther* as cultural phenomenon, most particularly quotations from the concluding chapter of Michael Eric Dyson's *What Truth Sounds Like: RFK, James Baldwin, and Our Unfinished Conversation about Race in America* (2018). Dyson's conclusion is called "Even If: Wakanda, Forever." I'm going to let these quotations largely speak for themselves without my gloss. Taken together, these excerpts ring like a sermon.

Dyson begins,

> I beg you, as the youth are wont to say these days, please don't judge me, but I've got a confession. I believe that most of the ills that I address in this book—the racism, the sexism, the homophobia— . . . might all be solved if we all took a trip to Wakanda. I know, I know, it's cheesy that I'm capitulating to the hype around a blockbuster superhero film, surrendering the high aesthetic moral ground to a piece of popular entertainment. . . . But . . . everything about *Black Panther* is right, timely, and, dare I say, prophetic—even black prophecy at its best—a visual witness to the aspiration and ideals we harbor in our black chests when we let our imaginations roam free.[53]

Further, Dyson describes the movie as "a fictional version of what our society can't provide us every day—a place where race is not an issue and our blackness is taken for granted."[54] "Wakanda is the name of our paradise and possibility," Dyson says. "Wakanda is the place of our unapologetic blackness, a blackness that is beautiful and ugly, that is uplifting and destructive, that is peaceful and violent, that is, in a word, human in all its glory and grief . . . [with] the infinite possibilities, and any and all options available to the human being. . . . In Wakanda, we finally get the chance to just be."[55]

He continues, "We went to see *Black Panther* time and again because time and again we had to remind ourselves that the denial of our beauty, time and again, is not real. That what is real is what we see projected as a fantasy, but which we know, in our hearts, in our black bodies, to be true. We are that great. We are that intelligent."[56] "Wakanda exists because what we should have is not here. Justice. Truth. Love." "Wakanda is Black Love," Dyson proclaims. "Wakanda is Black Brilliance," and "Wakanda is Black Blackness." By the latter, he means, "Not a blackness manufactured by others to satisfy their lust for our coolness, our suave, our earthiness, our grittiness, our sensuality, our sexiness."[57]

Perhaps most ringingly, he says,

Wakanda is where [murdered child] Trayvon [Martin] reigns as a King. As a Warrior. Most important, as a Man. Because he made it past a youth that is forever in peril in a culture that doesn't prize our breathing.

Wakanda is our insistence that we will choose how to be black. Wakanda is our insistence that we will choose what to be black about.

Hint: everything.

Wakanda is our refusal to let others tell us what is important to us. About us. For us.

Wakanda is our refusal to anymore pretend that what is happening to us in the real world, in real time, is really real. *This* is the illusion. This— this notion that oppression is natural, that violence is inevitable, that hate is normal, that whiteness is a birthright, that subordination is good, that empire is a goal, that control is a virtue—this is what is unnatural, false, fake, undesirable, should be banned and bashed and banished.[58]

And finally Dyson adds a statement apropos of our investigation of fantasy-acts: "Is it sad that all of this was inspired by a movie? In a way, perhaps, but then works of art have always inspired us to see ourselves in ways that aren't permitted when ruthless and narrow versions of reality pass for truth. . . . So, yes. It may seem silly, or kitschy, or needy, or downright desperate. Makes no difference. Wakanda exists in our minds and souls because our minds and souls have never existed as they should."[59]

I'm marshaling Dyson's paean to the movie's inspiration in part because it captures something of my own affective response to the movie (though of course my perspective is that of a person who doesn't assume that comic books or popular movies or the melding thereof automatically land in the category of the "cheesy" from which they must be rescued, or that to engage these seriously involves evading the pitfalls of a "surrender" of "high" "aesthetic" "moral" "ground"). Dyson's of course was not the only response of the black intelligentsia and literati to the 2018 movie, which generated a spirited and passionate ongoing series of responses in social media and editorial pages on a variety of platforms. Among the forty-four-plus stories the *Times* published headlining the movie is Salamishah Tillet's article "'Black Panther' Brings Hope, Hype, and Pride." There among the things said about the movie by prominent black New Yorkers, Tillet quotes,

> "Wakanda is a kind of black utopia in our fight against colonialism and imperial control of black land and black people by white people," said Deirdre Hollman, a founder of the annual Black Comic Book Festival at the Schomburg Center for Research in Black Culture in Harlem. "To the black imagination, that means everything. In a comic book, it is a reality, and through a major motion picture, it's even more tangibly and artistically a reality that we can explore for ourselves. There's so much power that's drawn from the notion that there was a community, a nation that resisted colonization and infiltration and subjugation."[60]

And, "For Frederick Joseph, a marketing consultant who created the #BlackPantherChallenge, a GoFundMe campaign to buy tickets so youngsters can see 'Black Panther' in theaters, the complexity of Wakanda takes on new meaning in our current moment. Compared with President Trump's disparagement of Haiti and African nations, he said, 'You have Wakanda as a place of Afro-futurism, of what African nations can be or what they could have been and still be had colonialism not taken place.'"[61] Of particular interest to me, in Dyson's published remarks and in the observations produced by interviews in Tillet's article, is the sway, the power, of the wholly fantastical *place* of Wakanda in what Dyson et al. find meaningful about the movie: Wakanda fittingly *is* nowhere since it is a utopia, because as we know, Thomas More's styling of "utopia" was a political fantasy conceit named for its meaning, "no-place."

The other reason I'm starting with Dyson is to provide a useful contrast to the work of the accomplished novelist and now comics creator Nnedi Okorafor, a Nigerian American writer whose publications, including the young-adult series *Binti* (2015–2019) and *Akata Witch* (2017–2018), the adult fantasy novel *Who Fears Death* (2014)—the latter reportedly being made into an HBO series with the adaptive assistance of *Game of Thrones* creator George R. R. Martin—have garnered wide critical acclaim and popular success. She is the winner of the World Fantasy Award, the Hugo Award, and the Nebula Award, the highest honors in the fields of sci-fi, fantasy, and speculative fiction.

Okorafor has written a Black Panther miniseries called *Long Live the King*, and an ongoing superhero comics series called *Shuri*, which centers the Black Panther's sister.[62]

In Okorafor and Dyson we see an intriguing, and arguably productive, divergence in how a fantasy entertainment initially created by two white, Jewish American comics creators sparks political imagination. Okorafor's and Dyson's differing views on Wakanda illustrate a fact—which we might otherwise consider a challenge, politically speaking—that theorists of the African diaspora such as Brent Hayes Edwards, Kenneth Warren, and Natasha Omise'eke Tinsley, among others, have rendered de rigueur in African-diaspora cultural studies: This fact is that a unity of viewpoint among members of the diaspora, the wide-flung dispersal of peoples of identified African descent across the globe, is elusive if not impossible, since different, even if overlapping, histories of engagement with the slave trade and colonialism and their aftermaths, have produced very different ways of cognizing the evils of antiblackness and of the despoiling of African peoples, and very different methods for addressing these evils.

Dyson's riff on Lee and Kirby's (and McGregor's and Reginald Hudlin's and Ta-Nahesi Coates's) Wakanda is not only the more effusive and optimistic and *fan*-like of the two writers I'm juxtaposing (where a fan is most receptive to, and likely to generate, fantasies of their own based on fantasy templates provided by fantasy stories). Dyson's view also emphasizes in useful ways the degree to which Wakanda is *American* in conception (in much the same way a superhero is conceived from a white point of view, as discussed earlier), and the degree to which Wakanda was at its inception and in much of its present glory a dream about the dream of Africa. This of course is the prettified (but nonetheless not inaccurate) language: the "dream of Africa" was always first an imperialist's dream—the dream of exploitable coffers of agricultural and older-world cultural wealth as viewed by the hungry eyes of conquering ancient-world Rome—which was then overlaid by a settler-colonizer's dream in the depredations that reached their nadir in the "scramble for Africa." "Africa," too, in this sense was (and is) a kind of no-place insofar as the continental name and its invocation's too-hasty reduction of myriad cultures, histories, nations, peoples, and terrain to a single "dark" entity is a product of political imagining—the sinister, ruthlessly antihuman political imagination of a place that is an endlessly exploitable resource.

In the 2018 collection of the Marvel Comics limited series (which originally appeared in digital form) *Black Panther: Long Live the King*, Okorafor appends a "Hello, Black Panther fans!" afterword. In a few paragraphs, Okorafor notes what she thought of the Black Panther figure when she was invited to write the limited series, as a Nigerian American author of speculative fiction usually centered in various African locales and almost always from the perspectives of characters on the African continent.

Okorafor's assessment of the Panther is skeptical and critical rather than inspired in the mode of Dyson. Wakanda for her is a fantasy place that does not immediately or most prominently offer chances to reimagine possibilities with regard to blackness and its perpetually embattled political and ontological crises. For her, the concept of Wakanda raises thorny but generative questions about the siting of the imaginary nation in *Africa*, with a recognition of how the continent is too often imagined as a place about which one can have summary and indeed monolithic knowledge. This conception of Wakanda is less utopian than practically political—and thus Okorafor's chosen title for the series foregrounds the imagination of Wakanda's governmental structure.

"I came into this [writing the series] looking at King T'Challa and Wakanda out of the side of my eye," she admits. "I'm Igbo"—Okorafor breaks to explain to readers that this is a Nigerian ethnic group, which should usefully remind us that neither she nor her editors at Marvel presume that *Black Panther* comics readers are at all knowledgeable about real places and real peoples in Africa. "Amongst the Igbo," she continues, "there's a popular saying, 'Igbo enwe eze,' which means, 'The Igbo have no king.' Being a more democratic society consisting of many small independent communities, historically, Igbos never had centralized government or royalty. I've grown up hearing this phrase and between this and also being an American, any type of monarchy gets my side-eye of disapproval, . . . even a mythical one."[63]

While Dyson views "a visit to Wakanda"—Wakanda as envisioned by Ryan Coogler and the filmmakers of the *Panther* movie—as a method for thinking and therefore practicing problack freedom, Okorafor sees her own visit as a contemporary cocreator of the Black Panther's ongoing fantasy story not as travel to an imaginary home or political paradise— not, therefore, as an exultant "return" to a place of home, the dream of any diasporan—but as travel to a site in need of repair, a place that is an unsatisfying, perhaps even damaged, imagination in need of revision in order to better serve the desires its fantasy stokes. "Writing BLACK PANTHER felt like visiting a country for the first time, and not as a tourist, but *as a diplomat*. I couldn't be passive during my visit."[64]

(Lest any of us smugly suppose that Okorafor's diplomat-visit metaphor extends the disbelief-suspension inherent to working with an imaginary place into absurdity, note that (1) apart from the many, many evocations of Wakanda on T-shirts, iPhone cases, posters, and other paraphernalia that one can chance upon nearly anywhere, Wakanda was briefly listed by the US government as a trading partner of the United States—albeit as a beta test of a governmental online tracking system used by the USDA[65]—and note also (2) the tenacious hold of imaginary places even beyond More's paradigmatic Utopia, as evinced by Alberto Manguel and Gianni Guadalupi's *The Dictionary of Imaginary Places*, first published in 1980 and expanded and revised twenty years later with multiple printings; Umberto Eco's *The Book of Legendary Lands* [2013]; and Laura Miller's *Literary Wonderlands: A Journey through the Greatest Fictional Worlds Ever Created* [2016].)

Okorafor "visits" Wakanda cognizant of its shortcomings, aware of what it doesn't do: she considers the present-day political implications of the idea that Wakanda is removed from the history of African colonization and concomitantly was immune to the devastation of the slave trade, the twin modes of scatter that initiated the African diaspora. As suggested earlier, in fact these are fantasy conceits that neither Jack Kirby nor Stan Lee, the creators of the character and of the country, explicitly engaged, and they may never have given extensive thought to these conceits: the Kirby/Lee Wakanda was a "hidden" nation primarily in that it masqueraded as an undeveloped patch of jungle, revealed to be a paradise of sci-fi technology when the Fantastic Four are invited to the country to be prey in Panther's test of his martial skills (figure 2.15). The original conceit had little to do with any imaginative divergence from the *history* that produces blackness but rather to do with the narrative *surprise* and imaginative leap—the fantasy—that an African "tribal" people *could* be something other than primitive.

Thus the Kirby/Lee conception of Wakanda partakes for its narrative power of the construction of an "Africa" that is synonymous with "darkness" and "primitive," with the jungle and the wild, and carries the assumption that this is the common characteristic of the entire continent. That Wakanda should be a place of the future rather than of the "primitive" past is a well-intentioned and rather progressive vision, to be sure—and, as noted earlier, we can see such a narrative ploy as partially aligning the character Black Panther with the future-oriented temporality of the (otherwise white-identified) superhero concept. We might guess too that Lee and Kirby's progressive imagination here took some of its cues from the wave of African independence struggles post–World War II, which introduced into the visual and cognitive lexicon what would at the time have appeared to any "educated" white American eye to be the wholly novel and nearly fantastic image and notion of a black African leader who didn't wear a loincloth and headdress. In this sense, Wakanda is a kind of *avant la lettre* Afro-futurist conception.

But nevertheless for Lee and Kirby, the fantasy of Wakanda is completely dependent on the fantasy of a "naturally" "undeveloped or underdeveloped" and predictably monolithic "Africa." In figure 2.16, an image that appeared two issues prior to Kirby's rendering of the huge metallic panther in figure 2.15, we see that despite the narrative revela-

Figure 2.15. Stan Lee writes Mr. Fantastic marveling in the world of Marvel Comics that "a scene like this"—presumably referring to the monumental metallic table of refreshments, the apparent opulence of the setting, and the command performance of "the world's most renowned pianist"—could occur "in the heart of the jungle!" (*Fantastic Four* #54, September 1966)

tion of technology antithetical to the comics creators' views of "Africa," the visual imagination of the place of Wakanda is still firmly ensconced in, and repeats, the established assumption of Africans as "primitive."

Of these Kirby images in "some of the very first Black Panther comics," Okorafor is quoted in an interview as saying—diplomatically, perhaps?—"Heh, those were interesting."[66]

Such visual renderings were refined in various ways over the years through successive additions, extensions, and revisions of the Panther story in the hands of other artists and writers (mostly white American but sometimes black American), with an effect of ever-deepening entrenchment of the idea of rich, technologically superior Wakanda as a hidden society, a secret miniworld removed from all else.

A digression here on the matter of Wakanda monarchy: Wakanda's secret, technologically superior miniworld status makes it not unlike other Marvel Comics imaginary sites: Dr. Doom's Latveria, of which he is king, or the Sub-Mariner's undersea Atlantis, of which he is king, or Black Bolt's Attilan of the Inhumans, of which he too has almost always since the character's invention in *Fantastic Four* been king. Okorafor gives Wakanda's monarchical government the side-eye, and that same feature has aroused the critical attention via storytelling revision of recent *Black Panther* writer Ta-Nahesi Coates, who worked in his version of the Panther to undercut the monarchy and democratize Wakanda's governance. The *New York Times* film reviewer Manohla Dargis, no fan of superhero movies (so much so that I wonder why the *Times* continues to send her to review them), takes up this same antimonarchical stance in her otherwise uncharacteristically approving review of Coogler's *Black Panther.* "The movie . . . rather too breezily establishes Wakanda as a militaristic monarchy that is nevertheless fair and democratic," Dargis writes.[67]

Since it doesn't seem as politically pressing to mark one's antimonarchical position in the 2010s as it would have in the 1810s or 1910s, I assume that Okorafor, Coates, and Dargis raise their objections precisely because they're approaching Wakanda in a manner parallel to Dyson—if not as a guide to how to feel and how to be as Wakanda is for Dyson, then as a Thomas More–style guide to the actual political constitution of a utopia. Their criticisms do not, however, account for how the convention of monarchy in superhero-comic-book storytelling functions. The selection of government structure in these cases has, I think, somewhat

Figure 2.16. The more familiar visual conception of "primitive Africa" is the first peek at Wakanda. Note the modern weaponry and the hint of futuristic devices at the bottom left. (*Fantastic Four* #52, July 1966)

less to do with any thinking-through of the relative features of monarchy and democracy than with the narrative necessity of explaining these particular characters' *difference* from other heroes and of course from real, ordinary humans. (Lee and Kirby were the originators of Dr. Doom and Black Bolt and had formative hands in the Silver Age elaboration of the Sub-Mariner.)

Black Bolt and Sub-Mariner are representative of a different species (Inhumans and Atlanteans), which is of course just a conceit for an alternate vision of humanity. Dr. Doom and the Black Panther are *representative* of different, hidden nations, which is of course just a conceit for an alternate vision of how and under what arrangements humans might live. Such alternate visions are the meat of speculative fictions. There's a narrative economy in having characters who come from an imaginary site that is meant to serve as a world with different assumptions than our own arrive on the page as that world's singular ruler, rather than having to provide readers with a complicated description of that world it-self. In effect, by making the characters monarchs, you world-make and character-create in the same flourish. We should see this monarchical feature as a storytelling device that the medium and genre beg for, not as a product of monarchical political sympathies: in a medium where the visual representation of a different, alternate world must manifest itself in a collection of single panels of art, often amounting to less than and almost never more than a couple of pages in any given issue, and at the same time in a genre where the superheroes' travel to other worlds at base necessarily provides an occasion and a setting for them to fight someone, the representational payoff and entertainment value of paus-ing to draw or to textually describe a functioning democracy (or radical anarchy or some other preferable nonauthoritarian governmental ar-rangement) is not high—and the effect of dull familiarity that one might achieve by referring to the Sub-Mariner as "the president / prime minis-ter of Atlantis" presents no greatly appealing dramatic choice.

Thoughtful reconsiderations of the imaginary government of an imaginary nation are on the one hand a luxury afforded by the fact of characters' and titles' elongated production, which invites constant revi-sion and retelling. On the other hand, these retoolings of governmental structure are perhaps a near necessity of the built-in demand for revi-sion that such elongated production entails: if you are telling the story of an imaginary nation for fifty years and more, chances are it will look like an appealing narrative device to shake things up from time to time. (One now-conventional aspect of superhero comics that flows from these commercial imperatives, and which I as a fanboy do not love in the least, is the constant recourse on the part of Marvel and DC to (1) destroy Paradise Island, Asgard, Attilan, Atlantis, etc. for ever-cheaper thrills, only to rebuild them to be ready for the next destruction; and (2) to kill superheroes off with great hype and ever-lesser thrills, only to "resurrect" them later with the mise-en-scène of the characters' lives slightly rearranged, their costumes or power sets tweaked, and every-thing else exactly the same as it was when the character became popular enough for the editors to think they could squeeze some extra sales out of fake-killing them.)

Thoughtful consideration of how *Wakanda*, specifically, can be said to have existed in our world and in relation to "Africa" and its history, is something I would argue that might well have been undertaken in the conception of the Black Panther character, because, as readers of *Black Panther* comics have since seen, it might have been accomplished with relative narrative economy (several pages' worth of panels and less than a full modern issue), even if the implications of such a move take longer to unfold. Don McGregor, progressive as he was, did not rethink Wakanda in relation to the actual history that produces blackness or the histories of African nations. It was when Reginald Hudlin came along to write *Black Panther* in 2005 that these histories were woven into the retelling of Black Panther stories, and thus changed Black Panther's conception as a superhero. Here, then, we see a pattern of *black* creators from other media or genres of representation, engaging in their own fantasy-act creative activity, twining the whorls of their own new renditions around the ever more obscured source material (the source material is ever more obscured in that it is *not*, finally, Lee and Kirby's Black Panther that leads Dyson to the sermonic heights of "Wakanda is Black Love" but Coogler et al.'s retelling of Lee and Kirby).

Hudlin along with artist John Romita Jr. articulated a vision of Wakanda as a place where, obviously, slavery couldn't have happened and, obviously, colonialism could not have been established. He took the conceit of Wakanda as a hidden secret society personified in the Black Panther and made it a kind of maroon society, except reversing the historical exigencies that produce marronage:

In a seventeen-page sequence in *Black Panther* #1 (accounted in Marvel Comics history as "Volume 4," being the fourth run of Black Panther–centered comics including McGregor's *Jungle Action*, which is "Volume 1"), Hudlin and Romita Jr. depict in wide-screen filmic panels two temporal moments: In the first, during the fifth century AD, spear-bearing African men try to invade the fabled land of Wakanda, only to die in droves, slain by unseen warriors who leave a lone survivor to spread the legend of Wakanda's martial fierceness. In the second sequence, pale Europeans in the nineteenth century bring the firearms they have every reason to expect will be superior weaponry—including one of the feared Gatling guns—to the same Wakandan border. The European invaders kill some tribesmen, carry off some booty, and then spy a giant panther statue from afar. The panther statue heralds the arrival of a man wearing a version of the Black Panther's costume (in fact, a costume that hails

Jack Kirby's original discarded drawings for the character that became the Panther). This nineteenth-century Black Panther warns the Europeans before unleashing the firepower of a futuristic Kirby-esque weapon on them; and they all die, except one, who is left to carry the news of Wakanda's indomitability back to the would-be colonizers.

The first trade paperback collections of Hudlin's *Black Panther*, published in the 2000s, typically bound about five or six single issues together. The opening page of the trade paperback would provide a short introduction to the character. The first of these, for the collection *Black Panther: Bad Mutha* (note the obvious *Shaft*, masculine-Blaxploitation shout-out), reads, "*previously*: THERE ARE SOME PLACES YOU JUST DON'T MESS WITH. WAKANDA IS ONE OF THEM. SINCE THE DAWN OF TIME, THAT AFRICAN WARRIOR NATION HAS BEEN SENDING WOULD-BE CONQUERORS HOME IN BODY BAGS. WHILE THE REST OF AFRICA GOT CARVED UP LIKE A CHRISTMAS TURKEY BY THE REST OF THE WORLD, WAKANDA'S CULTURAL EVOLUTION HAS GONE UNCHECKED FOR CENTURIES, UNFETTERED BY THE YOKE OF COLONIALISM. THE RESULT: A HI-TECH, RESOURCE-RICH, ECOLOGICALLY SOUND PARADISE THAT MAKES THE REST OF THE WORLD SEEM PRIMITIVE BY COMPARISON."[68]

In a later issue, *Black Panther Annual* #1 from 2008, Hudlin collaborates with artists Larry Stroman and Ken Lashley to tell the story of a future Wakanda. In "Black to the Future," the mutant Storm—the *other* African Marvel superhero, a Kenyan American whose membership in the best-selling, in-its-own-right cultural phenomenon *X-Men* series made her unquestionably the most popular black superhero, until Coogler's film—tells one of the children she has in her marriage with T'Challa about the history of Wakanda. "As you know, Wakanda has not involved itself in the affairs of other nations unless it was absolutely necessary," she says in a text box tucked into the corner of yet another wide-screen panel where unidentified African people labor in the vicinity of huts. "The rise of *European slavery* sorely tested that policy," she admits.[69] Wakanda itself of course easily repelled any attempts to invade or enslave its people, but Storm describes a debate about how best Wakanda should respond to the continent's devastation. "These developments threaten the long-term interests of Wakanda," a Panther-

monarch of the past announces. "They cannot go unchecked." Storm
then describes how Wakandans at first infiltrated slave markets to buy
Africans who were then "brought back" to Wakanda, "where they were
trained for military acts." A long guerilla war ensued, with Europeans
initially unable to locate their African adversary. Eventually, however,
Wakanda—or rather, its monarch—decided that it would have to go to
war against the whole world to end the slave trade. "Maybe [Wakanda]
would have won" the war, Storm explains. "Maybe it would have lost.
But the very act of attacking all of the major western powers *and* their
puppet states in Africa would have required a ruthlessness that would
threaten the moral fiber of the nation. Instead, the decision was made
to take a long view. Even if it took centuries, the world would eventually
learn that the Wakandan way is the correct path. And if not, God bless
them, for they would not survive."[70]

In staging an answer to a question not raised in the comics but easy
enough to ask for most black fans of the Panther—*Why didn't Wakanda
stop the slave-trade?*, a version of the same question we noted must dog
the black superhero: *If the hero is so powerful, why doesn't he or she end
the oppression of black people?*—Hudlin provides the basis for the dramatic opposition of T'Challa and Erik Killmonger in the movie *Black
Panther*. Most importantly, Hudlin gives Wakanda a history it never
had, even during the thoughtful McGregor-penned run. Indeed, in the
Lee/Kirby origin story for Black Panther, while the Wakandans seem
for some undetermined span of time to have stood guardian over "the
Eternal Peak," which was actually a mound of the precious mythical ore
"vibranium," their technological prowess seems only of recent vintage,
a result of the prodigious brain power of T'Challa, who was driven to
take revenge after watching the murder of his father, T'Chaka (another
version of the Batman story, then), the "greatest chieftain of all" (but
not a king). Such people would surely have been as subject as any other
to the depredations and exploitation of colonialism and the slave trade;
again, it is only the "surprise" of technological advance—dependent in
Lee/Kirby on the concept of vibranium—that marks Wakanda out for a
departure from the mythical "dark" "primitivity" of "Africa."

Thus Hudlin's Wakanda—a Wakanda that is not explicitly visual-
ized onscreen but surely is the imagined historical background for
Coogler's—is, as I see it, a sovereign maroon society. Rather than a

162 CAN THE BLACK SUPERHERO BE?

refuge created by people fleeing enslavement, Wakanda is a refuge for those who, having been born into the safety of immense martial prowess, need never have fled but need only stay put, or a refuge for those whom Wakandans deign to rescue: it's a refuge *from* history, an imaginative conceit that—for Dyson at least and presumably for many who flocked to and thrilled in the movie—serves as a maroon state of the imagination.

For Okorafor, though, this refuge from history signifies as a state of privilege. She writes, "I feel like I know T'Challa now," having written the series *Long Live the King*: "I've seen him face his privilege, and get checked about it."[71] The singular possessive pronoun suggests Okorafor means the monarchical privilege that she, Coates, and Dargis find so troubling, but really hers is an indictment of the imaginary nation of which T'Challa is, in the usual comic-book terms, a synecdoche. Hudlin's collection précis underlines this. The "tagline" that introduces the Black Panther isn't about the Panther and his great powers or scientific genius: it's about Wakanda and *its* superiority to the rest of the planet. (The recognition that Black Panther is a synecdoche for Wakanda should lessen, if not purge us altogether, of eighteenth- and nineteenth-century worries about the tyranny of kings.)

The privilege, then, that Okorafor sees the need to check is not quite white privilege, for it isn't based on race: it's *non-African* privilege, in that it describes unearned rewards based on Wakanda's imaginative siting in an Africa the history of which it refuses—and a history for which, as Okorafor sees it, Wakanda refuses responsibility. Evidently Okorafor is no more convinced of the efficacy or morality of "Black to the Future" Storm's "long view" than Michael B. Jordan's eloquent Killmonger is in the movie.

In the movie, Wakanda's privilege is called out by the half-Wakandan exile Killmonger's explicit fury that Wakanda not only never intervened to save him and his father from the perils they endured as black people in America, but that it hasn't used its technological prowess to effect revolutionary change on behalf of the world's oppressed peoples. Killmonger's is a view that one might say is definitionally African *American*, one that probably has to be sited in places that lie on the other side of the Atlantic or of the Mediterranean. Indeed, one definition of diaspora in diaspora theory is that the far-flung communities in exile from their homeland can at least imaginatively, if not politically or militarily, appeal to the protection of their mother country (or flee back to it) if they're mistreated abroad.

The observation of Wakanda's splendid isolation and the puncturing of its privilege is a running theme in Okorafor's series *Shuri*, which started in late 2018 and stars T'Challa's technological-wizard sister. This version of Shuri is almost entirely based on the Ryan Coogler film version. In the comics prior to the movie, Shuri was a highly able member of the royal family who was capable of taking on the mantle of the Black Panther at need and wielding the position's considerable superheroic powers, but she was not necessarily a genius tech geek, as she became in Coogler's rendition of her and as she is in Okorafor's comic.

Okorafor's vision as it's articulated in *Shuri* takes a view of Wakanda's privilege, as it were, from African shores. A great deal of the revision of the Panther mythos she undertook early in the series was to connect Wakanda to Africa, to bring Wakanda into the flow of African history *now*. Whereas Killmonger in the film chastises Wakanda's isolation as a failure to act against antiblackness, that is, to act for black people worldwide but especially black people in the United States, Okorafor's *Shuri* implants story lines and dialogue that mount an implicit and sometimes fully explicit criticism of how such a "mythical" country ought to be held accountable for having failed to offer aid and succor to its fellow *Africans* on the continent.

One of the initial multi-issue plots has T'Challa go missing when a spacecraft that Shuri has designed to facilitate Wakanda's successful entry into the space race mysteriously disappears. Shuri is urged to take up the mantle of the Black Panther in her brother's absence. She does so not as a ruling autocrat, since Wakanda under Ta-Nehisi Coates's dominion has been transformed into a constitutional monarchy, but rather as a symbol of Wakandan power and superheroic problem-solving acumen around whom the Wakandan people can rally. As Shuri searches for her brother and fights off new extraterrestrial threats that menace not just Wakanda but other places on the continent like Timbuktu, two "secret" gatherings of counselors emerge from the shadows to aid Shuri: one is a gathering of Wakandan women who call their group "the Elephant Trunk" and say they are working with Queen Mother Ramonda as a kind of shadow cabinet of advisers in times of crisis (figure 2.17).

Figure 2.17. In *Shuri* #1 (December 2018), Nnedi Okorafor with artist Leonardo Romero has Queen Mother Ramonda summon her daughter Shuri to a meeting of the Elephant Trunk advisers in T'Challa's absence.

The other secret council is "Egungun," named after one of the traditions of Nigerian masquerade.[72] The Egungun council announce themselves to be a "Pan-African alliance," "a seed group of . . . 'Africa Forever,' a two-way flow of information and resources between Wakanda and the rest of Africa" (figure 2.18).[73] "Africa Forever" as a slogan is obviously a revision of the phrase made so resonant in the Coogler film and among its fans and the array of paraphernalia celebrating the film: "Wakanda Forever."

One of the notes sounded in the dialogue that Shuri and Okoye the Wakandan Dora Milaje warrior have in the Egungun meetings with other Africans is how arrogant Wakandans have been. When the Egungun's establishment of a two-way flow of resources is announced, Okoye asks, "What could Wakanda need from you all?" Another member of the council reports, "Something's happening in Mali. No one's alerting you? Heh. Maybe the news isn't important enough for you Wakandans" (figure 2.19). The needling continues when another Egungun member wryly notes that it's easy for the council to hide in a Wakandan community center, since Wakandans, the continental narcissists, seem not to value community (figure 2.20).

Figure 2.18. Dora Milaje warrior Okoye (a character also featured in the movie) meets the Pan-African Egungun council. (*Shuri* #4, March 2019; Nnedi Okorafor, writer; Leonardo Romero, artist)

Figure 2.19. The members of the Egungun retort to Wakandan arrogance. (*Shuri* #4, March 2019; Nnedi Okorafor, writer; Leonardo Romero, artist)

Figure 2.20. The Egungun explains its name and meeting place to Shuri. (*Shuri* #4, March 2019; Nnedi Okorafor, writer; Leonardo Romero, artist)

The "secret" councilors of both the Egungun and the Elephant Trunk are a microcosmic analogue within Okorafor's revision of the Black Panther mythos for the "secret" nation of Wakanda itself. The two councils serve to open the secret and turn it upside down. They function in the story as mechanisms, appendages almost, for completing the implicit reversal of the maroon idea that Wakanda has become: now the conduit of resources, the pathway to greater freedom, is to run *from* Wakanda the secret nation *to* the proximate places from which Wakanda has historically hidden. "The Egungun was created to bring together all the disparate parts of Africa. . . . Africa is a false creation that over time grew a soul. It still needs a unifying symbol," the council avers. "Who better than the absent child returned home?" This question figures Wakanda as at once the diasporic exile and the maroon. "Princess Shuri . . . Bring Wakanda back to us" (figures 2.21 and 2.22).[74]

Okorafor's is an articulation of the continent of Africa as a product of imagination, as being its own diaspora of sorts, if by "diaspora" we can refer less to scattering, displacement, and exile, and more to a far-flung network of diverse communities aware of overlapping if distinct histories: as one member of the Egungun secret group says, "Africa is quite . . . big. And it has worlds to offer."[75] Implicit here is that Africa is a fecund source of imaginary worlds, and that Wakanda is not only or even primarily an imaginative site for dreaming a defeat of antiblackness but one for for dreaming a healing of the histories of dispossession and depredation that created the at once politically real and politically mythical "Africa."

Okorafor scales up Wakanda from Lee and Kirby's "strange gripping legend of the nation of Wakanda" to a more familiar dream of Pan-Africanism, from a nation of borders and a maroon redoubt to "nation" as Fanon sought to redefine it in *The Wretched of the Earth*: which is to say "nation" as the expression of peoples united in the ongoing task of a revolution that will achieve self-government and liberation from domination for all—nation that knows no racial limit and no geographical boundary beyond those of the atmosphere of the planet itself. Fanon recognizes this process of revolution to be in all practical terms unrelenting and unending and that the possibilities of its failure—of the success of counterrevolution—are nigh infinite. It's easier for Okorafor to represent this Fanonian idea in *Shuri*. Why? One reason of course is that

Figures 2.21 and 2.22. The Egungun asks Shuri to make the Black Panther a symbol of African unity and power. (*Shuri* #5, April 2019; Nnedi Okorafor, writer; Leonardo Romero, artist)

Okorafor is creating art/entertainment. Another is that she is doing so in the medium of the superhero comic book.

I've argued that white supremacy is not inherent to the concept of the superhero or even necessarily to the representational conventions of stories in superhero comics, but is more accurately ascribed to failures, willful or weak-minded, of political imagination on the part of various comics creators. Here I'll amend that observation to say that although white supremacy is not necessarily inherent to the concept or the conventions of superhero comics, there are limitations inherent to the *form* of superhero comics, and practiced in the conventions of superhero comics storytelling, that lend themselves to the form's practical repetition and accession to white supremacy.

These limitations are in part limitations that I suspect—but cannot say for certain—that no art form can escape: the limitations imposed on any artistic creation by its creator's inescapable immersion in, and indeed their personal expression of, a world of discourse that renders meaning through the identification, nominalization, and hierarchical valuation of terms of difference. In part, then, I'm only restating in other language what I noted before and that anyone can observe: that the racism of the world in which artists create infects them, they are themselves in various ways and degrees racist, and their work will in some measure reflect or at least refract this fact.

But this set of limitations, which we have reason to suppose is universal, finds a particular *formal* expression in comics' central (but not wholly defining or pervasive) reliance on *sequence*: the sequence of panels, of units of time, arranged to suggest the flow of linear temporal progression; the material binding of these reproduced panels into comic *books* or *issues*, which suggest a "complete" *episode*. Since innovations introduced by Marvel Comics under Lee's auspices and others during the 1960s, the scope of superhero comics' sequentiality multiplied, as these single issues themselves became significantly sequenced into multipart stories, linking with stories that preceded it and that followed it, and with stories staged as "occurring" concurrently: for example, the Avengers fight another group of superheroes, the Defenders, over the course of several issues appearing in both *Avengers* and *Defenders* comics; concurrently, over the course of many issues, Captain Marvel encounters and fights the mad death-obsessed god Thanos, whom the Avengers also fight in one of their issues subsequent to their fight with the Defenders. As Stan Lee, writing in 1993, observes of the *Fantastic Four* comics that introduced Galactus, "Never . . . had any super-hero sagas prior to that time made such exciting use of the mini-series formula, one of Marvel's most successful innovations, a formula that the television industry has since adopted and brought into worldwide prominence."[76]

The form of superhero comics, as discussed earlier, became paradigmatically a form of producing sequences of stories, of retelling and revising those stories (with the expectation of reader rereading). In this sense, sequence produces the effect of duration in time, and sequence with the effect of duration in time and linear progression produces the *effect of history*. Superman is not alive, but he "has" a history; or to clarify for our purposes, he "is" the repeated practical expression via text and image of the history of the character's representation. We may say that this formal and conventional investment in the production of the effect of history makes comics pliable, perhaps even well fitted, to the parlaying of any project of racial supremacy. This is because a project of racial supremacy (or indeed of any other supremacy premised on social category) cannot be mounted without a step beyond identification and nominalization of race (or other social category). It must place what it identifies into a hierarchy: x is superior to *not-x*—which is to arrange a metaphorical *sequence* of identifications with an emphasis on precedence-as-value and value-as-precedence. In this regard again, comics are not unique among art or representational forms, since many also rely on the production of a narrative effect.

But, as I've also noted, it is also centrally the case concerning the reading/seeing of comics that sequence can only be suggestive and can be defied, and that linear progression may be utterly ignored. This means that the very form that allows comics to buttress projects of white supremacy by producing the effect of history is also the set of formal properties, and the kinds of reading that those formal properties both demand and enable, that can defy or ignore or challenge white-supremacist projects, if the creator of the comic—like Nnedi Okorafor in *Shuri*—and/or the reader is motivated to mount that challenge.

To bring us back to earlier observations in this chapter regarding comics' layering of time and comics' disarrangement of temporality: the ever-lengthening history that is the *effect* of issues produced, distributed, and sold as episodes within a sequence (again, repeating the sequential arrangement within the comics issues themselves)—the endless retellings and revisions of origin stories, for example—invites comics readers' participation, that is, their active fantasy, their active invention of alternate pathways for story procession or active invention of untold stories that "happen," as it were, between issues, fully as much as such comics-reader participation is mandated and necessary *within* the story at the site of the gutter. The *form* of "reading" inculcated in an encounter with any individual comics issue—any individual sequential arrangement of panels that come to an "end"—establishes the foundation for, sows the seeds of, inventive participation across the whole span of sequential arrangement, a kind of participation, of fantasy-act, that necessarily uses but also exceeds and sometimes obscures beyond retrieval the source material of the comic, that is, the original sequence, itself. This is, again as noted earlier, how comics are always practically (in the encounter of reading/seeing) and always potentially (in the form) *queer*.

Thus it is the practical and formal queerness of the Black Panther and Wakanda, with its "history" that nonetheless produces a "strange gripping," queer kind of blackness—which is nothing less than the practical and formal queerness of the superhero comic—that enables the relative ease with which Okorafor can scale up from nation to pan-nation in her *Shuri* series. The panel is always *at least* (if not more) a springboard for imagination at the site of the gutter; the comic is always at least a springboard for imagination well beyond the material confines and story content of the comic itself.

3

Erotic Fantasy-Acts

The Art of Desire

Queer futurity does not underplay desire. In fact it is all about desire, desire for both larger semiabstractions such as a better world or freedom but also, more immediately, better relations within the social that include better sex and more pleasure.
—Jose Muñoz, *Cruising Utopia: The Then and There of Queer Futurity*

Alan Moore has authored many of the most critically lauded and arguably genre-defining or at least trendsetting comics of the past three-plus decades: Moore's revamping of the second- or third-tier horror comic *Swamp Thing* into the front rank of comic-book art paved the way for the crossover of Neil Gaiman's *Sandman* (also a revamp) from comic book to literary phenomenon. Moore's mid-1980s *Watchmen* changed superhero storytelling to a degree not achieved since Stan Lee and Jack Kirby's innovations in the 1960s and spawned various adaptations— Moore would call them thefts—in film and television after the turn of the millennium. Moore's *V for Vendetta* and *The League of Extraordinary Gentlemen* have also seen adaptation. And short assays of icons Superman and Batman from Moore's pen yet remain milestones in those characters' ongoing stories, influencing successive waves of writers.

If anyone has earned a right to speak and be heard about superheroes, then, it's Moore. Given that Moore's *Watchmen*, a deconstruction of superheroes that overshadows all deconstructions, "reveals" beloved heroic characters not unlike Batman, Superman, Doc Savage, and others to be racists, rapists, paranoids, narcissists, and mass murderers, it is perhaps not surprising—if nevertheless deflating for fans, especially for those of the Black Panther's movie adaptation—that Moore, in a headline-making 2016 interview, was less than sanguine about the genre to which he has given so much thought and contributed so many rich and compelling stories.

"What was the impact of popular heroes comic books in our culture?" the interviewer Raphael Sassaki inquires. "Why are people fascinated by alternative realities?" Moore replies,

> I think the impact of superheroes on popular culture is both tremendously embarrassing and not a little worrying. While these characters were originally perfectly suited to stimulating the imaginations of their twelve or thirteen year-old audience, today's franchised übermenschen, aimed at a supposedly adult audience, seem to be serving some kind of different function, and fulfilling different needs. Primarily, mass-market superhero movies seem to be abetting an audience who do not wish to relinquish their grip on (a) their relatively reassuring childhoods, or (b) the relatively reassuring 20th century. The continuing popularity of these movies to me suggests some kind of deliberate, self-imposed state of emotional arrest, combined with a numbing condition of cultural stasis that can be witnessed in comics, movies, popular music and, indeed, right across the cultural spectrum. The superheroes themselves—largely written and drawn by creators who have never stood up for their own rights against the companies that employ them, much less the rights of a Jack Kirby or Jerry Siegel or Joe Shuster—would seem to be largely employed as cowardice compensators, perhaps a bit like the handgun on the nightstand.

He adds, "I would also remark that save for a smattering of non-white characters (and non-white creators) these books and these iconic characters are still very much white supremacist dreams of the master race. In fact, I think that a good argument can be made for D. W. Griffith's *Birth of a Nation* as the first American superhero movie, and the point of origin for all those capes and masks."[1]

Make no mistake—as my critical encounter with comics yet again entwines comics form with the forms and history of cinema—that Moore sees the hoods and robes of the racist "heroic" Klan in *Birth of a Nation* as the precursors for superheroes' function and look, the figures from whose conceptual outlines, we might say, Siegel and Shuster's imagination traced Superman and his ilk.

On the one hand, a recognition that superhero comics are as deeply informed by the project and history of white supremacy as well nigh everything else in and of the modern world can be no surprise from the vantage point, central in the undertaking of this book, of black studies. Most of the foregoing two chapters wrestle with this very problem. And from that view, Moore's pithy rendering does little more than summon to a stage less customarily attended to the same grim stupefaction with which we must always, and always inadequately, reckon the costs and effects of the project of white supremacy in blood, bodies, misery, and mangled minds.

On the other hand, the larger part of the undertaking of this book has of course been to show that Moore's "very good argument" does not and cannot tell the *whole* story of superhero comics. There are two elements that Moore does not account for, that I have been discussing: One, which Moore diminishes intellectually via recourse to measure of their *numbers*, is the element of the "smattering of non-white characters." I have been arguing such characters are not marginal but significant, indeed perhaps central, when we describe them by dislodging the emphasis on whiteness in the adjective "nonwhite" to mark these characters' *conceptually* impactful *blackness*. These conceptual impacts ought not be measured by numbers alone. And two, which Moore does not even mention probably because he's not positioned to speak of it, is the element of the imaginative possibilities that Sassaki's question about alternative realities and their fascination point toward but that Moore does not address—especially the imaginative possibilities propagated from the comic-book page for the black or nonwhite reader and fan.

This latter obviously concerns me, and I am positioned to speak of it; but the account of it is less personal than it is a phenomenological account of reading/viewing the superhero comic, which thus describes the ontology of reading/viewing the superhero comic: which I have been discussing as a fantasy-act, its minor *doing* and its major *being*. Fantasy-acts may respond to and thus never fully escape their "point of origin," as Moore designates D. W. Griffith's cinematic fantasy to be the origin for superheroes; but they also are not confined to or contained by the origins with which they dance and that, in the involutions exemplified by a phenomenological description of superhero-comics reading, they always obscure, often mitigate, and may transform.

I quote Moore's hammering of the genre I love here not to restate my departure from his conclusions about superhero comics but to refocus my phenomenological account and to further hone it. I can better see what are the stakes or the core elements of my own account when held up to Moore's account, which stands at a useful angle to mine.

Moore makes use of a not-uncommon critical judgment—often just barely masked as neutral observation—which is that superhero comics are "originally" for *children*. This, we may recall, was also Frederic Wertham's concern and Frantz Fanon's. For Moore, even today's "supposedly adult" audience, he implies, are not *actually* adults but must really be children intellectually and perhaps politically, because their attachment to comics in their "original" aim indicates that these adult readers cannot relinquish their "relatively reassuring childhoods."

This too is a statement that makes scant gesture toward understanding black children, children of color, girl children, or queer children, whose childhoods, statistically more vulnerable to the deprivations of poverty, racism, antiblackness, misogyny, sexism, homophobia, and transphobia, do not necessarily—I might say, rarely manage to and, in my own anecdotal knowledge, never do—conjure up the word "reassuring" as their chief adjective. I'm not certain, either, based on the various representations of white, straight, cisgender male adolescence I've encountered in film, television, and literature, that *their* childhoods make for very reassuring memories either; but then this is a position Moore can speak of, which I cannot. And again, historically, the one hundred million copies of comics sold per month during the Golden Age included a hefty portion of young (white) men who did not qualify as child soldiers but were, rather, young adults.

Moore, Wertham, and Fanon for different reasons and to differing ends make central the child in their analyses of superhero comics. I would say they overemphasize the child to the detriment of our understanding of superhero comics' history. But while I depart from many of their conclusions and quibble with their historiographical hermeneutics, I find what they assume useful now as I come back to the child in my own account of reading/viewing blackness in superhero comics as the exemplar of fantasy-acts. The child as I see it is not Lee Edelman's futurity-invoking child that enslaves the present or even Kathryn Bond Stockton's queer child. Rather, I see the child as it relates to superhero-comics reading according to what I see as common to the figure of the child in Wertham's and Fanon's and Moore's analyses: the child's *structural* position within an account of reading superhero comics fuller than those that these three propose.

For Wertham and Fanon, the child is dangerously guided toward identifications with superhero figures that threaten the order of society, or (for Fanon) that threaten the potentially affirming, empowering integrity of the black child's self-conception. For Moore, nostalgia for childhood experience is a conduit transporting the adult reader back into the "reassuring" order of white supremacy (such a description is a fine rendering of Trumpism; and so it is no surprise that Moore articulates it in a 2016 interview). Ironically Moore's remembered and sought-after child helps solidify the "order" that Wertham in particular fears the child's reading of superhero comics threatens, though Wertham wants guarantees along the lines of normative gender and sexuality, while the order Moore perceives—which he doesn't endorse—is an order of racial hierarchy. In all three, reading/viewing comics, via identification or imaginative affiliation, imputes or implies a process of self-transformation and self-making—such self always being tethered to and impossible to cleave from a *world* also in the process of transforming and being made to accommodate it.

Thus I see the child as a *position* that galvanizes our attention to the processes of *identification*. The parts of the processes of identification that I want to emphasize are those that organize around or have as their motor and mechanism the operation of *desire*. "Desire" here denominates an orientation toward myriad vectors of possibility, the possibilities of what one might "be" or what one might enact. Desire, just as we know it in its common meanings of ordinary speech, might be about dreaming ideals (which must be ideals because they don't exist): the desire, no doubt, for the ideal of "whiteness" and its "innocence" and "purity" that Moore rightly decries. But I also mean to evoke another common valence of desire, which is the yearning for and movement toward proximity to other bodies, the desire for the embodied activation of the social—*erotic* desire. Recall Jonathan Dollimore's neat proposition: "The necessary identifications of male bonding—'I desire to be like you'—produce an intensity of admiration some of which just cannot help but transform into deviant desire. . . . And it occurs so easily—

almost passively—requiring little more than a relinquishing of the *effort* of emulation, the erasure of '*to be like*' and the surrender to what remains: '*I desire . . . you*'; thus: 'I desire (to be like) you.'"[2]

This position of the *child* I'm thinking of as marking the potential (and potentially potent) activation of possibilities for imaginative self-making and social-world-making does not depend on or necessitate any developmental trajectory or metaphor of "growth." The child here need not be, and is probably not, a child by measure of years and is not to be adequately described in terms that diminish them as the lesser, immature version of the adult.

It is important to note the racial character of this child position in my phenomenological account. (I am less sure that it's important to note the gender character at this point, though as I consider specific texts later, this arena will be more clearly marked.) This child bears an indelible relationship to whiteness—and therefore also to blackness; and vice versa—but this child is not positioned *as* white. Let me underline this: I have argued that the history of the superhero figure makes the figure definitionally white, and that all manner of changes in both name and conception must be effected to render the figure otherwise. In this respect, I concur with Moore.

But the position of the reader/viewer of superhero comics, the position from which fantasy-acts emanate, is *not* by definition white. Indeed, I hazard that this child cannot "be" white, at least not wholly. The child-position I'm trying to describe is not innocent, because the child is not blank and unwritten, not an infant tabula rasa (if such can even be said to exist or to be captured in language). But it is precisely this kind of innocence that whiteness strives for—even if it, too, also always fails to stabilize it.

This child-position arrives to read and view her superhero comic marked by the families and societies of her world. This child has been initiated into a world of discourse, of symbols and images, and is—borrowing from Lacan by way of Bersani—the expression and product of that world. (As Bersani writes and I quoted earlier, "We are born into various families of singularity that connect us to all the forms that have, as it were, always anticipated our coming, our presence.")[3] This child's fantasies would not and cannot take flight without her submersion into this world and her expression of it. Because of this, she is definitionally *not* fully in accord with, nor can she fully hold, the position of *whiteness*, with its irresolvable turn toward blank innocence and fruitless aim to achieve the endless pure potentiality truly granted only to divinity.

To recur to Bersani, "Whiteness . . . [figures] an indefinitely prolonged possibility of possibility."[4] Such indefinite prolonged possibility is not possible for anyone to hold. To the extent that it can be successful, it is dependent on the blackness that it (unsuccessfully) cordons off or abjects in order to define itself, yet it needs to always maintain its relationship to that blackness it avers that it despises; it must always hold blackness in sight. The racialized universe as Fanon describes it seeks, but only intermittently and unstably finds, a kind of frozen tableau of the Hegelian Master-Slave dialectic. In Hegel's account, this dialectic between Master and Slave is inherently unstable, with positions that cannot be maintained. As I see it, even *if* or even *when* my child-position reads/views their superhero comic with the desire of a white supremacist, finding succor in the genre's predicates as Moore describes them, or if and when they are interpellated into such a desire by those predicates, the position cannot hold its wished-for whiteness. Possibility is not prolonged, because its forms are chosen. Its form is Superman; and then it is whatever form of Superman the reader's imagination develops, whether this is seeing or imagining oneself as a version of Superman, or seeing or imagining oneself in a world that would facilitate one's interaction with Superman; and each of these forms is multiplied by the succession of different stories and different writers', artists', and eras' versions of Superman, fan art, fan fiction, and fan interaction. Even if the choosing of form activates a quest *for* indefinite possibility, the quest cannot be initiated without recognition that the object of the quest is lost. Remember what Ernst Bloch said about the utopian imagination: "If we had not already gone beyond the barriers, we could not even perceive them as barriers," Bloch says to Adorno.[5] Likewise, if we (or *you*; this may not be a desire I share) had not already lost the dream of whiteness and its indefinitely prolonged possibility, we could not rouse ourselves to quest for it.

The Superman and Psychopathology

If the desire for whiteness and its reassurances of innocence is evoked but stymied in superhero comics—and, as I discuss further shortly, such desire is as much undercut and transformed as it is unremitting—the *other* valence of desire I've noted, erotic desire, with its connection to sociality, instead flourishes in superhero comics. Superhero comics, I argue, stimulate, call up, evoke, precisely what they do not, as a rule, explicitly depict (notably, they do not explicitly depict in a pictorial medium): the erotic as the feeling of, the perception of, not sexuality but sex. For a number of readers—perhaps many? here, neither numbers sold nor opinion surveys would suffice to accurately count—the sex that superhero comics evoke, in part precisely because of its codedness and covertness, is abnormal or shameful (this is why it is hidden), and thus nonnormative and thus *queer* sex. A lot of people, in other words, fear or think, and thus read and view, superheroes as queer or "homosexual."

Hitherto I've been interested in discussing how comics, and superhero comics in particular, partake of queerness in their *form*. Now I want to consider the ways in which superhero comics—if considered phenomenologically—are rife with the content of queer sex and sexuality.

Earlier I linked Moore's calling out of the white supremacy in superhero comics (and movies) to Fanon's—a pairing that I imagine Moore would not find odious—and through Fanon to Wertham and *Seduction of the Innocent*—a pairing to which I guess Moore would object. But while Moore probably parts company with Wertham precisely as regards Wertham's homophobic indictment of comics, both Wertham's and Fanon's ways of analyzing comics—their innovative calls to take comics *seriously*—owe a considerable debt to a deeply, indeed rabidly, homophobic attack on American comics by Gershon Legman in 1948.

Carol Tilley, in her deep dive into what Wertham claimed was wrong about Wonder Woman and the character's "lesbianism"—which, again, occasioned US Senate hearings about the malign effects of comics reading and led to the development of the Comics Code Authority—discusses how Wertham and Legman, the latter an autodidact folklorist, were close associates, with Legman playing an important role in the development of Wertham's thinking on the subject of comics. Wertham, Tilley reports, invited Legman to speak at the 1948 symposium on "The Psychopathology of Comic Books." "Legman's paper, 'The Comic Books and the Public,' was largely a precis of his essay 'Not for Children,' which appeared in his book *Love & Death* the following year," Tilley says.

"Judging from the hundreds of notes detailing conversations between Wertham and Legman, along with the letters spanning the decades from the 1940s through the 1970s that are part of Wertham's manuscript holdings at the Library of Congress, Legman also served as a significant source of insight and information about comic books for the psychiatrist [Wertham]."[6]

Closely attentive readers of Fanon's 1952 *Black Skin, White Masks* may recognize "The Psychopathology of Comic Books" as a title cited in a long quotation by Fanon in the chapter "The Black Man and Psychopathology." There Legman's article is cited under a French title, untranslated in either the Philcox or the older Markmann English translation as "Psychopathologie des comics." This was an article published in 1949 in a French journal identified as *Temps Modernes*. However, *Les Temps Modernes* was a journal published by Fanon interlocutor Jean-Paul Sartre, and Sartre had translated the Legman essay into French from its original English.[7] The original article, "The Psychopathology of the Comics"—not to be confused with the Wertham symposium of a similar name—appeared in the English-language journal *Neurotica* in its Autumn 1948 issue. The original article was itself adapted from a lecture given by Gershon in which he read part of the then-unpublished *Love & Death* to the American Association for the Advancement of Psychotherapy.

In "The Psychopathology of the Comics," Legman comes to much the same conclusion about the racial politics of superhero comics as Moore does seventy years later. "It is . . . [the] ability to transcend all human law, and be honored for it instead of punished, that makes the Superman formula so successful," Legman observes.

> He takes the crime for granted, and then spends thirty pages violently avenging it. He can fly, he can see through brick walls, he can stop the sun in its orbit like a second Joshua; and all this godlike power he focuses on some two-bit criminal or crackpot, who hasn't even pulled a trigger yet but is only threatening to. Giant the Jack-killer. And of course, all of Superman's violence . . . [is] on the side of right. . . . And this obvious flimflam suffices to blind parents & teachers to the glaring fact that not only Superman, and his even more violent imitators, invest violence with righteousness and prestige . . . but that the Superman formula is essentially lynching.[8]

Finally, "The truth is that the Superman formula is, in every particular, the exact opposite of what it pretends to be. Instead of teaching obedience to law, Superman glorifies the 'right' of the individual to take that law into his own hands. Instead of preaching the 100% Americanism that he and his cruder imitators express in hangmen's suits of red-white-&-blue, Superman . . . is really peddling a philosophy of 'hooded justice' in no way distinguishable from that of Hitler and the Ku Klux Klan."[9] Despite his invocation of the Klan, Legman doesn't tarry long with superhero comics' associations with lynching—a metonymy that Legman mostly attacks for lynching's lessons in extralegal justice, more so than its targeting of black people, the caricatured depiction of whom Legman does not list among comics' evils in his twenty-eight-page screed. He is concerned with fascist undertones and fascist iconography, finding them so replete that he guesses that comics (or perhaps their creators, since comics do not possess actual minds) "are not unconscious of their function as pilot-plants for the fascist state." We find in superhero comics, Legman says, "the same appeal to pagan gods for unearned powers" as we find in Nazism; we find crypto-swastikas in Captain Marvel's and the Lone Ranger's monograms; we find "the same glorification of uniforms, riding boots, and crushed caps."[10]

It is with this observation of superhero comics' sartorial creative choices that Legman begins to unveil a more insidious series of covert lessons imparted to young readers by superhero comics. Legman's diagnosis of the psychopathology of comics overlaps, or might even be the same as, his diagnosis of the psychopathology of fascism: for both, what is psychopathological is the substitution of "normal" or healthy sexuality (or depictions thereof) with violent behavior and "perverse" sexuality. Yes, there is an odious presence of anti-Semitism in superhero comics as befits their possibly "not unconscious" Nazi leanings, but this receives only a single mention: "All the more sinister villains have 'Jewish' noses," Legman observes. "In some cases the hook-nose is the only way to tell the equally bloodthirsty villain and (snub-nosed) hero apart."[11] More glaring than such racial tropes, and a matter to which Legman devotes the next seven pages of his article, is that in superhero comics just as in Nazism, "there is the same undercurrent of homosexuality and sado-masochism."[12] Homosexuality and sadomasochism are, in the comics and perhaps also in Legman's imagination, largely the same thing; and to the point, both are very much the stuff of Nazism.

Legman finds a plethora of elements in superhero comics that he deems obviously homosexual. He reels off a list of these, which, frankly, having perused a fair number of reprinted collections of Golden Age comics, I find baffling to read, since I see little indication of them in the comics. Legman derides "the obvious faggotry of men kissing one another and saying 'I love you,' and then flying off through space against orgasm backgrounds of red and purple." Such kisses and avowals of love I have yet to discover examples of in Golden Age (or Silver Age or Bronze Age or Dark Age) comics, but at least Legman tells us what the "knockout colors" that Stan Lee hoped to use to disguise the first inter-racial kiss in mainstream comics *really* mean: they're the color codes of orgasms. Equally problematic but so ubiquitous as to cease to be truly important, Legman claims, are lamentable deviations from gender pro-priety: "the transvestist scenes in every kind of comic-book" and the common appearance of "long-haired western killers with tight pants."[13]

"The homosexual element" of superhero comics—indeed, it seems, of comics in general—can also be observed in other figurations that Leg-man deems to rise to the level of comics tropes: "the explicit Samurai subservience of the inevitable little-boy helpers—theoretically iden-tification shoe-horns for children not quite bold enough to identify themselves with Superprig himself . . . [and] the fainting adulation of thick necks, ham fists, and well-filled jock straps; the draggy capes and costumes, the shamanistic talismans and superstitions that turn a sissi-fied clerk into a one-man flying lynchmob with biceps bigger than his brain."[14]

Jock straps and biceps and drag, oh my! I'll come back to consider a couple of Legman's list items shortly. For now, I want to show that what Legman sees as a profusion of tropes within the comics, what he sees and reads on countless pages, leads him to conclude that he can know the sexual character of the comics' creators. As his analysis balloons into a diatribe, Legman huffs about "the two comic-book companies staffed entirely by homosexuals and operating out of our most phal-liform skyscraper"[15]—thus revealing a conspiratorial, metonymic link-age between comics storytelling tropes, perverse sexuality, and sinister politics that is so profound, so overdetermining, that its presence can be discerned in the architecture of the New York City skyline.

Yet as saturated as the superhero comic is with sexual and gender deviance, winking its evil eye at the impressionable young reader from every panel, the true "homosexual element lies somewhat deeper."[16] Naturally it would; hidden depths are ever the domain of the "homosexual." And where does this element lie? It lies in the comics' inculcation in the child of lessons of Oedipal failure. The bamboozled boy-reader learns from Superman not to rise to his Oedipal duty (and the girl-reader, though wisely spurning the comics featuring male superheroes, supposedly, gets led astray into man-hating lesbianism by Wonder Woman).

> The *really important homosexuality* of the Superman theme—*as deep in the hub of the formula as the clothes and kisses are at the periphery*—is in the lynching pattern itself, in the weak and fearful righteousness with which it achieves its wrong. No matter how bad criminals (or even crime-comics) may be, in identifying himself with them the child does consummate his Oedipean dream of strength: the criminal does break through his environment. The Supermen, the Supersleuths, the Supercops do not. They align themselves always on the side of law, authority, the father; and accept their power passively from a bearded above. They are not competing—not for the forbidden mother, not for any other reward. Like Wild Bill Hickok, our own homosexual hero out thar where men were men—with his long silk stockings and his Lesbian side-kick, Calamity Jane—they are too unvirile to throw off fear, and kill as criminals. Instead, unseen and unsuspected in some corner, they put on a black mask, a sheriff's badge and a Superman suit, and do all their killing on the side of the law.[17]

First, Superman and his imitators teach children to become fascist lynchers by acting as vigilantes outside the law; and their iconography is fascist and therefore homosexual. A couple of pages later, Superman and his imitators are homosexual because they act—but they don't really act; they "act" passively—only *on the side of the law*, which is the side of the Father, against the criminal, who by contrast has the guts to take the reins of the Oedipal dilemma and compete with Father; and opposition to the criminal, especially, perhaps, given the criminal's "Jewish nose," can be seen as covertly fascist.

There is a response to the illogic and contradiction of Legman's analysis that would answer the rather obvious call to psychoanalyze this speaker before the 1948 gathering of the American Association for the Advancement of Psychotherapy. *If you see "homosexuality" everywhere, including the form of the building where the comics are made, then . . .* But I'll take a pass on this response, tempting as it is. I focus on Legman here for two reasons: One, as is probably evident, is that I want to offer up to the ridicule it deserves the thought of a person who influenced the direction of US Senate hearings and who powerfully changed the development of the comics industry by making a fearmongering argument for censorship. (Legman's argument was also potentially for legal actions worse than censorship: Legman writes with chilling flippancy, "That the publishers, editors, artists, and writers of comic-books are degenerates and belong in jail, goes without saying.")[18]

Two, I reproduce Legman's calumnies (again, as a person influential in the development of the superhero genre and the comics medium) in order to underline that a phenomenological account of reading superhero comics—for this arguably is what Legman is doing, trying to describe what reading/viewing comics fundamentally *is*, the ontology of such reading—centralizes the *active, conscious invention, imagination,* and *fantasy* of the reader. Reading/viewing comics requires and invites *closure* at multiple levels, not just within the story but surrounding the story and across its many stories. This invention, this readerly participation and fantasy, moreover, is often an expression of the reader's eros and is often sexual in content.

Legman himself is a fabulous example of this phenomenon. Let us return to one of the tropes Legman identifies. He observes hypermuscled bodies—ham fists and thick necks and biceps bigger than Clark Kent's brain. Fair enough. We all see these, as my quotations of Jeffrey Brown in chapter 2 indicate. But Legman also sees something a bit more elusive: "well-filled jock straps." Legman notes, "The Supermen have ridiculously over-inflated genitals."[19]

Really?

The prospect of seeing how Golden Age comics artists drew overinflated genitals and well-filled jock straps is titillating. When I read Legman, I wondered if maybe in my admittedly somewhat dispirited past perusal of Golden Age comics (I take little pleasure, and only the most jaded interest, in encountering Whitewash and his ilk), I'd missed something. I subsequently searched for drawn bulges in Golden Age comics featuring Superman, Batman, Captain America, the Human Torch, the Sub-Mariner, and the Boy Commandos, as well as lesser-known figures like the Patriot, the Whizzer, Microman, the Falcon, Mantor the Magician, Jack Frost, the Vagabond, the Defender, Major Liberty, Rockman, and even the rather promisingly named—from a Legman perspective— Corporal Dix. I saw nary a one. That is, unless I tried to inflate with my imagination what sometimes but mostly *doesn't* appear as at most a bit of ink shading or some lines that indicate a silken ripple where the outside-worn trunks meet the leggings of the superhero's costume.

Superheroes in the Golden Age, like superheroes in the Silver Age, tended almost invariably to be drawn with the smooth, bumpless crotches one finds in Barbie and Ken dolls; such is the well-established convention, preceding even the watchful redactions of the Comics Code Authority. (The conventions have loosened but not disappeared in the present: it is sometimes, though not often, possible in contemporary superhero comics to see folds represented in the drawings of some male characters' costumed crotches and little bump-outs in profile that suggest the presence of genitalia. In the November 2018 issue of *Batman: Damned*—a short series published under the rubric of DC Comics' "Black Label," intended for "mature readers"—artist Lee Bermejo shows us a naked Bruce Wayne striding nude through the deep shadows of the Batcave to choose his fighting gear. In not one but two contiguous panels, readers can see the shadowed outline of Wayne's circumcised penis. This artful play with shadow was controversial, of course, and those penile outlines disappeared from the hardcover edition of the comic, which collects all the issues of the limited series.) My copies of the Golden Age stories are in reprints on glossy cardstock paper, with reinvigorated coloring and inking, so that I'm probably seeing more than Legman could have beheld in the cheap newsprint four-color pixels of the original comics.

That Legman did see what I deem to be entirely hieroglyphical indications of large genitalia in those same comics interests me. Is this not, then, a version of *closure*—a reading whereby a suggestion of a possibility provides the invitation, the foundation, and maybe the template for an imagined presence or movement? That Legman *imagines*, not to put too fine a point on it, a lot of dick depicted on the pages of his superhero comics suggests that the unacknowledged discourse or foundational concept of the superhero is not, or at least is not only, white supremacy, as Alan Moore claims; what is underacknowledged but is insistently suggested is the presence of genitals and sex happening, though these are nowhere on the page.

Some sixty years later, Douglas Wolk gives testimony to the presence of sex in superhero comics as he provides his own analysis of many of the most intriguing creations in the comic-book universe, in *Reading Comics* (2007). This is, mind, an analysis far more *straight* in what it sees and what it looks for than Legman's, lacking Legman's powers to conjure phalluses. Wolk provides one way of accounting for the erotic stimulus provided by Superman and his superheroic brethren. He identifies the *look* of the superhero as a key component of the figure's appeal. Wolk writes of the default style of most cartoonists drawing superheroes,

> It's designed to read clearly and to provoke the strongest possible somatic response. You're supposed to react to it with your body before you think about it. Most of its characters, especially the heroic ones, are drawn to look as "sexy" as possible—wasp waists, big breasts, and flowing hair on women; rippling muscles on men. . . . The style gives a sense of even the most everyday actions and interactions being charged with sex, power, and beauty. Most of all, generic mainstream drawing is doggedly quasi-realistic—or, rather, it's realness pumped up a little, into something whose every aspect is cooler and sexier than the reality we readers are stuck with.[20]

Perhaps, then, the depiction of "pumped up," better-than-reality bodies, even bodies of doll-like smoothness, functions not unlike the gutter between panels: asking, even demanding, that the reader supply the anatomical completion of the imagined figure, such that "cooler and sexier" than real fulfills its teasing promise, Comics Code Authority and conventions of comics be damned.

This interplay of absence and presence, the one evoking the other as though illustrating the dynamics of a classic psychoanalytic fetish, in the minds of readers, and the ultimately political work accomplished in readers' minds by what the creators of comics withhold and what they supply, is what Fanon finds of interest when he quotes Legman. Wisely neglecting the greater part of Legman's claims, Fanon selects the very end of Legman's analysis in order to reveal the antiblack identification into which black (male) comics readers are seduced. Fanon's quotation of Legman is translated by Philcox thus:

> Envisaging the repercussions of these [violent] comic books on American culture, the author [Legman] continues, "The question remains whether this maniacal obsession with violence and death is the substitute for a repressed sexuality or whether its function is rather to channel along the path left open by sexual repression both the child's and the adult's desire to aggress against the economic and social structure that with their free consent corrupts them. In both cases, the cause of the corruption, whether sexual or economic, is essential; that is why as long as we are unable to tackle this fundamental repression, any attack waged against simple escape devices such as comic books will remain futile."[21]

But remember that Philcox has translated Fanon's (borrowing Sartre's) translation of English into French back into English. The original quotation in Legman's article reads this way:

> It is an open question whether the maniacal fixation on violence and death in all our mass-produced fantasies is a substitution for a censored sexuality, or is, to a greater degree, intended to siphon off—into avenues of perversion opened up by the censorship of sex—the aggression felt by children and adults against the social & economic structure by which and to which they allow themselves to be distorted. In either case the distorting element is basic, whether sexual or economic, and until we are prepared to come to grips with these basic repressions, any attack on mere escape-mechanisms like comic books must be futile.[22]

Thus, we see that Sartre and Fanon have translated the first instance of what Legman calls "censorship" into what Legman only later in the paragraph refers to as "repression."[23] Probably this makes Legman, whom, as we have seen, is far from consistent, more coherent. But censorship in English generally describes a political and legal process, and certainly the word refers to such in Legman's article, since he is discussing at length all kinds of parent groups and librarian associations and Catholic decency watchdogs engaged in the purging of (hetero)sexual references in comics, while at the same time leaving intact and intensifying the depictions of violence. "Repression" we might think rather as referring to a psychological process that responds to political demand, and a politics that refracts psychological processes. Moreover, "repression," as our Foucault-trained ears prick up reflexively to note, supposes a Freud-inspired preexisting fund of sexuality that reacts like a sensitive hydraulic system to various pressures that warp its "natural" expression and development.

The meanings accruing to "censorship" rather than "repression" are where I want to direct our attention in assembling a phenomenological account of superhero-comics reading as fantasy-act. Legman, however much he gets things twisted, tries to account for what has been expunged from the page (good, healthy, normal heterosexual sex) and what has taken its place (violence and sexual perversion). For him, in this cause lie readable the effects of reading/viewing the comic. His map of cause to effect draws only a straight line (however ironic such a description may be). Comics reading for Legman is a direction to imitation or some other form of inculcation; that is, "I see/read it; therefore, I will or I must do it" or "I see/read a version of it; therefore, I am inured to or unfazed by it wherever or however it appears." I'm interested, rather, in mapping the process of comics reading along the lines of, "I see it; therefore, it inspires my imagination." What, then, might it mean that imagination is sparked by a form that routinely engages in "censorship" of direct depiction of a *queer* sexuality that it otherwise evokes? Or, to mind our Foucauldian dogma, what might it mean that imagination is sparked by a form that routinely engages in shaping and bringing into consciousness a sphere of being that we call queer sexuality by ostentatiously censoring direct references to it?

Big Black Super-Black

To hazard partial answers to these questions, I will examine imagery of black male characters as implicit or explicit superheroes in pornographic comics. Rather than framing these depictions by reference to pornographic comics in general, I read these gay porn comics as they converse with the genre from which these cartoons derive their visual codes: mainstream superhero comics.

It should be unnecessary in the context of this book's concerns to mount any special pleading that explains why I'm discussing comics centrally featuring black characters. Nevertheless, it's worth noting that the porn superhero-esque characters I've chosen to consider are black as well as sexually queer, because these comic strips implicitly bring to the fore *both* the underacknowledged projects of white supremacy undergirding superhero comics and the underacknowledged discourse of homoerotics undergirding superhero comics.

That these figures are black male rather than black female characters does require some explanation. First, the homoerotic dynamics evoked in superhero comics are largely evoked in relation to male bodies (or rather, to the drawn effect of cisgender male embodiment, where the figures drawn are of course not actually alive, were never born, and are not embodied but are suggested as having bodies). Here we can recur to Jeffrey A. Brown: "comic book superheroes represent an acceptable, albeit obviously extreme, model of hypermasculinity."[24]

Second, the relative paucity of black female characters appearing in a superhero idiom in porn comics—and, from my anecdotal experience, their relative paucity in porn comics, period—while it contrasts sharply with a quite significant presence of black women in photovisual, film, and online-video pornography, is probably not unconnected to wider cultural dynamics identified by black feminist critiques (overlapping with antipornographic feminist critiques) of the representation of black women. Such critiques have demonstrated how representations of black women have had a structural position within the modern world as always-already pornotropes, tending toward, if not outright, caricatures. Jennifer C. Nash in *The Black Body in Ecstasy* (2014) provides a lucid overview of black women's figuration in pornography and of critical responses to it, observing, "Black women's projection on the hard-core pornographic screen has concerned black feminists precisely because it has been imagined to make explicit the exploitation that representation already inflicts on black women."[25] As Hortense Spillers describes, under the various practices and processes of the transatlantic slave trade and chattel slavery in the Americas, black people, but black women particularly, were transformed from whatever subject positions they may have enjoyed among African peoples to a kind of cultural resource (as well as, of course, a physical labor source), especially evident in the visual tropes routinely deployed to represent them: "the captured sexualities" of enslaved black women, she writes, "provide a physical and biological expression of 'otherness'; . . . [and] as a category of 'otherness,' the captive body translates into a potential for pornotroping and embodies sheer physical powerlessness that slides into a more general 'powerlessness.'"[26]

The profusion of black women's pornotroping across representational forms and genres has thus facilitated blackness becoming and appearing as "a pornographic fantasy."[27] Challenging or at least complicating this well-articulated critique of black women in pornographic representation, Nash's work, along with Mireille Miller-Young's (*A Taste for Brown Sugar: Black Women in Pornography*, 2014) and Ariane Cruz's (*The Color of Kink: Black Women, BDSM, and Pornography*, 2016), has tracked the myriad ways that black women as sex workers, performers, artists, and consumers of pornography at once work against and within these constraints, showing how "black pleasures can include sexual and erotic pleasures in racialization, *even when* (and perhaps *precisely because*) racialization is painful, and . . . the racialized pornographic screen is a site that makes . . . visible the complex relationship between race and embodied pleasures."[28] Yet the screen seems so far to have had a different historical trajectory from the porn comic-strip page, even as the two overlap significantly today in the explosion of online comics: the fantasy of *power* that superhero comics trade in via images of "hypermasculinity" has as yet not been coupled with pornographic cartoons featuring black female characters to the same extent that the two have been paired with regard to black male characters (even as the latter does not comprise a huge proportion of porn comics with superhero references).

As we'll see, there are advantages and disadvantages to having a racialized presence in the worlds of queer porn comics, payoffs as well as losses.

* * *

The creators and consumers of gay erotic cartoons have had an ongoing love affair with superhero comics. Felix Lance Falkon, an early observer of these comics, describes the artist Graewolf (a pseudonym for Falkon himself) as a paradigmatic gay erotica cartoonist in the following terms: "The greatest influence on his [Graewolf's] development was the comic books—Superman, Captain Marvel, and the rest—for he taught himself drawing by tracing various well-muscled comic book heroes, leaving off clothing and adding erections of male organs. . . . Although he can build up a drawing from a sketch of his own, he is still most at ease working closely—perhaps too closely—with his reference material."[29] Rupert Kinnard's superhero-esque cape-wearing character the Brown Bomber (named after the boxer Joe Louis), acclaimed as the first avowedly gay African American character in comics, began appearing in Kinnard's comic strip in Cornell College's student newspaper in 1977. Kinnard describes in the documentary film *No Straight Lines: The Rise of Queer Comics* how in the early development of his cartooning he gained notoriety among childhood friends as the boy who could draw superhero favorites like Spider-Man, Batman, and the Hulk. Kinnard narrates that as time progressed, "I moved on to a slightly embarrassing part of that period, where I would sometimes draw these superheroes in these erotic acts."[30]

If early gay cartoonists, whether or not they were publicly producing erotica, honed their craft via quietly imitating and then revising superhero-comics iconography, in effect supplying and undressing the well-filled jocks that Legman only feverishly imagined, then the past two decades of comics have brought these previously censored and underground imaginations into full visibility. We see clearly homoerotic versions of Batman and Robin in almost all of Joe Phillips's superhero images in his monographs, calendars, comic strips, and DVDs, for example, and read an at-length exploration of a superhero-sidekick romantic relationship (albeit between partners of comparable age) in Chayne Avery and Russell Garcia's *Boy Meets Hero* (2008), as well as enjoy exuberant renditions of either the dynamic duo or Batman alone (he does have a distinct top daddy appeal) in the collected volumes of art by Glen Hanson and Patrick Fillion. There is even a Superman-Batman romantic duo—à la the now widely known Kirk-Spock "slash" fan-fiction phenomenon (the still-burgeoning genre embraces every other conceivable TV show or movie franchise pairing)—which is of prominence in the mainstream superhero-comics world: popular and critically acclaimed writer Warren Ellis's creation of the characters Apollo and Midnighter, first for Wildstorm Comics and now appearing in DC Comics. Apollo and Midnighter are superheroes with clear references in their powers to Superman and Batman. Ellis, cheekily, in collaboration with artist Bryan

Hitch, revealed the two powerhouses to be lovers in an early issue of the *The Authority*, when they kissed.

Here again is Falkon on the early underground of gay-themed graphic work:

> The interest in the muscular physique as a subject for homoerotic art work . . . can be attributed to several sources. The ancient Greeks have a direct hand, through their surviving works, notably sculptures. . . . Another major cause . . . is the proliferation of comic book superheroes—Superman and his myriad of descendants—in costumes that usually revealed every line of their musculature. . . . On the other hand, the regular masked-hero comic books are strangely prudish in some ways, for they are drawn without any appreciable genital bulge and lack nipples even when shown bare-chested. Regardless of the intent of the artists, however, the comic-book heroes do much to establish clean-cut musculature as a virility symbol among adolescent boys, and even more important, to establish that symbol in pictorial form—as a *drawing*.[31]

Falkon's emphasis on the sexiness of superheroic figures being the achieved effect of *drawing* is noteworthy for us because it grounds us again in the recognition of how central the activity of fantasy is in the production and reception of superhero comics, whether their queer sexual content is censored or set free. Queer and gay porn comics are on the one hand more *realistic* than superhero comics—they show what prudish conventions and the Comics Code Authority dictate cannot be shown, in the form of exposed nipples, pubic hair, schlongs that are prodigies. On the other hand, through this very "realism," they draw attention to their being achieved, *drawn*, the results of imagination, since few "real" people are so muscular and so outrageously gifted in genital size.

As Thomas Waugh, a seasoned observer of pornographic photographs and pornographic cartoons, argues, porn comics are a fantastic, *nonindexical* genre of representation: "Graphics offer *a richer spectrum of fantasy* than do indexical images like photographs, often in inverse proportion to their importance as documentary evidence."[32] The richness of this spectrum is conveyed by a variety of representational techniques: Deborah Shamoon, writing about early Japanese boy-love *yaoi* comics (manga featuring tales of male homoerotic or homosexual relation-ships), notes, "Boy-love comics . . . feature a strong fantasy element. . . . Many boy-love stories have a fantastic, historic, or futuristic setting."[33] This same element of the fantastic distinguishes what Shamoon observes of Japanese pornographic manga aimed at female readers (which is not necessarily or exclusively homoerotic or homosexual). Shamoon notes that the biggest difference between these comics—widely consumed in Japan for a period—and the "frenzy of the visible" indicative of filmic porn is the ingenious methods used to show aspects of sexual acts or experience that are not visible to the eye: for example, signifying the wetness of a female character's vagina and thus the level of her arousal by drawing what are plainly droplets of moisture throughout the panel, so that the scene itself is drenched; or indicating penetration via tricks such as cutting away from panels depicting the "action" much as a porn film would depict it, to panels where a woman's skin appears to be trans-parent and the reader can see the penis or fingers within the body.[34]

Black male characters are of course relative rarities in the corpus of gay erotic cartoons, as they are in the mainstream superhero comics that have claimed my attention in this book. But insofar as they do ap-pear, with their pedigree in the fantasy sex of porn comics and in the sex-saturated fantasies of power in superhero comics, the articulation of "black" and "superhero" in queer porn cartoons endows us with *fanta-sies of blackness* that are otherwise concealed or censored in superhero comics proper. In the next section, I discuss the dimensions of these intentionally, deliberately unreal figurations of blackness that illustrate the *minor doing* and *major being* that I've attributed to fantasy-acts as (1) evoking and stoking readers' investments in the deeply problematic and yet imaginatively fecund imago of the Big Black Dick and (2) in-sinuating into readers' imagination—perhaps their being?—a desiring relationship for blackness that pushes the affirmation of blackness that we see in both Negrophilia and its political opposite Black-Is-Beautiful cultural advocacy to its limit, and perhaps beyond.

Black Dick Power

Let's look at the black male figure in pornographic comic strips of the cartoonists Belasco and David Barnes, whose work almost exclusively focuses on black characters, and Patrick Fillion, whose images are multiracial. All of these strips feature explicitly erotic black male superheroic figures or actual superheroes. In these images, the physical appeal and desirability of the characters—a fundamental characteristic, too, of mainstream male superheroes, but not generally acknowledged in fandom or deployed as a plot or thematic device—is emphasized, though it is also true that their beauty and desirability is bound up with, or at least cannot be extricated from, familiar racist images of black male hypersexuality.

The porn-comic genre is meant to sexually arouse, and Belasco's, Fillion's, and Barnes's presentation of the characters as objects of desire, as well as possible (though, as noted earlier, far from necessary) identification—sites for the reader to sexually fantasize, like porn in any medium—renders them, within the terms of the genre, analogous to the hero in superhero comics. Whether the black superhero is a reference providing a foundation for how we read the porn comic or the porn comic protagonist is explicitly a black superhero, in fictional worlds where what would be a battle in mainstream superhero comics becomes the sexual act in sex comics (or the sexual act becomes the conclusion of a truncated version of such a battle), the black male character's sexual or erotic desirability is itself a form of *power*, not unlike superspeed or laser vision.

It should be noted that how we recognize, feel, and assess the presence and operation of *power* in the context of a pornographic gay male comic already illustrates the ways in which that concept must always, understood properly, be seen as relative in a scale of measurement that also designates the not-powerful, and that therefore the content of power is not absolute but malleable, that in the blink of an eye the subject is subjected and an object, too. These characters (again, possible figures for identification as well as objects on the page to be desired or to prompt *as-if* fantasies of possession of them) are black male figures with big black dicks (BBDs), and thus ultramasculine in a way confirming the common linkage between the black male body and threatening (as well as desirable) violent masculinity; at the same time, that they are black male figures means the erection/castration paradox is in play, and the characters are "pussies" as well as human-shaped apparati for BBDs. And at the same time, too, since these representations are of all-male sexual worlds, another doubling is functioning, which Leo Bersani describes when he tells us that gay male fantasies work to both establish and disestablish masculinism, since such fantasies worship at the altar of phallic masculinity but also never cease to feel the appeal of masculinity's violation (insofar as to be penetrated—as a male figure in a gay male fantasy can be and often will be—is to become or to risk becoming nonmasculine and/or feminine).[35]

That these paradoxes and confusions of signification should be at work in a supposedly simple genre where penises are enormous and where conventions of representation satisfy the wish for power with the fantasy of shooting lethal rays from one's fingers or eyes is curious, to be sure. But it points to the way that exaggeration and caricature— which are in large part the work of the comics genre—are useful forms of analysis and revelation, and it underlines as well the heterogeneity and plasticity of what *appears* as though it is a rock-solid element of our human reality, like blackness.

Belasco is probably the most historically prominent of gay-male-comics artists whose work features black men. In addition to the collection of many of his strips called *The Brothers of New Essex: Afro Erotic Adventures* (2000), his strips, poster art, and illustrations have appeared in black gay publications like *GBM*, in porn magazines, in ads for clubs and events, and as cover art for editions of James Earl Hardy's popular *B-Boy Blues*, since the early 1990s. A fan of cartoonists such as Tom of Finland and the Hun, Belasco, a commercial artist, hungered for "more imagery exploring a wider range of African American men" than he saw in those artists' work or in popular culture generally. "Mind you," he notes, "this was only shortly after the onslaught of all that Mapplethorpe hoopla and way before the advent of Tyson Beckford, D'angelo, Taye Diggs and many more who represent the plethora of striking images of black masculinity. The fact that people responded so strongly to my Marvel comic-y rendered examples of b-boys, ruffnecks and buppies in all honesty floored me and I've been obsessed with telling these sordid little tales ever since."[36]

Belasco's primary Marvel comic-y protagonist is Boo, a broad-shouldered, sculpted-physique, earrings- and baseball-cap-wearing Apollo who would in current parlance probably be called, appreciatively, a "thug." Boo does indeed get involved in a number of "sordid" adventures, looking like a far lovelier and more overtly sexual version of Luke Cage. One of his forays, in the strips "Boo: Pleasure n' Pain" and "Hard Knox," finds Boo whisked off to a subterranean all-but-magical place where a band of black men whose clothing looks as though it were inspired by Earth, Wind & Fire album covers practice BDSM, and have captured Boo so that he will perform for their pleasure. Boo, heroically, endures his spankings and other trials but gets the sexual better of his fellow performers and eventually defeats the wizard-y warlock-y master, precipitating a general revolt among the captives and S/M brethren against the master's cruelty. Boo, the captors, and the captives all have a lot of fun in the bargain.

Another strip, "When the Master Commands," features the character Oasis, an exotic dancer and "the most scandalous brother in New Essex!" This strip takes the superheroic subtext of Boo's adventures a step further. Belasco's homage and debt to Marvel comics is evident in the strip's opening (figure 3.1), which is like the splash page of a '60s or '70s Marvel comic, surrounding a large-panel rendering of the "hero" with text that enumerates his various "powers"—Oasis's primary puissance being his immense sexual attractiveness, as is evident by Belasco's rendering Oasis nude and erect. "Hard of body, head and dick, watch as Oasis gets in way over his head (both of them) in his first spine-tingling, pulse-pounding, dick-throbbing adventures!!!!"[37] This list of noun-gerund adjectives is familiar to any reader of Marvel comics from the '60s and '70s, as its adrenaline-pumped style is pure Stan Lee.

Oasis touches off a melee at the strip club because the club patrons become obstreperous in their zeal to sample his wares, and as a result, he gets fired. Just as the splash page warns, "that body gets him [Oasis] into more trouble than his brain can handle sometimes!"[38] Needing work, Oasis answers an ad for a sex worker willing to play out the fantasies of a recluse who lives in a suburban mansion. Once Oasis arrives at the mansion, he is told to wait naked for the "master's" approach, whereupon the lights are doused, Oasis slips and falls hard in the darkness, and he awakens to find a shadowy figure licking him all over and generally having his way with him—treatment that hits Oasis's "hot spots."

Oasis wonders whether his assailant, who's wearing a "strange body suit," is black. A panel shows the mysterious man's hands, partially gloved, grasping Oasis's buttocks, and a thought balloon lets us in on Oasis's sex-worker-cum-rape-victim process: "He's got some big-ass hands! I wonder . . ." On to the next panel, where we see Oasis's body pressed up against the shadowy body-shape next to him, and see two very swollen erections. ". . . I was right. Big-ass dick, too! He's black." The

Figure 3.1. Belasco's Lee/Kirby-style splash page—with a wet Oasis.

bodysuit in shadow with penis unsheathed proceeds to force a blowjob from Oasis and soon showers Oasis's face with lovingly detailed tendrils of ejaculate—which upsets Oasis, who was more or less fine with the forced fellatio but finds the unexpected cum-facial to be disrespectful. But no matter, Oasis falls asleep, muttering, "Everything is blurry . . . Your . . . dick . . . was . . . DRUGGED?!"[39]

Strange bodysuits, sleep-inducing powers—Mr. Big Black in the Bodysuit clearly bears the hallmarks of supervillainy. But he's a porn supervillain, revealed to be black by his fulfillment of black-man-is-a-big-penis cultural conjury (and he's all the more so since the nearly-full-body-sheath makes him something of a walking black phallic symbol).

When the master finally reveals himself in the light, he is in fact attired in a form-fitting, face-concealing bodysuit replete with spikes running along the head, shoulders, ass, and crotch. He tells Oasis, "I wasn't always the master. I was taught by the first master . . ." The picture of the first master on the wall, we see, is a ringer for Oasis. Now the current master wishes to teach Oasis to be a master as he himself was taught. This task involves Oasis's elaborate submission: Oasis's brief for the evening is to navigate "the maze of temptation" in the catacombs beneath the mansion. "If you can navigate your way out without succumbing to its carnal pleasures, i.e. cumming," the master warns, ". . . you will be released . . . However, if you fall prey to lust and spill your seed, you lose and will be mine to do with as I please . . ."[40]

Oasis then prepares himself for his heroic task by donning his own version of superhero togs (figure 3.2). This skimpy costume, more Wonder Woman bathing suit than Superman long johns, is a curious development, since Oasis will not need clothes to have sex. It serves to

Figure 3.2. Oasis prepares for the evening's battle.

Figure 3.3. The master as human vibrator.

underline the strip's conscious reference to superhero comics. Subsequent to dressing this way, Oasis has sex of various configurations with several of the catacombs' lusty denizens—one-on-ones and a three-way, getting expertly sucked, getting brutally fucked, and imperiously fucking others: all comprising a quick set of Herculean labors. Oasis triumphs over each "temptation" he meets by making his partner or partners ejaculate with his superior sexual skills and overwhelming allure, while he successfully manages his (black and) blue balls.

At the end of the strip, Oasis finally faces the master himself, who reveals that his supervillain suit has been adapted to transform him into a human vibrator ("The former master, my beloved Demetri, left me an array of tools to handle young bucks like you")[41]—thus completing the master's transformation into walking Big Black Dick (figure 3.3).

After the master and Oasis fight, the master tries to fuck Oasis into submission. Oasis finds the pleasure of the master's suit-powered thrusts to be so intense that he risks dying "from ecstasy." But Oasis finds a way to turn the tables, and, applying techniques of "erotic suffocation" in which his sex skills have made him proficient, he chokes the master into unconsciousness (figure 3.4). But in addition to defeating the evil master, Oasis also has other interests, and he continues to ride the big black cyborg dick. "This dick feels sooo goood!" he cries, in a panel that shows us Oasis's penis in the foreground, nearly as large as his head and dripping with pre-cum, though it is the master's unseen penis that is being spoken of—and Oasis orgasms, at last.[42]

Oasis's ejaculate, like the rest of him, seems to be superhuman, since its mysterious properties are such that contact with the master's bodysuit fries the suit's system and completes the defeat of the master—so we see from the electric lightning-like lines frizzing around the master's splayed limbs in the panel where Oasis sprays over him. Oasis's ejaculate, his sexuality, is *power*, thus almost bearing a divine valence in the universe of superhero comics, where lightning and electricity are frequently the province of gods and mutants. According to the rules of the game as first established, Oasis's ejaculation was to seal him into submission and defeat. But the rules are upended: the master who was once not a master and learned submission to become a master falls, while the captive

Figure 3.4. Oasis triumphs over the master.

hero triumphs, defeats his captor, and gains his freedom, thus breaking the cycle of mastery and submission through "losing"—though losing is orgasm, and it is by means of the glory of Oasis's sexual skills and his Helen-like inducement of maddening desire that his triumph has been achieved. The borderlines between masculine-penetrator and feminine-penetrated, between domination and submission, master and slave—and of course the inescapable reference of these terms, in a context where black characters appear, to the history of slavery in the Americas[43]—are all crossed and blurred, even as each piece of them is touched upon and stroked to Oasis's pleasure and, presumably, stroked too for the fantasizing pleasure of the reader.

Patrick Fillion is a white Canadian cartoonist whose work has been widely reproduced in a variety of venues where illustrations of sexualized male figures appear—anthologies of gay art, beautifully produced monographs, and a wide array of porn magazines. He is also the creator and impresario of a line of digital and print comic books, *Class Comics*, featuring lavishly illustrated stories of gay male characters (*Class Comics* publishes the work of a number of creators). Fillion's characters include callboys, cops, strippers, aliens, demons, and most prominently, a large number of superheroes bearing names like Naked Justice.

The surprise—if we compare Fillion's universe to that of gay male porn films and mainstream superhero comics—is how frequently black male characters appear: a lot. In fact, one of Fillion's hardback collections of cartoon illustrations is called *Hot Chocolate* and is exclusively devoted to his drawings of black men. In figures 3.5 and 3.6, you can see that while Fillion's black men are always sporting outsized members (again, often larger than the characters' heads!) in an apparent fulfillment of the reduction to BBD that figurations of Blade and Black Panther conceal behind images of fright and horror, they are also illustrated as beautiful, via soft lines and the rendering of dreamy, romantic, happy expressions. (It must be noted, too, that *all* of Fillion's characters, whatever their race or species, have penises longer and fatter than even Tom of Finland's.)

One of Fillion's stable of superhero creations is a character called Space Cadet. Like many of Fillion's heroes, he's gloriously good-looking and hugely endowed, and he's also black, with blond hair. Space Cadet in his earliest appearances as a secondary character—and sex partner—in

Figure 3.5. From Patrick Fillion's collection *Hot Chocolate*.

Figure 3.6. More of Patrick Fillion's *Hot Chocolate*.

the adventures of Naked Justice (a red-headed solar-powered hunk whose lover was Latinx Ghostboy) wore an ungainly fishbowl helmet and sported a laser pistol and seemed to have the vague power set reminiscent of the classic mainstream Silver Age superhero Adam Strange, one of many "spaceman" creations inspired by the Cold War competition for space flight in the '50s and '60s. But later Space Cadet moved to center stage, getting his own series, and he doffed the helmet and acquired jazzier powers involving "radiation bursts" shot straight from his fingers and eyes (and in a recent adventure, his penis). Arguably his chief power, though, is to be such an apparently delectable bottom that he attracts the attention of horny villains and interlopers. On the cover of *Rapture* #3 (figure 3.7), we see his costume torn from his body à la Luke Cage, though his expression, unlike Cage's painful-looking fury, is one of, well, rapture, as he's fondled from behind by a demonic satyr who appears to have his penis deep up Cadet's backside.

In the pages of the issue, we discover that the satyr, Vallan, has been spying on Space Cadet to determine whether he's powerful enough to serve as a champion in Vallan's realm, which is menaced by Baron Von Phallus. Space Cadet's subsequent trip to the land of the satyrs finds him constantly being fondled, molested, and mounted (he's stripped of his costume almost immediately—satyr customs and immigration at work, evidently). He's also constantly called "the dark one," as in "The dark one is glorious! What a magnificent warrior's physique he possesses!" and "We could play with the dark one and Jakoor . . . would never know" and "Forgive us, my lord . . . We could not resist the beauty of the dark one!" Though Space Cadet complains that the satyr, fairy, and centaur folk he's supposed to champion (but who've been busy having their way with him while he's comatose) should call him by his name (Byron) rather than "dark one," the very next line has Strider, the king of the centaurs, replying, "As you wish, dark one."[44] Later King Strider hits the double, saying, "You truly are a Nubian prince, dark one," to which Space Cadet replies, "Okay, fine . . . you can keep calling me 'dark one' . . . if you kiss me." The text caption after the two kiss makes the language of Strider's dialogue its own: Fillion writes, "Strider swoops Space Cadet into his arms, hungry to get at the Nubian hero's rigid member."[45]

Byron, needless to say, does not hail from the ancient land of Nubia or its present-day national locations: the descriptive refers to his color, his

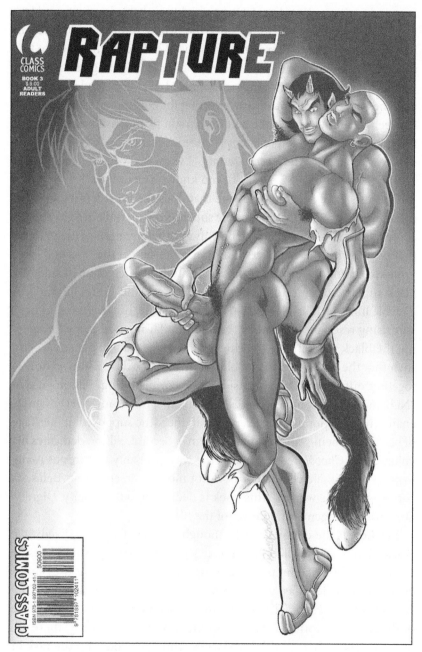

Figure 3.7. Patrick Fillion's Space Cadet in rapture.

race and heritage. Thus Space Cadet's highly fuckable loveliness is *black* fuckable loveliness—and we see this, too, where Cadet faces the villain Icecap. Icecap has been lured to come out of hiding by the smell of Cadet's free-hanging cock, and he wastes no time highlighting verbally what we can *see*, which is the two characters' racial difference (indeed, Icecap's whiteness is so unrealistically extreme that the confrontation seems to be between villainous ice people and heroic sun people, as though plucked from a simplistic version of a '90s Afrocentric fantasy). "Oh, groovy! It's my favorite fudgesickle!" Icecap taunts. "I've missed you! You're the tastiest chocolate sundae I've ever had, you know!" (figure 3.8).[46]

The insistence here on language that does the unnecessary work of racial marking—and that makes the superhero-supervillain fight a racial confrontation—seems at first to be only another iteration of the practice that began with the racialized naming of heroes in the '60s and '70s. From this point of view, the conceptualization and depiction of an erotic black superhero figure differs between Belasco and Fillion along predictable lines, insider-black versus outsider-white. But there are perhaps surprising resonances between the two, similar methods of reconfiguring the black male image to achieve a *desirable black* male superhero, such that the view from inside blackness to black desirability is not altogether different from the outside view. For one thing, Fillion's use of "Nubian" takes up (and eroticizes) naming that has its most recent provenance in then-popular Afrocentric parlance (the supposed ur-heritage of black folks being "the original Nubian"). Second, Fillion dedicates his volume *Hot Chocolate*—which, by the way, probably features as many distinct black male characters as, if not more than, appear in Belasco's corpus—in these words: "This book is dedicated to the Beauty, Dignity, Strength, Intelligence and Power of the Black Man."[47]

Key here is the definite article, though it remains uncapitalized: "*the* Black Man"—an appellation that is designated from a position outside blackness or black communities but that of course also has its uses enunciated from inside—as in this comment in Belasco's foreword to *The Brothers of New Essex*: "The stories in this book only scratch the surface of the kinds of erotic tales I have in my head to tell. Luckily, there are other artists such as . . . David Barnes who have taken up the task of providing stories and imagery that explore the sexuality of *the black gay* (or same-gender loving . . . take your pick!) *male*."[48]

Figure 3.8. Space Cadet and the ultrawhite villain Icecap confront each other.

All of this is on one level a demonstration of how the discourse of racialization has worked in the case of African-diasporic slavery and its aftermath: a hodgepodge of peoples naming their heritages with a variety of different names get called "black," are forced to internalize this name, and later assert their presence, designate their historical experience, and demand redress for injustice using the names and terms they have acquired, the names that were central instruments in their subjugation.

In Belasco's Oasis story, the villainous master, sheathed in a black shadow-suit, identified as African American by the size of his dick felt in the dark, and hyped up by the suit to be a human vibrator, *is* the Big Black Dick. Oasis is the black *hero*, who also has a big dick: one set of values (a protagonist's centrality, heroism, desirability) becomes visible in part because it is broken off and distanced from a more exaggerated—and, in typical binary fashion, less attractive (the suit isn't cute)—and problematic set of values (the über-dick, the bestial), which must come along with the black male figure. Oasis ejaculates—in symbolic terms, he is able to summon his own vital energy, the stuff of his genetic being, and it saves the day for him, though he has been told to keep it in check in order to survive—while riding the big black dick, which is a creation of the suit and which is thus artificial in the story, as a way of pointing to its chimerical nature in reality.

A comic strip by David Barnes, whom Belasco names as a cotraveler, provides an illustration of how this circuit of naming is also a circuit of ways of looking, and of ways of conceiving fantasy. It performs a different, but instructive, working with the split characteristics of the black male figure.

One of Barnes's main characters is Radio Raheem. Raheem appears in Barnes's zine *The Erotic Adventures of Radio Raheem*. Raheem is not a superhero, but his status is superheroic in the sense that he is the focus of the strip and his desirability is of such fantastic proportions that I deem it superhuman. Raheem is described in a splash page thus: "He's part black, part Puerto-Rican, he's young and full of cum . . . He's a homeboy, he's a playboy . . . He will rock your world . . ."[49] I therefore treat Raheem as a superhero-like character here.

In the strip "At the Gym," Raheem rocks the world of the lucky folks who happen to be present when he goes to work out. Note in figure 3.9 that while the story turns entirely on Raheem's appeal, Barnes's style is

Figure 3.9. David Barnes's "Raheem Ramos" cruises the gym.

less hyperreal in the Marvel Way than Belasco's and Fillion's; it is instead more sketch-like, calling you to fill out the missing dimensions with your own imagination.

Barnes's style might mean that Raheem's positioning as a paragon of desirability—as the locus of erotic fantasy for the reader—is not as aesthetically apparent as Boo's, Oasis's, or Space Cadet's. Rather, it is established by the other characters' response to him. In this vein, the culminating panel of figure 3.10 catches the attention: Who are the two voyeur characters, extreme right and left, in the panel?

The two observing characters are white, while the sexual performers are black, and this of course is underlined by the younger man's line, which spills out of the borders of the panel, "God, I love black men!" Neither of these figures plays any other part in the story or has any other dialogue. The older man appears here and nowhere else. The younger character appears prior to this moment, watching Raheem's shorts bulge (figure 3.11)—though this appearance is ambiguous, since the similarity between this character's face and the young voyeur in the shower is not pronounced; both simply appear to be "white," as evinced by the rendering of the two figures' hair.

Figure 3.10. Raheem and his trick are observed in the shower.

This younger of the two shower-voyeur characters appears again—
less ambiguously—after the cum-shot panel, standing around watching
as the imminent arrival of the gym manager brings the play and exhibition to a close (figure 3.12).

Why are these white characters included?

To establish the response that Raheem garners, his power over men.
The fact that they are voyeurs rather than participants might be a nod
to the reader, a way to represent us in the story so that, as promised,
Raheem rocks *your* world.

But it is surely significant that these voyeurs, and by extension perhaps *you* the reader, are white. There's a considerable amount of *watching*, it seems, when black male characters are in the center of the porn
comic, since Vallan watches Space Cadet, and Oasis gets observed at
different times in his story, by the master and his servants or captives. In

Figure 3.11. The voyeur in a singlet watches Raheem in the weight room.

Figure 3.12. The young white voyeur watches Raheem and his beau, Aaron, watch the off-panel gym manager watching.

"At the Gym," Raheem engages in exhibitionistic sex with Aaron, is duly watched by the unnamed white voyeurs in the shower and in the weight room, and then is watched by an unseen gym manager. In this way, we may surmise that the element of *surveillance*, which is a fundamental practice enforcing white supremacy, and the resultant effect of *enclosure*, are recognized as conditions under which the blackness of black men takes meaning, even in a porn comic. Barnes's story makes a recurring black male character the protagonist and focus of the erotic and sexual desires activated in the story, but the story also represents as structural elements a kind of racialized framing for the setting in which that desire is activated—black bodies surveilled; black bodies as *objects* of a gaze that is Negrophilic, yes, but therefore also Negrophobic.

If Belasco's inclusion of Barnes in the project he describes for his creation of Boo and Oasis et al. is an accurate description of Barnes's oeuvre—the project of providing "more imagery exploring a wider range of African American men" as cartoon templates of erotic fantasy, then the line "God, I love black men!" seems to be a core statement of Barnes's strip. It surely responds to and follows the famous late-1980s motto, "Black men loving black men is the revolutionary act," a line that is ritually repeated in Marlon Riggs's 1989 documentary *Tongues Untied* and that itself echoed Joseph Beam's exhortatory, "Black men loving Black men is a call to action, an acknowledgment of responsibility."[50] To come to "love black men" with an exclamatory and divinity-beseeching fervor is an encapsulation of the tendency of Barnes's strip and the object of its drive. The line confirms the desirability and lovability not just of Raheem but of Raheem and his gym paramour, Aaron, as representatives of black men in general, Raheem as *the* black man.

The line's position in the flow of the story is significant, too. Barnes writes/draws it spilling out of the panel into the gutter. This *might* be a "mistake" having to do with the problem of containing all the text and picture that Barnes needs for each temporal beat in the story that the panel represents. Barnes might have run out of room. But even if that's so, Barnes felt the need to have the line included in full, and to sacrifice the integrity of the panel to include it.

Reading this as a cartooning mistake, however, doesn't quite hold up. Breaking the line of a panel is a fairly conventional convention-breaker in comic-book art, where figures or effects spilling over panel lines con-

Figure 3.13. Raheem reveals himself, with a "THROB" that flows beyond the panel's bounds.

vey movement and dynamism or emphasize how what breaks the panel cannot be contained in a single temporal beat within the story, how it dominates what lies near it. The likely intentionality of the panel-line break is further suggested by the fact that the same spillage occurs only one other time in the nine-page strip, when the sound effect of Raheem's penis getting erect is too much to contain (figure 3.13).

This "THROB" helps tell us something about Barnes's similarly positioned "God, I love black men!" The word "throb" describes a movement we cannot actually see, of course. But the description of movement via a text word rendered in capital, visually hollow letters aligns it with the representation of sound effects in cartooning, something we routinely encounter in comics where fighting occurs and building walls come crashing down. This particular "THROB," then, is a movement unseen, but also a sound we could never hear. It's related to the "BOING!" and other such orthographical "sound" effects that flare above the head of the iconic character Archie Andrews when he sees Veronica and experiences a thunderbolt of desire that the Comics Code Authority (and perhaps the dictates of comedy) required to be dissimulated (figure 3.14).[51]

Both the statement "God, I love black men!"—exclamation, substitute for ejaculation, and revelation all at once—and the unhearable sound effect of a throbbing penis spill into the *gutters* of Barnes's strip. Both statement and sound effect thus represent something dynamic, something that exceeds its moment. One reading of this parallel is to see the

Figure 3.14. Archie Andrews experiences a typical moment of comic erotic excitement.

latter as informing, even causing the former: in such a reading, it is the BBD, the race-inflected and often or even mostly racist fantasy, that is the source of love. I think this line of cause and effect is operative, but the provenance of "I love black men!" in Beam's and Riggs's work—and thus the line's background and meaning in an exhortation to combat how antiblackness sows black community discord—tugs my attention in a different direction.

The gutter is where the reader of the comic supplies the imagination of what is not represented on the page. It is the invitation to and require-ment of the comics reader's dreaming. Both the love for black men and the unhearable sound effect of Raheem's penis's throb are directions, ori-entations, that Barnes gives us for the conscious dreaming inherent to comic-strip reading and viewing. Legman's filled-up jocks and inflated crotches that he never actually saw but nevertheless reported as ubiqui-tous give us an instructive, if also cautionary, example of how to track the significance of the unrepresented in comics. Barnes's textual and text-effect spillovers point us to qualities of blackness that are not seen, that perhaps cannot be *seen*, cannot be *captured* in the figural and picto-rial, qualities that lie beyond the visual field and the Fanon-described dictates of blackness apprehended via epidermalization—qualities of blackness suggested by the link between text and image that is the DNA of comics, qualities of blackness that one *loves*.

I see this as a love that at once coincides with, and is nonetheless out of scale with, embodied love—embodied love being that which exists in the temporal (the temporal is broken by the spillage out of the panel) and which conflates blackness-as-category with bodies-deemed-black. In a comic strip that tells a story about *physical* embodied love, the *metaphysical* and nontemporal is signified; but the two dimensions are linked, not cleaved. When we evoke the metaphysical not confined to the temporal, we are often invoking *gods* and divinity, which here we can for brevity's sake sign as a category denoting what is ineffable with respect to a system of representation. The young white voyeur's "God . . . !" signals the reader's brief transition into this category as one reads. The process I'm groping for here is where metaphor and metonymy bleed into, and then infuse, causality. This is another way of describing *magic*. Comics reading here *is* "magical thinking." But the dismissive judgment inherent to that phrase—for me, inaugurated in the diamond-faceted writing of Joan Didion and her memoir *The Year of Magical Thinking* (2007)—we must jettison in this context, in order to perceive the ontological features of what we are describing.

It is troubling, from an anti-antiblack perspective, to follow the pathway of Barnes's strip to an excessive, metaphysical physical love of blackness and black men through the perhaps-unwanted interposition of a white gaze. It is troubling if in all these strips, the desirability of the black male figure is most firmly established—might well even require—the construction of a white viewer recognizing it, even in a fantasy created from a position supposedly *in* blackness or within black communities.

Belasco, Barnes, and Fillion come from different racial positions as they create their fantasy figures, but once they enter the discourse of fantasy, visual and textual, and that discourse shapes them as much as they shape it, what is the degree of difference between them in how they *see* the black figure? How different truly are Belasco's and Barnes's conceptualization from Fillion's?

It may be that the appearance of a black male hero under the conditions established by superheroic fantasy fiction requires a distribution of the attributes of the stereotype(s) without which the blackness/maleness of a black male figure is nigh illegible: some other, related character or some part of the hero's core story or some part of his list of powers, some aspect of his appearance, must sign the bestial and/or monstrous and/or hypersexual and/or menacing and/or outlaw. This, we may consider, is not unlike the appearance of a black man with political power—I'm coming back, of course, to Obama, who as I noted in the introduction shaped the visions of black supermen in comic-book pages in the 2010s: the black man with political power, who, having come to be under conditions of sociality defined by antiblackness, and under the aegis of a political system that made its principal structural foundation the conjuring of (white) freedom out of its constitutive contrast with the enslavement of visibly "black" demi-citizens, and that established its post-emancipation definition of order and nation via the relentless restriction of the movement of black bodies and prosperity of black persons, must signify a fundamentally unstable contradiction that tends always toward impossibility: powerful but actually powerless; or powerless but covertly powerful—a president, but one ever restrained and on the cusp of castration; a revolutionary leader, but assassinated.

Barnes, Fillion, and Belasco similarly manage this tendency toward impossibility—and recall, we are encountering this impossibility in fantasy, where we might expect that "the resistance of the empirical world is eliminated," as Ernst Bloch says of art.[52] Management for Barnes et al. involves constructing within their tales a position *outside*, as it were, from which blackness can be valued as powerful and desirable. An outside-black or nonblack position must be shaped within the narrative and shaped *by* the flow of tableaux, for *seeing* black desirability, because the domination of ways of seeing and valuing would make such beauty otherwise invisible, or conceal it beneath the more familiar veneers of monstrosity and threat.

Regarding such hegemonies of seeing and valuing, we have an insightful comment by filmmaker Isaac Julien. Here he comments on the phenomenon of the so-called snow queen, the black gay man whose apparent preference for romantic or sexual object is white men. Julien calls himself a snow queen in an essay about his 1993 short film *The Attendant*, though his use of the colloquialism reveals a complexity in the phenomenon that users of the term rarely admit or even wish to know.

> In fact in this Western culture we have all grown up as snow queens—
> straights, as well as white queens. Western culture is in love with its own

(white) image. The upholding of an essential black identity is dependent upon an active avoidance of the psychic reality of black/white desire. . . . The out black snow queen draws attention to the fact of black desire for the white subject. . . . Fixed ideas about racial difference are brought into play by both black and white subjects in their everyday transactions, mediated on a sexual and racial anxiety which is internal to every subject and which is based on the insistent denial of the Other within ourselves.[53]

Julien's comment is of course to state in a (somewhat) different context exactly what Fanon says when he declares that there is only one destiny for the black man, and it is to become white.[54]

The dictates of the snow queen world mean that the *difference* of the black figure is inescapable, a given: blackness will be an object in the discursive eye, and it will be alien, though it can also, with effort, be a beautiful object, a gorgeous alien. I return briefly here to LaPlanche and Pontalis's definition of "phantasy," referenced in the introduction. Recall that, "It is not an *object* that the subject imagines and aims at" in phantasy, they note, "but rather a *sequence* in which the subject has his own part to play and in which permutations of roles and attributions are possible. . . . The primary function of phantasy [is as] the *mise-en-scène* of desire."[55]

Presumably any number of desires are at work for which a black superhero fantasy in porn comics provides the mise-en-scène. I want to suggest that among them, what is being structured and set in motion in these fantasies is a desire *for* blackness in its beauty, for blackness it-"self," as a tangible, consumable object, which cannot become such an object unless its consolidation also renders us the fantasizers, through participation in the artist's fantasies, as also thereby separated from blackness, whether or not we "are" black. We are then as readers all positioned as *nonblack* desiring blackness in these strips.

This returns us to the Julien formulation that we are all snow queens; but with these comic strips, we are snow queens whose melancholic attachment to a blackness that our very entry into a racialized world required us to abject turns around to greedily imbibe that blackness from which it has been alienated. Of course, the likely *outside* available—in a snow-queen world—is the white position that sees blackness (and creates it) as different, whether desirable or repellent. And then insofar as the image, flat on the page, two-dimensional, is the gateway to and the frame for this fantasy, is not the produced experience, however fleeting, one of *having* the privileges of whiteness? Doing whiteness in a minor key, occupying and being it in a major key? Which is in part to say to have the position of being unobserved observer, the unmarked presence, a momentary plenitude to be found in an actually—within the terms of the fantasy—consummated or fulfilled relation to *necessarily* (for the process to work) idealized blackness.

Clearly this is a good-news, bad-news observation: such effects we can see as utopian, because they model for us a reality in which a certain kind of privilege—an erotic privilege, a privilege to eroticize and enjoy—becomes common. Linda Williams makes an analogous observation in writing about depictions of interracial lust in porn and in the mainstream film *Mandingo* (1975). Williams notes that such depictions regularly exploit racist stereotypes in order to create pleasure for all viewers: "The excitement of interracial lust—for both blacks and whites—depends on a basic knowledge of the white racist scenario of white virgin / black beast. But the pleasure generated by the scenario does not necessarily need to *believe* in the scenario. Rather, we might say that there is a kind of knowing flirtation with the archaic beliefs of racial stereotypes. . . . The pleasure of sexual-racial difference once available to white masters alone are now available to all." Williams adds, "though not equally to all," which of course is the easy-enough-to-see bad news, since we find here limits that we probably don't want even to utopian *imagining* in our fantasies: limits that appear in the narrowness of a conceptual structure, of a widely held cultural fantasmatic, that cannot find any more free, empowered, connected-to-pleasure position than that of "white."[56]

This analyzes and describes our inescapably racist or race-informed ways of looking and erotic fantasizing. But before we fall too far down the deep, deep well of this particular despair, I would like to point out that even where we have to be interpellated into something like whiteness to see and desire blackness, we are at the same time seeing the conjunction of supposedly disjunct elements: *power* and blackness, *beauty* and blackness, *superhero* and blackness.

For there is another layer to the achievement of the representation of black desirability, subtending the apparently necessary construction of an outside-black or nonblack viewership, a layer that even Oasis's villain helps us recognize: this is the way in which the black male figure can be or is powerful, desirable, even worshipful via its operation as a surplus, an excess, a double. We can discern the valuation of the surplus in an element of homosexual desire, which might not from a certain vantage be love of the *same* so much as it is love of *more*—that is, I love dicks. It is not enough that *I* have one. I have to "have" in whatever way possible many, many more, too. For Belasco and Barnes, creating from the point of view within a social position identified as black, black is or becomes gorgeous, loved, revered, but as *more* than their own, as an excess of blackness that appears in their creations in the mode of exaggeration: the master villain in the Oasis story. Or it appears as a transcendent value, a cobbling together of meanings that cohere into something like the divine—and by "divine" here, I mean to designate by way of nominative placeholder something that does not exist or cannot be measured in the human scale, something that is consummately a *figure* acknowledged to be larger than life (a dick that's *that* big! cum that's like lightning!) and operating as a container for a variety of aspirations, desires and wishes: *the* Black Man to whose Beauty and so on Fillion dedicates his work; the generalized "I love black men!" ejaculation that arises from watching two of the type fuck and that overspills the boundaries of the page.

It is this black-beauty-as-excess-and-surplus that, of course, a medium steeped in the fantastic like comics is particularly primed to facilitate our experience of: we can *do* it only in a minor key, perhaps, but we can *be* it, experience it as part of our reading.

This intimation of self-making or self-transformation I now turn to in conclusion.

Conclusion

On Becoming Fantastical

If this world would finally just "be allowed to breathe" and were set free, . . . this would provide some space for such richly prospective doubt and the decisive incentive toward utopia that is the meaning of Brecht's short sentence, "Something's missing." This sentence . . . is one of the most profound that Brecht ever wrote. . . . What is this "something"? If it is not allowed to be cast in a picture, then I shall portray it as in the process of being (seiend). But one should not be allowed to eliminate it as if it really did not exist.
—Ernst Bloch, "Something's Missing"

Because parlous times not only ever were but probably ever will be, I sometimes find myself wanting to step into the shoes of Eviline, the Wicked Witch of the West in *The Wiz* (1978), whose most famous line (for me, anyway) was not Elphaba's lament "Oh, what a world!" but a rather more diva demand: "Don't nobody bring me no bad news."

I began writing this book in the months following that foulness Trump's Electoral College win in 2016. As I conclude, I hear helicopters buzzing overhead as they patrol to watch signs of protest that have erupted across the nation in the wake of George Floyd's murder by police, and myriad repercussions and threats of further devastation due to the COVID-19 pandemic ooze like rancid sludge through our lives. Clearly my desire to emulate Eviline has been, and will remain, as ineffective as hers was in *The Wiz*. No surprise there. Certainly, keeping the news of the tide at bay does nothing to prevent the deluge from taking you under.

But this we must suppose a woman as worldly as Eviline surely knew, and as I think of her now, I can see that hers was no reimagination of

King Cnut's futile command against the elements, but a different and more feasible, if still overwhelmingly challenging, demand: that others help her in *keeping her attention on what empowers rather than dispirits her*. Such a demand does not propose that it can solve, say, the ubiquity of antiblackness, or suppose it can exist without reference to antiblackness; but it does say that sometimes (well, Eviline being a diva, for her, most all the time) it would like to train the powers of its mind on antiblackness's defeat—or just on the relief of antiblackness's absence. In many ways, this book has been an exercise in testing whether and how things in and of this world—active fantasy, and its exemplar and ready-to-hand instrument and method, superhero comics—can help focus our minds (my mind) beyond the world, to think in the mind, and thus to live in the body, *as if* something is different, to think and to live and thus to *be*, for just a moment, *something different*, a "something" we see in light of, rather than refusing to know, as Brecht through Bloch articulates in the epigraph, that "something's missing."

I'll tell a personal story—personal in a way but highly impersonal in its most significant dimensions—to illustrate my Eveline's strategy. Some bad news that Eviline's example could not help me stop sailed in among the everyday flotilla on March 19, 2018, courtesy of that great bearer of bad tidings, the *New York Times* (an institution about which I often have an inclination similar to Eviline's, to slay the messenger). The headline of the story said, "Extensive Data Shows Punishing Reach of Racism for Black Boys." The story reported the findings of a study undertaken by researchers at Stanford, Harvard, and the Census Bureau, which showed that the income inequality between blacks and whites in the United States is "entirely driven" by inequality between the divergent prospective earning power of black boys and white boys. "Black men consistently earn less than white men, whether they're raised poor or rich," and "most white men raised in wealthy families will stay rich or upper middle class as adults, but black boys raised in similarly rich households will not," two searing graphics summarized. The research "traced the lives of millions of children" and was based on earnings and demographic data of nearly every American child in their late thirties as of 2018. It found that large income gaps exist between black and white men of similar background (though not black and white women of similar background). "Even when children grow up next to each other with parents who earn similar incomes"—correcting, therefore, for residential factors—"black boys fare worse than white boys in 99 percent of America."[1]

Sometimes bad news of this sort finds itself discussed in my family's group text messages. Rarely—never, I think, except this once—is such news accompanied by a sense of wonder and a dollop of relief for any family member, as this bit of news was. My sister passed along to my father and me via text a link to the story, with a heartfelt statement of amazement and gratitude that we two are, apparently, in the 1 percent. Granted, of course, I have not been for some time in my late thirties, and so the statistical portrait offered by the researchers doesn't include me, though it is not unreasonable to suppose—we certainly supposed this when we all read the story—that something approaching these statistics, whether worse or better, obtains for older generations.

But whatever the generational fit of the statistics, it does not tell our story. I was raised in a middle-class household (a class position by no means easily obtained by my father and mother, who are the children or grandchildren of Deep South sharecroppers), was educated at Stanford (as my sister was) and Yale, and—at least as of this writing—am solidly in the middle and, by some counts, the upper-middle class. Whether my earning is roughly equal to that of white men similarly situated is not something I know. But I haven't experienced any economic class decline relative to my father or to my childhood. This story, then, like many of the statistics-bound and anecdotal stories told about the pasts and fates of black men in the United States that I've read or heard in various news outlets since I was a teenager, from the *New York Times* to the *New Republic* to National Public Radio's *This American Life*—of jail and prison time, of struggles to succeed academically (the perils of being "an affirmative-action baby" and other such diminishments), and so on—does not describe any significant portion, or any portion at all, of my life.

I don't know why this is so, and it's with no small bit of reluctance that I'm willing to recount my statistical outlier status. I felt no great responsibility or sense of achievement for this outcome (again, an outcome so far). Definitely I felt and feel no gratitude to the system that has so relentlessly and viciously robbed 99 percent of my brethren of education and/or opportunity in order to redistribute their life chances to white males—and evidently, to me and to the rest of that remaining 1 percent.

I couldn't receive my sister's congratulations with any grace. I attributed my having escaped the clutches of this particular racist punishment to statistical luck. Though the *luck*, really, is my parents' *doing*.

My father was similarly circumspect in response to my sister's observation. Regarding the study's findings, he texted back, "I've known about this since I was seven years old."

My sister and I were both curious to know exactly *how* my father perceived "this" in his specific circumstances, growing up on a sharecropper farm in Shreveport in northern Louisiana in the middle of the twentieth century. We supposed it had to do with our grandparents' parenting and with his childhood observation of life under quotidian Jim Crow, his being subjected even in an indirect way to Jim Crow's violence and its hate. We conjectured that he became knowledgeable, and perhaps precociously began to plot his way through the minefield of being young, black, and male, via an osmotic absorption of the general social atmosphere, some process not unlike any child's absorption of, say, the tensions and conflicts of divorcing parents, even when the child has no idea of anything involved in the conduct of adult relationships. These seemed likely explanations, from the essentially ignorant distance we could view my father's life. Northern Louisiana, we knew, is the Klaniest of Klan country. My father, we supposed, could see *Birth of a Nation* play out in his home county.

Probably all our suppositions did rightly identify contributing factors. But when, more than a year later, we remembered to pose the question to him—*How did you* know *when you were seven?*—he mentioned none of these factors in reply.

My father's answer surprised me. Though given everything I've written in this book, it shouldn't have.

I recorded his answer and transcribe a portion of it here.

How did he know? "At that age, seven years old," he said, "I probably had a real active imagination or something. I used to read all these comic books. . . . I read . . . all those, I guess, superpeople. They didn't call them superheroes then. I used to read not so much that stuff that used to be in the newspapers. It must have been those superheroes. . . . I used to collect those things. I had all that stuff."[2]

This surprising answer—a part of the surprise being that I never knew my father had collected comics when he was young just as I did—I don't suppose to be an exhaustive answer, listing all the factors at work. I don't suppose his answer either to map the lineal clarity of a cause-and-effect relationship between his reading and collecting superhero comics and his knowledge of the malignant forces operating to fleece, if not to destroy, him. (This is a knowledge we should not fail to recognize as traumatizing to acquire, whether at age seven or seventeen.) It is, however, an answer that reflects what he remembers, and how causes and effects are linked, in however possibly circuitous or truncated a fashion, in his memory. He understood the fate our racist, antiblack, anti-black-male world planned for him. He understood it and thus was facilitated in navigating it, as he remembers it, because his imagination was primed by reading superhero comics.

My father didn't remember the names of the comics he read, or of the specific characters whose adventures he read, or what name he or "they" used to categorize those characters; he repeated several times that he has no recollection of them being called superheroes, though he does recall that the characteristic of these figures that most stays with him in memory is that they were "really strong."[3]

But these comics would be the same superhero comics that Legman and Wertham, and even Fanon following Legman, found to be so deleterious to the young mind. My father turned seven in 1948, as it happens in the very same month that dates the *Neurotica* issue in which Legman's "Psychopathology of the Comics" was first published.

I return to Legman now, not because I think Legman's *right* about reading superhero comics, but because the process he describes of reading comics has some useful explanatory power, even if the outcome of that process is not necessarily, always, or perhaps ever, really, what Legman thinks the outcome is.

Legman maintains that comics inure their readers to depictions of violence and thus to the acceptance of violence. "All comic books without exception," Legman says—ever the neutral nuanced reporter is Legman—"are principally, if not wholly, devoted to violence."[4] The consistent depiction of so many violent acts and so many weapons, Legman claims—"toy guns and fireworks, advertised in the back pages of the comics—cap-shooters, b-b rifles (with manufacturer's enscrolled Bill of Rights), paralysis pistols, crank'emup tommyguns, six-inch cannon-crackers, and ray-gats emitting a spark a foot and a half long"—produce for child readers, Legman says, "The Universal Military Training of the mind." "The effect, if not the intention, has been to raise up an entire generation of adolescents—twenty million of them—who have felt, thousands upon thousands of times, all the sensations and emotions of committing murder, except pulling the trigger," Legman writes.[5]

For purposes of illustration, I want to pause to consider this last remark: What could conceivably be the logical distinction between how Legman's child reader perceives pulling the trigger and all the other acts he reads and sees, if in fact reading/seeing these acts is enough to feel "all the sensations and emotions of committing murder"? Logically there cannot really be a distinction, unless there's an ontological distinction between a depiction of holding a gun and a depiction of pulling the trigger. Such a distinction lies only between the act of holding the gun and the act of pulling the trigger, not in the two-dimensional representation of these acts. Legman can only be using "pulling the trigger" as the synecdoche for actually murdering someone: the one thing the child reader/viewer hasn't felt out of all the acts he or she reads of and views is actually murdering one of the characters. But still there cannot logically be a distinction. If the premise is that reading/viewing the act of murder automatically causes—not allows, causes—the reader to *feel*, to experience all the sensations of murder, this cannot be clearly enough distinguished on an emotional and sensational level from the commission of murder via pulling the trigger. The distinction could only be a legal distinction—the child is guilty of a murder or isn't—and a consequential distinction: there is a murdered person or there isn't.

What is potentially useful here for us is that Legman, in rather sloppily overstating his case, is nevertheless pointing toward a *dynamic* he identifies with comic books that we have, via Bersani, also identified with fantasy: that of there being difficult distinctions to draw between material experience and fantasy experience, at the level of "sensations and emotions." This reformulates the claim I am making about fantasy-acts as constituting minor forms of doing—the child who reads/views the comic book obviously *didn't* kill anyone—and constituting significant forms of *being*, in that surely a great part of the stuff of human *being* is the embodied experience of, and animation by, "sensations and emotions."

We should note regarding the former part of this formulation that Legman proceeds, as the level of his diatribe intensifies, to argue that in fact every child-murderer—whoever these may be; he doesn't bother to cite any evidence—claims he murdered under the influence of comic books. "No matter how many children commit killings exactly imitated from comic-books," Legman says, "and [then] produce the comics to prove it, psychiatrists and educators can always be found to say that the child was neurotic in the first place."[6] Thus, in Legman's understanding, reading/viewing the comic *is* just a step away from, and thus essentially *almost* tantamount to, committing murder.

This after all is the only-slightly-hidden implication of the very portion of his lecture that Fanon cites and that Fanon avers as truth: the reading/viewing of a comic book with its fantastic content inures the reader to violence—for Fanon, to violence against enemies or black men deemed the monstrous negative face of the human; thus, the violence of antiblackness—and it prepares them to commit such violence. Unlike Fanon, I don't accept Legman's understanding of the process and effect of reading/viewing comic-book narratives. But I'm intrigued by the prospect that a small pinch of their oversalted analysis might have critical purchase—that is, Legman and Fanon are perceiving, even if probably misrepresenting and simplifying, a complex relationship between fantasy and *doing* or *acting* that, even if minor, is not negligible and that carries a *weight* that I want in this book to account for, to feel the heft of. This weight complements the *being* of "sensations and emotions" that Legman identifies in the reading/viewing of comics and that I see as part of fantasy-acts.

Legman estimates that given the cheap price of comics—just a dime in the 1940s—and national distribution, each American child consumes "ten to a dozen of these *pamphlets*," which, as a pamphlet usually aims to do, educates them: for Legman, the education is in Universal Military Mind-Training. Given at least one violent act per page of every comic, an estimate that Legman says is highly conservative, this provides "a minimum supply, to every child old enough to look at pictures, of three hundred scenes of beating, shooting, strangling, torture, and blood per month, or ten a day if he reads each comic-book only once." The deleterious impact on children is entirely to be blamed on the volume of children's exposure. "With repetition like that, you can teach a child anything: that black is white, to stand on his head, eat hair—anything."[7]

My father did parlay his college ROTC training to build a career for himself in the US military—this is why I began chapter 1 staring at an image of Nubia in a military-base bookstore in 1973. So maybe Legman is onto something there? Although even if he is, Legman is certainly not thinking of black children reading comics any more than Alan Moore is thinking of queer children reading superhero comics in his condemnation of them. My father "chose" the military because it was one avenue of employment open to black men that was not menial labor, and it promised a career pathway with enough regulation to mitigate the effects of racism among one's white employers. My father always told my sister and me that in the military, you get promoted if you meet or surpass various clear benchmarks, not because your superior officer likes you or feels comfortable having a beer with you; military officials have to justify *not* promoting you with written efficiency reports, he often said, and though this by no means eliminated racism or racist decisions in the officer corps, it made racist decisions somewhat more difficult to sustain. My father's narration of his choice of the military involved a cold-eyed assessment of racism in the workplace, more than it did an inurement to committing violent acts begun by reading comics. His career selection involved a recognition of the antiblack violence baked in, as it were, to daily life in US society, more than a primary exposure to generalized violence in comics. Indeed, as he narrates it, comics provided assistance in coming to that recognition.

Vis-à-vis Legman's assertion that with the volume of repetition in comics you can teach a child *anything*, we might see the scope of what can be taught—and in my father's case, was taught—as wider and more complex than Legman proposes. My father remembers that comics facilitated his "real active imagination"—active imagination thus providing a capacity to perceive what might otherwise be obscure, as much as it provides the capacity to reinvent the real. Perhaps "with repetition like that," you could teach a child not only about Jim Crow—a teaching that Legman has no brief for but that the presence of Whitewash Jones and his ilk, and their manifest degradation, might well accomplish— but about the capacity for strength and inventiveness in navigating the constraints of Jim Crow. Perhaps that kind of repetition could teach a child to settle his attention on what *isn't there* in the world and to tone his imaginative muscles such that he could envision and begin to live *as if* his world were different. Perhaps it could teach him to *be* a superhero, under some other name because the condition and the terms of such being cannot be adequately captured by the label superhero.

This is because a reader's engagement with a story premised on fantasy can—maybe must—transform the being of the reader into a fantastic being. So at least Jean-Paul Sartre says.

Sartre says this in an essay called "Aminadab: Or the Fantastic Considered as a Language," published in 1947. Thus, Sartre's thoughts arrive to him around the same time that Legman's thoughts about comics coalesce, during the same crucial years of my father's "active imagination" and his dawning realization of the world's antiblackness.

"Aminadab" is a kind of meditative review of Maurice Blanchot's novel *Aminadab* (1942), a work bearing "an extraordinary resemblance" in Sartre's eyes to the fiction of Franz Kafka. In considering them together, Sartre makes striking observations about twentieth-century literature that centrally features fantastic elements.

The fantastic in literature presents a baffling and profound series of challenges, Sartre deems. "One doesn't make occasional allowances for the fantastical," he decides. "Either it doesn't exist or it extends to the whole of the universe." As a result of the requirements that reading the fantastic makes of the reader, its upending of a reader's expectations and a reader's learned ways of decoding conventions of representation, Sartre finds that the reader him- or herself is transformed. "The circle must be closed: no one can enter the world of dreams other than by sleeping; similarly, *no one can enter the world of the fantastic other than by becoming fantastical themselves.*"[8]

For Sartre, this "becoming fantastical" is a function of the genealogy and evolution of the fantastic in Western literature. In the epochs of literary representation where "we thought it possible to escape the human condition by asceticism, mysticism, the metaphysical disciplines or the practice of poetry"—prior to the European Enlightenment, presumably—"the genre of fantasy had a clearly defined role to fulfill," which was to manifest "our human power to transcend the human." "We strove to create a world not this world," he says, differentiating this kind of creation from the fictive dreaming of what we might call *alternative realities*; for this historical genre of fantasy made no reference, he says, to "this world." This historical genre was a world of "inhuman" figures, like angels. Now, however—now in 1947—fantasy has "only one fantastical object . . . : man. Not the man of religion and spiritualism, who is only half-committed to the things of this world, but given man, natural man, social man." Such man "is a microcosm" of "the world, the whole of nature: in him alone can the whole of spellbound nature be revealed. . . . Not in his body . . . but in his total reality as *homo faber, homo sapiens*." The fantastic has humanized itself, Sartre says. "It has rid itself, it seems, of all its trickery. There is nothing up its sleeve now and we recognize that the footprint on the shore is our own. No succubi, no ghosts, no weeping fountains. . . . For contemporary man, the fantastic is now just one way among a hundred others of reflecting back his own image."[9]

This move at the heart of fantastic literature away from reference to nonhumanity and toward "transcribing the human condition," and thus a kind of reinscription or revision of the human, is why the reader becomes fantastical.[10] The angel is no more. Now there is "the hero," who is our guide and who, though he might in the diegesis of the work be transported from our world to the fantastic one, has to become a fantastical creature, without any familiar logic governing his actions, wants, desires, or purposes that we can divine: "So we are forced, by the very laws of the novel, to espouse a viewpoint that is not our own, to condemn without comprehending and to contemplate with no surprise things that astound us. . . . We fall into line, because we *are* the hero and reason with him."[11] But since "there cannot be any *fantastical* events, because the fantastic can exist only as a universe," Sartre notes, "if I were fantastical and inhabited a fantastical world, I could in no way regard it as such"; rather, "I" would be—I am, I become—fantastical myself.[12]

Sartre intimates that what fantastic narrative accomplishes is, via the reader's accepted invitation to participate in it, a transformation of the reader's being into a fantastic being and, consequently or concomitantly, a transformation of the world into the fantastic world: "a world in which, while continuing to be inside it, I see myself from the outside. We can conceive this world only with evanescent, *self-destroying* concepts": "self-destroying" as in concepts that compel the abandonment of the terms by which the reader's self has hitherto been known and out of which it has been constructed.[13]

Sartre uses the example of walking into a cafe and seeing lots of implements (tables, utensils, benches, mirrors) as a way to illuminate what the operation of fantastic narrative, or the becoming of fantastic being, involves: in fantasy, all that is familiar is rendered strange; and of course, the strange, familiar. In the familiar, "real" world of the café, "Each [implement] . . . represents a piece of subjugated matter. Taken together, they are a part of a manifest order. And the meaning of their ordering is a purpose, an end—an end that is myself, or, rather, the man in me, the consumer that I am."[14] In the fantastic world, though, what is represented as "normal" is the loss of such order, a crossing-over into the disarray of instrumentality and purpose; we find "objects which of themselves show their instrumentality, but do so with a force of indiscipline and disorder, a kind of woolly independence that causes their purpose to elude us just when we think we have grasped it."[15] A door might open to a wall; or your meticulously recorded coffee order is followed by the waiter serving you an inkwell.

The hero who is you, the reader, becomes fantastical by having to internalize and endeavor to domesticate the inhuman or alien perspective formerly produced by the old fantasy genre's aim to represent the transcendent. In this alien but fully humanized and human perspective, the hero sees that all means and ends that appear to us as fixed have become radically contingent. "This brush is here in my hand. I merely have to pick it up to brush my clothes. But on the point of touching it, I stop. It is a brush seen from the outside. It is there in all its contingency; it refers to contingent ends, as seems to be the case to human eyes with the white pebble the ant stupidly pulls towards its hole. 'They brush their clothes every morning,' the Angel would say. And that is all it would take for the activity to seem obsessive and unintelligible."[16]

(Sartre, surely, given other references he makes in the essay, is referring to that "human" who is really a post-1492 European figure, busily accumulating his inherent attributes by depriving those whom he enslaves, colonizes, and slaughters of their attributes. My attempt here is to import the language of his reference with as little of this baggage as possible. When I use "human" here, I mean to say almost nothing about a supposedly autonomous Subject, endowed with rights by constitutions or Jehovah. I mean an embodied creature bearing the various perceptual and expressive apparatuses common to, but not limited to, our species.)

For Sartre, the author of fantasy in 1947 refuses the transcendent stance of the inhuman (the Angel, in his example) to permit "a ghost of transcendence" within immersion into the fantastic world, the world "turned upside down." "The *method* is clear . . . : since human activity, when seen from outside, seems upside down, Kafka and [Maurice] Blanchot, seeking to have us see our condition from the outside but without resorting to angels, have depicted a world turned upside down."[17]

My emphasis on "method" in the preceding quotation accrues its charge from Marxist engagements with the concept of method and from Sartre's own later *Search for a Method* (1963) (which as I understand it aims to reconcile individual action with Marxist collective-emphatic or economic-force-emphatic historical process). To describe the fantastic and fantasy as a *method* helps enrich my conception of fantasy-acts, but also helps situate fantasy as an instrumental interface with our common world (reality)—an instrument of means that might be this very method, but with ends that are opaque, that are queer, and that queer the relationships between act and effect, signifier and signified, means and ends. If these descriptions enlighten us as to the acts of fantasy, as to its activity, we see that fantasy's very operation might otherwise be described as queering: here, then, we have the recognition of fantasy as queer, the illumination of why Sedgwick might include "fantasists" among her antisexological list of queer positionalities.

Sartre of course is talking about reading fantasy in literature, in *high* literary form, not even the supposedly lower reaches of fantasy *genre* literature (which in 1947 still had seven years to wait for J. R. R. Tolkien's *The Lord of the Rings*). I'm looking at reading superhero comics, in many eyes the lowest genre of a low-culture form, as an example of the more general activity of fantasy. But as I conclude my phenomenological account, I argue that superhero comics illustrate and exemplify the fantastic *method* that Sartre theorizes. Superhero comics' closure processes entail not only the transformation of the reader's being but also a transformation of the reader's world.

Let's return once more to the ways comics represent time, as an example of what "being fantastical" via reading comics can entail: it can entail a queer and queering relationship to the temporal and to history.

In the introduction, I talked about wanting to emulate Almodóvar's pointed refusal to acknowledge Franco in his films. The Almodóvar tactic (refusal of the noxious recent past) we might place alongside Eveline's (refusal to attend to noxious reports of the even more recent past and present). Both involve an orientation toward knowledge of pasts that determine the present. Almodóvar's studied and flamboyant ignorance of the recent past of Franco in Spain, his work as a "conscious fantasist," is still of course a response to that past, and thus a mining of it. His refusal is generated by that past and has everything to do with that past. Almodóvar rewrites the past by fiat. But to rewrite is not to escape: this is where we can see again the misapprehension of common critical perspective that calls fantasy "escapism." Almodóvar has not escaped Franco. Almodóvar's position or tactic—not necessarily he himself but the figurative Almodóvar's position or tactic—is at once to *know* one is shaped by and founded on an inexorable past and to remold it: to remold the ground one walks on, as though shaping elaborate castles out of sand already set into recalcitrant figures, as though remolding one's own body's outline in an effort to affect one's stubborn internal organs.[18]

Comics, and not just superhero comics, provide a formal analogue of such an orientation toward the past, and thus they are a ready structure for enacting this kind, or mode, of relationship between present and past, which extends too to a relationship with the future. Comics provide a ready instrument for "becoming fantastical" with respect to the "real" experience of linear time.

If the notion of "closure" is that the reader supplies the connective tissue, the unseen movement and action that connects Panel A to Panel B, it is also possible for us as a phenomenological inquiry to perceive that "closure" is as much misnaming as it is aptly descriptive. What if, in the speed of reading/seeing, of moving through and across the story in whichever direction we choose, we do *not* "close," that is, we do not connect the panels, we don't make sense of their relation? What if we merely accept the transition between Panel A and Panel B and between Panel A and Panel C, without giving any thought to *how* they are connected or how they resolve into process? What if the movement between panels is a leap from one panel to the next?

To recap, in Scott McCloud's typology, this is what occurs in non sequitur transitions: panels do not clearly relate to one another—one, say, depicts a car driving on a highway; the next depicts a green lizard-woman making a passionate argument in a meeting of a parliament on a distant alien planet.

Yet what I've described is partly what we do in our encounter with comics even when the transition is mapped or intended as sequential, because the transition and the movement *isn't there*; it is only a blank space. What we *do* is akin to stacking the panels and images thereof or therein, one atop another. (This takes us back to Hilary Chute's observation: "Comics has the ability to powerfully *layer* moments of time.")[19] And/or we discard the foregoing panel to substitute it with another, where substitution is the only mental or imaginative gesture toward connectivity between them, where palimpsestic presence is all the closure that we notice (even as this palimpsestic presence is fully available to recovery, with a simple shift of eyes and attention).

The world of Panel A bears some relation to Panel B (which may not be anything other than contiguity, as in the case of non sequitur transitions), but we need not suppose, and often may not give enough time or imaginative space to consider, how Panel A changes *into* Panel B but rather simply see that change has occurred. This *might* take the form of mere repetition with a difference. And indeed repetition-with-a-difference is the most common form of comic-strip or comic-book narrative construction: Panel A shows the Thing with his fist upraised against a particular background—a cityscape, perhaps. Panel B shows the same cityscape background, the same position for the Thing, except that his arm is outstretched rather than raised, and broad curved lines suggest the force with which the Thing's apparently (but not actually) moving arm has displaced the air surrounding his body (though there is no air, and there is no body).

But the mind in encounter with the images and text does not require that there is any repetition of forms or background in order to apprehend a flow between Panel A or Panel B: only contiguity, only proximity. This is a relation in space that performs in imagination a relation in time.

(Moreover, reading in general takes place *in* time but is not *of* the time in which the reading occurs. Reading is of the time in the work, as an element of its necessary immersion—necessary in that it is not reading without such immersion. Reading's being *of* the time in the work is an element of that gainful loss of self and estrangement that Roland Barthes describes as the *jouissance* of reading.)[20]

These are properties of fantastical time, as opposed to linear or real or consensus time, with which one aligns or into which one merges as a reader, thus "becoming fantastical" via and for the duration of the act of reading. However, these fantastical properties merge too into *being*, even the being that we ascribe to our consensus reality. This form of reading, this closure that is not closure, belies the horizontal arrangement of the panels and the way they urge the reader toward sequence and linearity. The comics form aims to reflect linear progression, and it does, but not with absolute success. Where this queer timing invests reading, we have a model of stacking moments in time and of time—a model, that is, for our *actual* lived and embodied relations in time.

That is, we do not *see*—or perceive by any other apparatus—the *transition*, the *connection*, between a particular point in time (yesterday, an hour ago, ten months ago) and now. We do not see how they change; we simply move and perceive retrospectively a thread or a grain of transition and connection. Life may be understood as a series of panels, in which you only inhabit one panel at a time, and it's only that one that you *know*—and soon, very soon, you will no longer fully know it.

I have been trying to make the possibly laughable argument that reading superhero comic books is serious. By "serious," I do not mean the brutally and universally serious, like the possession and threat to use, or deployment of, nuclear weaponry; or like the bureaucratic operations that extend or withdraw the coverage of health insurance to a person suffering illness in a system that has ceded health to market forces; or like the violence of a lynch rope constricting a neck, a blunt instrument dashed against a skull. I do mean a range of relations to these very paradigms of the serious that can be described variously as: not unconnected to these serious things and events; despite these events; in light of these events; analogous to these events in structure or effect; existing in a non-contradicting way with these events; having an attenuated influence on persons or actions implicated in these events or actions; having a traceable influence on these actions; connected to these events or actions. By "serious," I mean sometimes all of these together, but far more frequently activating just one or two of these descriptive relations.

To take the converse of a statement I made earlier, superhero comics' closure processes entail not only the transformation of our world but self-transformation. The two foster each other and are thus mutually constitutive.

Imagining oneself as *super* does not leave the world imagined to contain or to accommodate the transformed super-you intact, but at the very least toggles some of that world's defining assumptions and characteristics. This becomes more potent the more sustained the imagination—that is, the more it endures in time and the more elaborate the imagination of you becomes.

This will be particularly true when the superhero character that is your template and that you imaginatively are—the means by which you imaginatively self-transform—is imagined as in some way black or imagined as partaking in the conditions of blackness. As discussed earlier, "black" and "superhero" entwine considerable reworkings of nomenclature in relation to meaning and of conceptual framework. As we have seen, this imagination of you need not begin with you but need only take someone else's imagination and publicizing of, say, the Black Panther and Wakanda as its fuel and its foundation. In turn, that imagination stabilizes into a creation that new creators successively revise, and these new creators are themselves readers and fans of the older versions of the character and world, have themselves taken flight in their own imaginations with and as the character and the character's transforming world, and receive the influence of other readers and fans who are not directly participating in the publicized version of the character's and world's elaboration.

You the reader transform your imagination of yourself in relation to this suite of processes. The potency and sustaining of this super-you *within* you—which is to say, the super-you that probably has no or limited access to publicity, except perhaps as online avatars or cosplay personae, but that also is to say the super-you *as* you—may be entirely ephemeral (because you invest little energy into it) or may boast not much more than the comparative weight of a pebble to Gibraltar. But it is significant as fantasy-acts are significant; it *is* a *working with* and *working of* self and the world—derealized being, unrealized being. *And* it is enmeshed with and inextricable from the web of the processes of imagination, stabilizing creation, and character/world elaboration, such that these fantasy-acts, individual as they may appear to be when we assess them, are as transindividuated, collective, and thus as potentially social as any expression of the discourse that inaugurates and animates the human world is. Which is to say, finally, that fantasy-acts are as much acts of life as any acts constituting life.

Tony Kushner wrote something beautiful for his character Prior Walter to say at the end of *Angels in America* (1992). Prior, remember, has been anointed by an Angel in the midst of times surely as dark as the current moment. What he says by way of farewell is, "You are fabulous creatures, each and every one. And I bless you: *More Life*."[21]

Following Kushner, I'll end with a paraphrase.

We can and do become fantastic creatures, each and every one.

I exhort you: more fantasy—which is more being and a little more doing—which is: *More* (perhaps better) *Life*.

ACKNOWLEDGMENTS

There are many people to thank for their help and inspiration in the completion of *Keeping It Unreal*—though, for me, the standard acknowledgments list always feels like inadequate gratitude for the myriad ways that things people have said or have written—or how I received the gift of their presence—lived in my consciousness as I wrote this book and helped bring the project to fruition.

I would like to thank Ramzi Fawaz, my collaborator in editing *American Literature*'s "Queer about Comics" special issue (June 2018). Working together on the special issue and getting to know Ramzi's pioneering work on superhero comics *The New Mutants* (2016), as well as our many, many conversations, were indispensable in my becoming conversant with comics studies and to the realization of this book.

Much gratitude also to two collective international groups of scholars, who heard and responded to parts of *Keeping It Unreal* and other work I've done on comics in the past decade: the fabulous members of a fabulous symposium on the African diaspora and visual culture, convened by my Berkeley African American Studies Department colleague Leigh Raiford, and Heike Raphael-Hernandez, in the Herrenhaus castle in Hannover, Germany, in 2014; and the members of the Practicing Refusal Collective/Sojourner Project, founded by Tina Campt and Saidiya Hartman.

While I've had the pleasure of ongoing conversation with the conferees of the Hannover symposium and the members of Practicing Refusal, single encounters and comments from audience members of lectures I gave as part of a black feminist speaker series at Columbia (thanks again to Saidiya Hartman), in the English Department at the University of Wisconsin–Madison (thanks again to Ramzi Fawaz), and at San Diego State (thanks to Yetta Howard) were inspiring and crucially important. My gratitude also to audiences at the "Black Currents Symposium" held at Northwestern University in 2012 and at the Ludwig Maximilian University of Munich, Germany, in 2010.

Thanks also for innumerable contributions to the development of my thought—and for the fantastic gift of making work actually fun—to all of my Berkeley colleagues but especially to my fellow members of the Black Room: Stephen Best, Nadia Ellis, Leigh Raiford, and Bryan Wagner.

A special thanks must go to Julie Carlson, whose characteristic generosity and encouragement made all the difference in turning my scattered interests in comics into a considered engagement with fantasy.

I would also like to thank the Mellon Foundation Project Grant for its support of research for *Keeping It Unreal*, and James Sime and all the fab folks at Isotope Comics in San Francisco for innumerable instances of assistance and years of nourishing conversations about comics.

The parts of chapters 2 and 3 discussing the superhero character Blade and gay erotic comics appeared in an earlier iteration as the essay "Big Black Beauty: Drawing and Naming the Black Male Figure in Superhero and Gay Porn Comics," in the anthology *Porn Archives* (2014). I owe a great debt of thanks to the editors of that volume, Tim Dean, Steven Ruszczycky, and David Squires.

The least adequate of all these inadequate thanks, and infinite gratitude, goes to my husband and best friend, Stephen Liacouras, last listed but always first in my thoughts.

NOTES

INTRODUCTION

1. Ibram X. Kendi, *Stamped from the Beginning: The Definitive History of Racist Ideas in America* (New York: Nation Books, 2016), 505.
2. My blithe and brief description of *la movida* of course fails to track the extensive scholarly and cultural-criticism debate about the extent, content, and meanings of *la movida* and whether in fact its developments should be characterized as a cultural movement or an "efflorescence," as I've termed it. See Gema Pérez Sánchez, *Queer Transitions in Contemporary Spanish Culture: From Franco to La Movida* (Albany: State University of New York Press, 2007), 1–10, 106–112. See also William J. Nichols and H. Rosi Song, eds., *Toward a Cultural Archive of La Movida: Back to the Future* (Madison, NJ: Fairleigh Dickinson University Press, 2014).
3. Pauline Kael, "Law of Desire: Manypeeplia Upsidownia," in *For Keeps* (New York: Dutton, 1994), 1132.
4. Pedro Almodóvar, *Almodóvar on Almodóvar*, ed. Frédéric Stauss, trans. Yves Baignéres and Sam Richard, rev. ed. (New York: Faber and Faber, 2006), 180. Almodóvar concludes, "Today I think it fitting that we don't forget that period, and remember that it wasn't so long ago." Though Almodóvar's gesture of refusing the memory of Franco is unique in my own thinking, this gesture—not unlike so many contributions that may appear to be the creation of singular genius—was apparently a hallmark of a significant portion of *la movida* politically engaged art. Michael Harrison, writing of the Barcelona-situated 1980s comic *Anarcoma*, notes, "Anarcoma and its original queer sensibility appear at a time when Spanish culture was attempting to emerge from the shadow of an oppressive dictatorship. A number of cultural texts of the time move specifically to forget the Franco period, and to re-create a sense of national cultural identity, in many cases by moving toward a kind of postmodern aesthetic that relies heavily on the primacy of images and eschews deep political discourse." Harrison, "The Queer Spaces and Fluid Bodies of Nazario's *Anarcoma*," *Postmodern Culture* 19, no. 3 (2009): 4.
5. Kael, "Law of Desire," 1133, ellipses in original.
6. Rosemary Jackson, *Fantasy: The Literature of Subversion* (New York: Routledge, 1981), 172, 173.
7. Frantz Fanon, *The Wretched of the Earth*, trans. Richard Philcox (1961; repr., New York: Grove, 2004), 20–21, emphasis added.
8. Lauren Berlant, *Cruel Optimism* (Durham, NC: Duke University Press), 122.

9. Jackson, *Fantasy*, 174–175, emphasis in original.

10. Jackson, 175.

11. "BDSM" stands for "bondage, discipline, sadism, and masochism"—or, more properly, the *D* and the *S* do double duty, so that *D* denotes "domination" and *S* denotes "submission" as well.

12. G. W. F. Hegel, *Phenomenology of Spirit*, trans. A. V. Miller (1807; repr., Oxford: Oxford University Press, 1977), 115.

13. Hegel, 116–117, emphasis in original.

14. Frantz Fanon, *Black Skin, White Masks*, trans. Richard Philcox (1952; repr., New York: Grove, 2008), 107, emphasis added.

15. Ernst Bloch, "Something's Missing: A Discussion between Ernst Bloch and Theodor W. Adorno on the Contradictions of Utopian Longing (1964)," in *The Utopian Function of Art and Literature*, trans. Jack Zipes and Frank Mecklenburg (Cambridge, MA: MIT Press, 1988), 12, 15.

16. Bloch states, "Hope is critical and can be disappointed. However, hope still nails a flag on the mast, even in decline, in that the decline is not accepted, even when this decline is still very strong. Hope is not confidence. Hope is surrounded by dangers. . . . Possibility is not hurray-patriotism. The opposite is also in the possible. The hindering element is also in the possible. The hindrance is implied in hope aside from the capacity to succeed" (17).

17. Frantz Fanon, *Black Skin, White Masks*, trans. Charles Lam Markmann (1952; repr., New York: Grove, 1967), 162n25.

18. Fanon, *Black Skin* (Philcox trans.), 203–204.

19. The reference to "*Y a bon Banania*" (translated in Charles Lam Markmann's earlier version as "sho' good eatin'"—but this is obviously not a literal translation) links the passage quoted in the main text to a more famous flight of rhetoric in "The Lived-Experience of the Black Man" chapter (somewhat more euphoniously and evocatively titled "The Fact of Blackness" for Markmann): "I was responsible not only for my body but also for my race and my ancestors. I cast an objective gaze over myself, discovered my blackness, my ethnic features; deafened by cannibalism, backwardness, fetishism, racial stigmas, slave traders, and above all, yes, above all, the grinning *Y a bon Banania*." Fanon (Philcox trans.), 92.

20. Norman Fischer, *Training in Compassion: Zen Teachings on the Practice of Lojong* (Boston: Shabhala, 2013) 54–55.

21. Bloch, "Something's Missing," 4, emphasis in original.

22. Ernst Bloch, "Art and Utopia," in *Utopian Function*, 110–111.

23. Karl Marx, "Letters from the *Franco-German Yearbooks*," in *Early Writings*, trans. Rodney Livingstone and Gregor Benton (London: Penguin, 1975), 209, emphasis added. Livingston and Benton translate the phrase as "dreamed of something." Zipes and Mecklenburg translate Bloch quoting Marx as "dreamed of a thing" (Bloch, "Art and Utopia," 110).

24. See the epigraph: "You might not like bein' who you are, but you better start likin' it, / because you sure can't be nobody else / In other words: I can't be you—ain't

no way, yeah–you can't be me / Well, that's how it is, sisters and brothas / . . . / It's the Law of the Land." The Temptations, "Law of the Land," written by Norman Whitfield, *Masterpiece* (Tamla Motown [UK], 1973).

25. Ursula K. Le Guin, "The Ones Who Walk Away from Omelas," in *The Unreal and the Real: Selected Stories of Ursula K. Le Guin*, vol. 2, *Outer Space, Inner Lands* (Easthampton, MA: Small Beer, 2012), 2.

26. Ernst Bloch, "Art and Society," in *Utopian Function*, 49.

27. Gayle Salamon, *The Life and Death of LaTisha King* (New York: New York University Press, 2018), 15–16.

28. See David Halperin, *How to Be Gay* (Cambridge, MA: Harvard University Press, 2012).

1. I AM NUBIA

1. By "sensed," I have to mean *feared*: the fears of annihilation with which antiblackness menaces those who are embodied as black.

2. Ernst Bloch, *The Principle of Hope*, vol. 1, trans. Neville Plaice, Stephen Plaice, and Paul Knight (1953; repr., Cambridge, MA: MIT Press, 1986), 214, emphasis in original.

3. Bloch, 215, 214.

4. Bloch, 215.

5. See Scott McCloud, *Understanding Comics: The Invisible Art* (New York: Harper-Collins, 1993), 60–74.

6. Put "gay fan art" prefaced by any superhero's name—but especially Batman—in your image search engine and see these very wishes transformed into their own joyously rendered drawings.

7. L. L. McKinney (writer) and Robyn Smith (artist), *Nubia: Real One* (Burbank, CA: DC Comics, 2021) 6. Also referenced: L. L. McKinney (writer) and Alitha Martinez (artist), "NUBIA in FUTURE STATE," in *Future State: Immortal Wonder Woman* #1 (March 2021): 25–46.

8. DC Entertainment Rights and Permissions, email to the author, November 11, 2015.

9. Heike Raphael-Hernandez, email to the author, November 13, 2015.

10. Deborah Elizabeth Whaley, *Black Women in Sequence: Re-Inking Comics, Graphic Novels, and Anime* (Seattle: University of Washington Press, 2016), 100.

11. I am not counting as a reappearance of the original Nubia a related character called "Nu'bia," which appeared in *Wonder Woman* comics beginning (briefly) in 2000. Though "Nu'bia" was a reiteration of the character Nubia, its overlap with the original character was confined to the correspondence between the two characters' skin color and the addition of an apostrophe to her name—evidently to make the name less offensive and more authentic, or to differentiate this new Nu'bia from the old Nubia. Nu'bia was an Amazon but not Diana's sister, and she possessed none of the Wonder Woman superpowers that the original Nubia supposedly shared in identical fashion with Diana. (L.L. McKinney's 2021 rendition

of Nubia, by contrast, does possess Wonder Woman's powers.) Grant Morrison, in addition to his *Final Crisis* Nubia-as–Wonder Woman, also features a black Amazon called "Nubia" in *Wonder Woman: Earth One* (Burbank, CA: DC Comics, 2016), another parallel-Earth alternate universe. Morrison's Earth-One Nubia is Queen Hippolyta's counselor and lover but is not a version of Wonder Woman, nor does she possess her powers. "Nubia" in Johnson's *Wonder Woman: Dead Earth* is a black Amazon character, a warrior who counsels Queen Hippolyta and tutors Diana in combat skills, but it is not clear whether this Nubia bears any similarity to the original other than the shared name, blackness, and martial prowess. See Daniel Warren Johnson (writer/artist), *Wonder Woman: Dead Earth* (Burbank, CA: DC Comics, 2020).

12. Phil Jimenez, email to the author, November 15, 2015.
13. Jimenez.
14. Kobena Mercer, *Welcome to the Jungle* (New York: Routledge, 1994), 200, 201, 200.
15. Phil Jimenez, introduction to *Wonder Woman by Phil Jimenez Omnibus* (Burbank, CA: DC Comics, 2019), 7.
16. For an illuminating and nuanced recent consideration of Wertham's argument specifically about Wonder Woman, see Carol L. Tilley, "A Regressive Formula of Perversity: Wertham and the Women of Comics," *Journal of Lesbian Studies* 22, no. 4 (2018): 1–19.
17. Frantz Fanon, *Black Skin, White Masks*, trans. Richard Philcox (1952; repr., New York: Grove, 2008), 124–126, first, fourth, fifth, and sixth emphases added.
18. Fanon, 17.
19. Tilley, "Regressive Formula of Perversity," 3.
20. Comichron, accessed July 24, 2019, www.comichron.com. The website banner reads, "COMICCHRON: A RESOURCE FOR COMICS RESEARCH!" and relies on reports and statistics provided by the primary comics distributor in North America, Diamond Comics Distributor.
21. Jonathan Dollimore, *Sexual Dissidence: Augustine to Wilde, Freud to Foucault* (Oxford: Oxford University Press, 1991), 305, emphasis in original.
22. Jean LaPlanche and Jean-Bertrand Pontalis, "Phantasy (or Fantasy)," in *The Language of Psycho-Analysis*, trans. Donald Nicholson-Smith (New York: Norton, 1973), 314.
23. LaPlanche and Pontalis, 318, emphasis in original.
24. Ramzi Fawaz, *The New Mutants: Superheroes and the Radical Imagination of American Comics* (New York: New York University Press, 2016), 22–23, emphasis in original.
25. This is a quotation from the unpublished draft of an essay titled "A Queer Sequence If There Ever Was One; or, The Comics Revolution in Literary Studies," which Fawaz provided to me in late 2018. Following is a citation for the published version of this essay, which does not include the exact quotation utilized in the main text: Ramzi Fawaz, "A Queer Sequence: Comics as a Disruptive Medium," *PMLA* 134, no. 3 (2019): 588–594.

26. Eve Kosofsky Sedgwick, "Queer and Now," in *Tendencies* (Durham, NC: Duke University Press, 1993), 8, emphasis in original.
27. Sedgwick, 9.
28. J. L. Austin, *How to Do Things with Words*, ed. J. O. Urmson and Marina Sbisá (Cambridge, MA: Harvard University Press, 1962), 5, accessed at https://web.stanford.edu.
29. Leo Bersani, "Psychoanalysis and the Aesthetic Subject," in *Is the Rectum a Grave? And Other Essays* (Chicago: University of Chicago Press, 2010), 149, emphasis added. The original essay appeared in *Critical Inquiry* 32 (Winter 2006): 161–174.
30. Bersani, 140.
31. Bersani, 144.
32. Bersani, 142.
33. Bersani, 142.
34. Bersani, 152.
35. Bersani, 140.
36. Bersani, 139–140, emphasis added.
37. Bersani, 142.
38. Bersani, 145, emphasis added.
39. Bersani, 141.
40. Bersani, 148.
41. Bersani, 149.
42. Bersani, 139, emphasis added.
43. Bersani, 146.
44. Bersani, 145.
45. Bersani, 148.
46. Bersani, 145.
47. Bersani, 148, emphasis added.
48. Bersani, 149.
49. Bersani, 147.
50. Bersani, 148, emphasis added.
51. Bersani, 147.
52. Bersani, 148.
53. Bersani, 147.
54. Bersani, 146.
55. Bersani, 149, emphasis added.
56. Toni Morrison, *The Origin of Others* (Cambridge, MA: Harvard University Press, 2017), 35–36.
57. Bersani, "Psychoanalysis and the Aesthetic Subject," 147.

2. CAN THE BLACK SUPERHERO *BE*?

1. Frantz Fanon, *Black Skin, White Masks*, trans. Richard Philcox (1952; repr., New York: Grove, 2008), 17, emphasis in original. Fanon's earlier translator Charles Lam Markmann renders this italicized bit of pidgin without italics but in quota-

tion marks, thus: "'Sho' good!'" Fanon, *Black Skin, White Masks*, trans. Charles Lam Markmann (1952; repr., New York: Grove, 1967), 34.

2. Fanon, *Black Skin* (Philcox trans.), 119.

3. Fanon, 131n15.

4. Gore Vidal, *Screening History* (Cambridge, MA: Harvard University Press, 1992), 1.

5. Vidal, 96.

6. Vidal, 96, emphasis in original.

7. W. J. T. Mitchell, "Comics as Media: Afterword," *Critical Inquiry* 40, no. 3 (Spring 2014): 255.

8. Mitchell, 259.

9. Mitchell, 263, emphasis added.

10. Mitchell, 256.

11. See Harry Brod, *Superman Is Jewish? How Comic Book Superheroes Came to Serve Truth, Justice, and the Jewish-American Way* (New York: Free Press, 2012).

12. See the illuminating introductory essay, "The Sweeter the Christmas," by Francis Gateward and John Jennings, in *The Blacker the Ink: Constructions of a Black Identity in Comics and Sequential Art*, ed. Gateward and Jennings (New Brunswick, NJ: Rutgers University Press, 2015), 1–15, especially 1–4.

13. See Noah Berlatsky, *Wonder Woman: Bondage and Feminism in the Marston/Peter Comics, 1941–1948* (New Brunswick, NJ: Rutgers University Press, 2015).

14. Jeffrey A. Brown, *Black Superheroes, Milestone Comics, and Their Fans* (Jackson: University Press of Mississippi, 2001), 178.

15. See my discussion of this matter in the context of Los Bros. Hernandez's marvelous comic, *Love and Rockets*. Darieck Scott, "Love, Rockets & Sex," *Americas Review* 22, nos. 3–4 (1994): 73–106.

16. Reginald Hudlin, "The Black Panther: A Historical Overview and A Look to the Future," in *Black Panther: Who Is Black Panther?*, by Hudlin (writer) and John Romita Jr. (art) (New York: Marvel, 2006), n.p. Capitalization emphasis in original, italicized emphasis added.

17. J. Reid Miller, *Stain Removal: Ethics and Race* (New York: Oxford University Press, 2016), 98, emphasis in original text.

18. Miller, 98, emphasis added.

19. See Hortense Spillers, "Mama's Baby, Papa's Maybe: An American Grammar Book" (1987), in *Black, White and In Color: Essays on Literature and Culture* (Chicago: University of Chicago Press, 2003), 206.

20. I have discussed this matter at length in *Extravagant Abjection: Blackness, Power and Sexuality in the African American Literary Imagination* (New York: New York University Press, 2010). See especially the introduction.

21. Fanon, *Black Skin* (Philcox trans.), 92, emphasis in original.

22. This was a problem faced by creators of Superman after World War II: while during the war there were evidently issues in which Superman beat up Hitler and essentially won the war or even prevented it before it started, later references to

World War II tried to align themselves with history by rewriting comic-book history to accommodate actual history—retconning, i.e., introducing new "retroactive continuity"—so that they erased Superman from the 1940s to begin his existence later. This is the most common choice, since Superman's "continuous" story has been restarted at least three times since the 1980s. In the 1970s, however, with a mere forty years of previous existence to explain, DC Comics' writers devised elaborate explanations of Hitler's possession of a powerful magical weapon that prevented Superman from landing in Festung Europa—since Superman's second big weakness after Kryptonite is supposed to be magic.

23. Fanon, *Black Skin* (Philcox trans.), xiv.
24. Fanon, 201.
25. Hillary Chute, *Why Comics? From Underground to Everywhere* (New York: HarperCollins, 2017), 24, first emphasis added, other emphases in original.
26. Mitchell, "Comics as Media," 264, emphasis added.
27. Dylan Horrocks, *Hicksville* (Montreal: Drawn and Quarterly, 2010), 84.
28. Horrocks, 84–86, emphasis in original.
29. Horrocks, 86.
30. Ashraf H. A. Rushdy, *Neo-Slave Narratives: Studies in the Social Logic of a Literary Form* (New York: Oxford University Press, 1999).
31. Saidiya Hartman, "Venus in Two Acts," *small axe* 26 (June 2008): 11.
32. Grant Morrison, *Supergods: What Masked Vigilantes, Miraculous Mutants, and a Sun God from Smallville Can Teach Us about Being Human* (New York: Spiegel and Grau, 2011), 162.
33. See Rey Chow, "The Politics of Admittance: Female Sexual Agency, Miscegenation, and the Formation of Community in Frantz Fanon," in *Frantz Fanon: Critical Perspectives*, ed. Anthony Alessandrini (New York: Routledge, 1999), 34–56. See also Samuel R. Delany, "Some Queer Notions about Race," in *Dangerous Liaisons: Blacks, Gays, and the Struggle for Equality*, ed. Eric Brandt (New York: New Press, 1999), 259–289.
34. Don McGregor, introduction to *Marvel Masterworks: Killraven*, vol. 1 (New York: Marvel, 2018), vi.
35. Morrison, *Supergods*, 156, 165.
36. Don McGregor, "Panther's Chronicles," in *Marvel Masterworks: The Black Panther*, vol. 1 (New York: Marvel, 2010), vi.
37. McGregor, introduction to *Killraven*, viii, emphasis added.
38. McGregor, ix.
39. McGregor, ix.
40. Ernst Bloch, *The Principle of Hope*, vol. 1, trans. Neville Plaice, Stephen Plaice and Paul Knight (1953; repr., Cambridge, MA: MIT Press, 1986), xvii.
41. Stan Lee, "A Combo That's Hard to Beat," in *Fantastic Four Omnibus*, vol. 2 (New York: Marvel, 2007), 548.
42. See Arlen Schumer, "The Origins of Kirby's Black Panther," in *Black Kirby Presents: In Search of the Motherboxx Connection Exhibition Catalogue*, ed. John

Jennings and Stacey Robinson (Buffalo: Black Kirby Collective, 2013), 121–125, especially 122.

43. Both interviews are quoted in *Kirby & Lee: Stuf' Said! The Jack Kirby Collector* 25, no. 75 (Winter 2019): 58.

44. See Schumer, "Origins of Kirby's Black Panther," 124.

45. This interview is cited as "Jan.-Feb. 1970 Stan Lee interview by Mike Bourne for *Changes* magazine (published April 15, 1970)," in *Kirby & Lee: Stuf' Said!*, 58.

46. Roy Thomas, "Absolutely Fab-ulous," in *Michael Chabon's The Escapist: Pulse-Pounding Thrills* (Milwaukie, OR: Dark Horse Books, 2018), 185.

47. McGregor, *Panther*, v.

48. McGregor, ix.

49. McGregor, v.

50. McGregor, vii, emphasis added.

51. Lee, "Combo That's Hard to Beat," 548, emphasis added.

52. See Martin Scorsese, "Martin Scorsese: I Said Marvel Movies Aren't Cinema. Let Me Explain," *New York Times*, November 4, 2019, www.nytimes.com. See also Ryan Lattanzio, "Francis Ford Coppola Says Marvel Movies Are 'Despicable,'" *IndieWire*, October 20, 2019, www.indiewire.com.

53. Michael Eric Dyson, *What Truth Sounds Like: RFK, James Baldwin, and Our Unfinished Conversation about Race in America* (New York: St. Martin's, 2018), 269–270.

54. Dyson, 270.

55. Dyson, 271.

56. Dyson, 272.

57. Dyson, 273.

58. Dyson, 276.

59. Dyson, 277.

60. Salamishah Tillet, "'Black Panther' Brings Hope, Hype, and Pride," *New York Times*, February 9, 2018, www.nytimes.com.

61. Tillet.

62. Okorafor also wrote another comics miniseries with her own original characters, called *LaGuardia*, about a travel ban on extraterrestrial immigration and two-way flows between the United States and Biafran activists in Nigeria.

63. Nnedi Okorafor, "Hello, Black Panther Fans!," in *Black Panther: Long Live the King*, by Okorafor (writer) and André Lima Arújo (artist) (New York: Marvel, 2018), n.p.

64. Okorafor, emphasis added.

65. See Laura M. Holson, "U.S.D.A. Lists Wakanda as Trading Partner," *New York Times*, February 19, 2019, www.nytimes.com.

66. Abdulkareem Baba Aminu, "Afrofuturista! The Fantastical Adventures of Nnedi Okorafor," *Full Bleed: The Comics & Culture Quarterly* 2 (2018): 53.

67. Manohla Dargis, "Review: 'Black Panther' Shakes Up the Marvel Universe," *New York Times*, February 6, 2018, www.nytimes.com.

68. Reginald Hudlin (writer) and Scot Eaton (artist), *Black Panther: Bad Mutha* (New York: Marvel, 2006), 3.
69. Reginald Hudlin (writer) and Larry Stroman and Ken Lashley (artists), *Black Panther: Back to Africa* (New York: Marvel, 2008), n.p., emphasis in original.
70. Hudlin, Stromand, and Lashley, n.p., emphasis in original.
71. Okorafor, "Hello, Black Panther Fans!," n.p.
72. I do not profess to fully understand the lineaments, much less the history, of Nigerian "masquerade," but it is a spiritual practice and cosmological feature that Okorafor also uses to significant effect in her *Akata Witch* series, where an albino Nigerian girl becomes initiated into a society of African witches.
73. Nnedi Okorafor (writer) and Leonardo Romero (artist), "Timbuktu," *Shuri* 4 (March 2019): 10.
74. Nnedi Okorafor (writer) and Leonardo Romero (artist), "The End of the Earth," *Shuri* 5 (April 2019): 21.
75. Okorafor and Romero, "Timbuktu," 10.
76. Stan Lee, "When Inspiration Struck," in *Fantastic Four Omnibus*, vol. 2, 292.

3. EROTIC FANTASY-ACTS

1. Raphael Sassaki, "Moore on Jerusalem, Eternalism, Anarchy and Herbie!," *Alan Moore World* (blog), accessed January 2020, https://alanmooreworld.blogspot.com.
2. Jonathan Dollimore, *Sexual Dissidence: Augustine to Wilde, Freud to Foucault* (Oxford: Oxford University Press, 1991), 305.
3. Leo Bersani, "Psychoanalysis and the Aesthetic Subject," in *Is the Rectum a Grave? And Other Essays* (Chicago: University of Chicago Press, 2010), 146.
4. Bersani, 152.
5. Ernst Bloch, "Something's Missing: A Discussion between Ernst Bloch and Theodor W. Adorno on the Contradictions of Utopian Longing (1964)," in *The Utopian Function of Art and Literature*, trans. Jack Zipes and Frank Mecklenburg (Cambridge, MA: MIT Press, 1988), 12.
6. Carol L. Tilley, "A Regressive Formula of Perversity: Wertham and the Women of Comics," *Journal of Lesbian Studies* 22, no. 4 (2018): 8.
7. My thanks to Claude Potts, a librarian at the Gardner Library at UC Berkeley, for alerting me to this provenance. Potts found a citation to the original Legman article, along with a notation describing Sartre's engagement with it, in Alexander C. T. Geppert, ed., *Imagining Outer Space: European Astroculture in the Twentieth Century* (New York: Palgrave Macmillan, 2012). This information appears in note 28 of Pierre Lagrange's "A Ghost in the Machine: How Sociology Tried to Explain (Away) American Flying Saucers and European Ghost Rockets, 1946–1947," 224–244.
8. Gershon Legman, "The Psychopathology of the Comics," *Neurotica* 3 (Autumn 1948): 14–15, reprinted in *Neurotica Issues 1–8* (London: Jay Landesman, 1981). Subsequent citations refer to the 1981 reprint version.

9. Legman, 16.
10. Legman, 18.
11. Legman, 18. Legman's observation here—like many of his observations—is arguable. The descriptive vagueness of "Jewish noses" renders their identification challenging at best in a representational form where noses are only indicated by ink-drawn lines and pixelated color effects. In addition, there is the fact that a great many Golden Age superheroes, like Captain America and nearly every other hero of Timely/Marvel, were most frequently featured in stories fighting Nazis and cruelly caricatured Japanese soldiers and saboteurs. For these Nazi and Japanese villains to often have demonstrably "Jewish noses" across the span of different artists' work would be a tremendous conspiratorial feat. Or else it would have to be the product of an association in the US cultural unconscious between Nazi villainy, Japanese caricatures, and visible "Jewishness" that, while not impossible, does not seem very likely.
12. Legman, 18.
13. Legman, 18.
14. Legman, 19.
15. Legman, 19.
16. Legman, 18.
17. Legman, 19, emphasis added.
18. Legman, 21.
19. Legman, 24.
20. Douglas Wolk, *Reading Comics: How Graphic Novels Work and What They Mean* (Cambridge, MA: Da Capo, 2007), 50.
21. Frantz Fanon, *Black Skin, White Masks*, trans. Richard Philcox (1952; repr., New York: Grove, 2008), 125–126.
22. Legman, "Psychopathology of the Comics," 29.
23. Markmann's 1967 translation is arguably more faithful to Legman. Markmann translates, "There is still no answer to the question whether this maniacal fixation on violence and death is the substitute for a forbidden sexuality or whether it does not rather serve the purpose of channeling, along a line left open by *sexual censorship*." Frantz Fanon, *Black Skin, White Masks*, trans. Charles Lam Markmann (1952; repr., New York: Grove, 1967), 147, emphasis added. Markmann preserves the word "censorship," but his appending "sexual" to it has a similar effect as Philcox's translation, ascribing a psychological process to what Legman is referring to as the result of political action.
24. Jeffrey A. Brown, *Black Superheroes, Milestone Comics, and Their Fans* (Jackson: University Press of Mississippi, 2001), 178.
25. Jennifer C. Nash, *The Black Body in Ecstasy: Reading Race, Reading Pornography* (Durham, NC: Duke University Press, 2014), 2.
26. Hortense Spillers, "Mama's Baby, Papa's Maybe: An American Grammar Book" (1987), in *Black, White, and In Color: Essays on American Literature and Culture* (Chicago: University of Chicago Press, 2003), 206.

27. Nash, *Black Body in Ecstasy*, 6.

28. Nash, 4, emphasis in original.

29. Felix Lance Falkon with Thomas Waugh, *Gay Art: A Historic Collection of Gay Art* (1972; repr., Vancouver: Arsenal Pulp, 2006), 121.

30. Rupert Kinnard, onscreen interview at 17:12, rough cut of *No Straight Lines: The Rise of Queer Comics*, directed by Vicki Kleinman (accessed with permission of the producer Justin Hall, May 2020).

31. Falkon with Waugh, *Gay Art*, 59, emphasis in original.

32. Thomas Waugh, *Out/Lines: Underground Gay Graphics Before Stonewall* (Vancouver: Arsenal Pulp, 2002), 20, emphasis added.

33. Deborah Shamoon, "Office Sluts and Rebel Flowers: The Pleasures of Japanese Pornographic Comics for Women," in *Porn Studies*, ed. Linda Williams (Durham, NC: Duke University Press, 2004), 86.

34. The latter technique is also used in Japanese gay manga, such as Gengoroh Tagame's glorious S/M fantasy—nevertheless taking place in a recognizably "real" world, its setting being family-owned restaurants—*Gunji*. See Gengoroh Tagame, *Gunji*, English ed. trans. Anne Ishii (Berlin: Bruno Gmünder, 2014), 59. I have also seen this technique taken up in Patrick Fillion's comic *Rapture*, which is discussed further in the main text. See Patrick Fillion, writer and artist, *Rapture* 2 (Canada: Class Comics, October 2006), 4.

35. See Leo Bersani, "Is the Rectum a Grave?," in *AIDS: Cultural Analysis, Cultural Activism*, ed. Douglas Crimp (Cambridge, MA: MIT Press, 1987), 222.

36. Belasco, foreword to *The Brothers of New Essex: Afro Erotic Adventures* (San Francisco: Cleis, 2000), n.p.

37. Belasco, 136.

38. Belasco, 136.

39. Belasco, 145, 146, ellipses in original.

40. Belasco, 156, ellipses in original.

41. Belasco, 169.

42. Belasco, 172.

43. See chapter 5 of my *Extravagant Abjection: Blackness, Power and Sexuality in the African American Literary Imagination* (New York: New York University Press, 2010).

44. Patrick Fillion, writer, *Space Cadet* #1, art by Bob Grey (Canada: Class Comics, April 2010), 6, 4, 8.

45. Fillion, 18, 19, ellipses in original.

46. Patrick Fillion, writer and artist, *Rapture* #3 (Canada: Class Comics, January 2009), 5.

47. Patrick Fillion, *Hot Chocolate* (Berlin: Bruno Gmünder Verlag, 2006), i.

48. Belasco, foreword to *Brothers of New Essex*, iii (emphasis added; first ellipses added, second ellipses in original).

49. David Barnes, "Raheem," in *Meatmen: An Anthology of Gay Male Comics*, vol. 22, ed. Winston Leyland (San Francisco: Leyland, 1998), 103, ellipses in original.

50. Joseph Beam, "Brother to Brother: Words from the Heart," in *In the Life: A Black Gay Anthology*, ed. Beam (Boston: Alyson, 1986), 242.

51. I do not know which of the many, many issues of the various *Archie* titles this panel sequence comes from. See https://boingboing.net, accessed June 2020.

52. Bloch, "Something's Missing," xvii.

53. Isaac Julien, "Confessions of a Snow Queen: Notes on the Making of *The Attendant*," in *The Film Art of Isaac Julien* (Annandale-on-Hudson, NY: Center for Curatorial Studies, Bard College, 2000), 82.

54. Fanon, *Black Skin* (Philcox trans.), xiv.

55. Jean LaPlanche and Jean-Bertrand Pontalis, "Phantasy (or Fantasy)," in *The Language of Psycho-Analysis*, trans. Donald Nicholson-Smith (New York: Norton, 1973), 318, emphasis in original.

56. Linda Williams, "Skin Flicks on the Racial Border: Pornography, Exploitation and Interracial Lust," in Williams, *Porn Studies*, 302, emphasis in original.

CONCLUSION

Epigraph: Ernst Bloch, "Something's Missing: A Discussion between Ernst Bloch and Theodor W. Adorno on the Contradictions of Utopian Longing (1964)," in *The Utopian Function of Art and Literature*, trans. Jack Zipes and Frank Mecklenburg (Cambridge, MA: MIT Press, 1988), 15.

1. Emily Badger, Claire Cain Miller, Adam Pearce, and Kevin Quealy, "Extensive Data Shows Punishing Reach of Racism for Black Boys," *New York Times*, March 19, 2018, www.nytimes.com.

2. Huey B. Scott, conversation with the author, October 4, 2019.

3. Scott.

4. Gershon Legman, "The Psychopathology of the Comics," *Neurotica* 3 (Autumn 1948): 7.

5. Legman, 8.

6. Legman, 25.

7. Legman, 7, emphasis added.

8. Jean-Paul Sartre, "Aminadab: Or the Fantastic Considered as a Language," in *Jean-Paul Sartre: Critical Essays*, trans. Chris Turner (1947; repr., London: Seagull Books, 2017), 188, 202, emphasis added. Originally in *Situations I: Essais critiques* (Paris: Gallimard, 1947).

9. Sartre, 192–193, emphasis in original.

10. Sartre, 192.

11. Sartre, 204, emphasis in original.

12. Sartre, 206, emphasis in original.

13. Sartre, 210, emphasis added.

14. Sartre, 194.

15. Sartre, 194–195.

16. Sartre, 208–209.

17. Sartre, 209, emphasis added.

18. This may speak to an idea I've broached before in *Extravagant Abjection: Blackness, Power and Sexuality in the African American Literary Imagination* (New York: New York University Press, 2010): it may not be possible to have anything other than an instrumental relationship to the past.

19. Hillary Chute, *Why Comics? From Underground to Everywhere* (New York: HarperCollins, 2017), 24.

20. See Roland Barthes, *The Pleasure of the Text*, trans. Richard Miller (New York: Hill and Wang, 1975).

21. Tony Kushner, *Angels in America: A Gay Fantasia on National Themes* (New York: Theatre Communications Group, 1995).

INDEX

Page numbers in italics indicate illustrations.

Action Comics #1, 47

Adam (comic), 3

Adams, Neal, *130*

Adam Strange (comic character), 204

Adorno, Theodor, 27, 33

aesthetic representation, 52

Affleck, Ben, 147

Africa: African diaspora, 151, 167; anticolonialism in, 11; in *Black Panther* (comic), 161; for culture, 62–63; in film, 164; history of, 143, 158–59; imagination of, 152–53, 167; politics of, 150–51; stereotypes of, 141–42, 152, *157*

African Americanist letters, 126–27

African American scholarship, 38

Afrocentric fantasy, 206

"Afro-fabulations" (Hartman and Nyong'o), 95

Afro-Futurism, 150–51

AIDS, 9

Akata Witch (comic/novel), 151

Algeria, 11

Almodóvar, Pedro, 7–10, 232–33, 241n4

alternate histories, 122, 127, 141

alternative reality, 229–30

Amazing Adventures (comic), 128–29, *130*, 131–34

Amazing Adventures featuring War of the Worlds (comic), 128–29, *130*, 131–32

anatomy, 185–87, 191–93, 195–96, 202, 213–14

Angels in America (Kushner), 237

antiblackness, 36–37, 43, 52, 57, 62; bias, 102; for Fanon, 227; as racism, 176; revenge for, 118; in United States, 7–8, 222; white supremacy and, 2

anticolonialism, 11

Antifa, 87

antiheroes, 101

anti-Semitism, 182

art: in *Black Skin, White Masks*, 89–90; for Bloch, 50–52, 216; censorship of, 188–89; fantasy as, 10–11; film as, 82; gay fan art, 243n6; in psychoanalysis, 80; violence in, 225–26

assumptions, 236

The Attendant (Julien), 216–17

Austin, J. L., 77–78

The Authority (comic), 192–93

Avengers (comic), 141, 169

Avengers (TV show), 58

Avery, Chayne, 192

Baker, Kyle, 58

Barbie dolls, 186

Barnes, David: with Belasco, 46, 212, 219; blackness for, 194–95, 206, 208–10, *209–11*, 212–16, *213*

Bates, Cary, 55–56

Batman (comic), 186

Batman (comic character), 86, 96, 118, 192–93

Batman (film), 147

BDSM (bondage, discipline, sadism, and masochism), 18, 181, 196–97, 242n11

being. *See* embodiment

Belasco: Barnes with, 46, 212, 219; blackness for, 194–202, *198–201*; fantasy for, 215; superheroes for, 208

Beloved (Morrison, T.), 1

Berlant, Lauren, 13, 18

Bersani, Leo, 44, 78–84, 178–79, 226

the Bible, 36

Binti (Okorafor), 151

Birth of a Nation (Griffith), 174, 224

Black Bolt (comic character), 157

Black culture, 90–92, 122–23, 216; *Blade* (comic) for, 45–46, 117; comics for, 70; masculinity in, 97–98, 100, 105; punishment in, 222–24; slavery for, 190–91

Black fantasy, 36–39, 51

Black feminists, 190–91

Black literature, 38

Black men. *See* masculinity

blackness: for Barnes, 194–95, 206, 208–10, *209–11*, 212–16, *213*; for Belasco, 194–202, *198–201*; in *Black Panther* (comic), 141–46, 151–54, 155, 156–62, *157*, 167, 168, 169–71; in *Black Panther* (film), 162–63; black women and, 49–50, 62–63; in comics, 3, *3–5*; criminality and, 101–2; desirable, 206, 216–19; embodiment of, 35, 78, 216–17; for Fanon, 121; in fantasy, 2, 23–24; imagination of, 30–31, 175; as lived experience, 29; for male gaze, 212; of Nubia, 56–58, *59*, 60–66; politics of, 11–12; in porn comics, 194–202, *198–201, 203*, 204, *205*, 206, *207*, 208–10, *209–11*, 212–19, *213–14*; queerness and, 39–40, 57, 66–67, 171; race and, 78–79, 117–19, *119*; significations of, 42; stereotypes of, 1–2, 95–99, 105, *106*, 107, *108–9*, 110–11, *112–14*, 115–16; for superheroes, 89–95, *93*, 100–104, 119–29, *130–31*, 131–37, *136*, 189–94, 236; unapologetic, 149; whiteness and, 102, 132; in *Wonder Woman*, 51–52

Black No More (Schuyler), 28

Black Panther (comic): Africa in, 161; blackness in, 141–46, 151–54, 155, 156–62, *157*, 167, *168*, 169–71; *Blade* compared to, 202; covers for, *112–13*; in culture, 45; history of, 132–34, 137–41; plots in, 163–64, *164–66*, 167; reiterations of, 97–98

Black Panther (film), 56; blackness in, 162–63; costumes in, 159–60; for fans, 173–74; *Fantastic Four* related to, 142; history of, 146–51; race in, 100; in United States, 97–98

"'Black Panther' Brings Hope, Hype, and Pride" (Tillet), 150

Black philosophical fiction, 40

Black Power movement, 6–7, 140

Black Skin, White Masks (Fanon), 23–24, 29, 68–69, 89–90, 122

Black Superheroes, Milestone Comics, and Their Fans (Brown), 96–97

Black Women in Sequence (Whaley), 56, 58, 60–61, 123

Blade (comic), 105, *106*, 107, *108–9*, 110–11; for Black culture, 45–46, 117; Black Panther compared to, 202; Superman compared to, 120

Blade (film), 105, *106*, 107, *108–9*, 110–11

Blanchot, Maurice, 232

Blaxploitation, 160

Bloch, Ernst, 27, 33, 36, 43, 242n16; art for, 50–52, 216; censorship for, 221–22; empiricism for, 137; utopia for, 179

Blue Marvel (comic character), 3

The Book of Legendary Lands (Eco), 153

Boomerang (film), 100

Boy Meets Hero (Avery and Garcia), 192

Brecht, Bertolt, 221–22

Brown, Jeffrey, 96–97, 99, 185

Bruce Wayne (comic character). *See* Batman

Burger, Dick (comic character), 124
Burton, Tim, 147

Captain America, 87
Captain Marvel (comic character), 98, 99, 169–70
Carmilla Frost (comic character), 132–36, *136*
censorship, 188–89, 222
Chabon, Michael, 141
children: for Comics Code Authority, 180–81; comics for, 176, 225–29; fantasy and, 16–17, 25, 37–38; identification for, 90, 93–94, 177–78; politics for, 222–23; psychology of, 70–71; race for, 178; racism for, 224–25; as readers, 178–79, 182–83; superheroes for, 176–77, 184–85
Christianity, 101–4
Chute, Hillary, 45, 123–24, 234
cisgender male embodiment, 190
civil rights, 140
Clark Kent (comic character). *See* Superman
Class Comics (Fillion), 202
closure, 53–54, 95, 186–187, 232–236
Coates, Ta-Nahesi, 97–98, 156, 162–63
Cockrum, Dave, 129
Colan, Gene, *106*
Cold War, 47–48, 204
colonialism, 11, 23
The Color of Kink (Cruz), 191
Colter, Mike, 111
"The Comic Books and the Public" (Legman), 180
Comic-Con, 139–40
comics: antiblackness in, 43; for Black culture, 70; blackness in, 3, 3–5; in *Black Skin, White Masks*, 68–69; for children, 176, 225–29; Cold War for, 204; costumes in, 60–61; for culture, 94, 135–36; episodes for, 170–71; eroticism in, 191–92, 206, 208–10,

209–11, 212–16, *213*; for Fanon, 68–70; fantasy in, 15, 85–88, 225, 233–37; film compared to, 93–95; history of, 89, 98, 119–29, *130–31, 131–37, 136,* 176–77; hypersexuality in, 215–16; in Japan, 193–94; as literature, 75–76; magical thinking in, 215; for Moore, 173–77, 179; Nubia in, *48,* 49–50, 55, 59; online, 191; philosophy in, 124–25; for popular culture, 68; porn, 194–202, *198–201,* 203, 204, *205,* 206, *207,* 208–10, *209–11,* 212–19, *213–14;* as products, 54–55; queerness in, 45–46, 74–76; race in, 57; for readers, 64–65, 71–72; realism in, 193, 251n34; sadomasochism in, 182–83; scholarship on, 74–76; sequentiality in, 123–24; sound effects in, 212–13, *213;* spatialization in, 126; stereotypes in, 92–93, *93;* storytelling in, 53, 157–58; taxonomy in, 65–66; in United States, 70, 153, 185; for women, 55–56. *See also specific topics*
Comics Code Authority, 44, 46, 134, 180–81, 193
comic strips, 124, *213*
consciousness, 22–24, 32, 81–83, 116, 127
consensus reality, 27–28, 235
Conway, Gerry, 132
Coogler, Ryan, 146–48, 153, 159, 164
Coppola, Francis Ford, 147
Corregidora (Jones), 126
costumes, 60–64, 90, 96, 139, 204; anatomy for, 186; in *Black Panther* (film), 159–60; masculinity in, 111, 115, 129
COVID-19, 221
criminality, 101–5, 118–20
critical fabulation, 127
critical race scholarship, 12–13
criticism, 7–16, 39, 57–58, 63
Cruel Optimism (Berlant), 13
Cruising Utopia (Muñoz), 173
Cruz, Ariane, 191

culture: Africa for, 62–63; *Black Panther* (comic) in, 45; Christianity in,
101–2; comics for, 94, 135–36; cultural
consciousness, 116; of Europe, 90;
fantasy-acts in, 41–46; gay, 9; human
existence related to, 19–20; information in, 92; military, 227–28; misogyny
in, 99; paradigms in, 117; popular,
68; queerness in, 121; race in, 19, 102;
racism in, 63; sexuality in, 26; Spider-
Man in, 141; superheroes for, 117–19,
119; unapologetic blackness in, 149; of
United States, 2, 70–71, 87; Western,
216–17; whiteness in, 46, 222–23; *X-
Men* (comic) for, 160. *See also* Black
culture

Daredevil (film), 147
Dargis, Manohla, 156, 162
Davis, Miles, 100
DC Comics, 55–60, 63, 133–35, 158. *See
also specific topics*
Deacon Frost (comic character), 107, 110
deconstruction, 173–74
Defenders (comic), 169
deities, 18–19, 21–22, 36
desire: desirable blackness, 206, 216–19;
erotic fantasy-acts and, 173–79; for
fantasy-acts, 84; for Fillion, 46, 192,
195; in gay porn, 189–94; homosexual,
219; Nubia related to, 86; objects of,
72–73, 217; for whiteness, 179–89. *See
also* porn comics; pornography
The Dictionary of Imaginary Places
(Manguel and Guadalupi), 153
disalienation, 122–23, 126
Djurdjevic, Marko, *109*
Dr. Doom (comic character), 115, 156–57
domination, 35, 120–21
Dyson, Michael Eric, 148–52, 159

Earth 2 (Taylor/Scott, N.), 5
Eco, Umberto, 153

Edelman, Lee, 176
"The Edge" (Hemphill), 89
education, 50, 223–24
Edwards, Brent Hayes, 151
Elektra (film), 147
Ellis, Warren, 192–93
Ellison, Ralph, 6
embodiment: of blackness, 35, 78, 216–17;
cisgender male, 190; of love, 214–15;
of masculinity, 110, 194–202, *198–201*,
203, *204*, *205*, *206*, *207*, *208–10*, *209–11*,
212–19, *213–14*; of race, 100–101; for
readers, 116
empiricism, 137, 216
enclosure, 212
Erik Killmonger (comic character),
161–63
The Erotic Adventures of Radio Raheem,
208–10, *209–11*, *212–16*, *213*
erotic fantasy-acts, 45–46, 173–79
eroticism, 187, 213; in comics, 191–92, 206,
208–10, *209–11*, *212–16*, *213*; in Oasis,
197–202, *198–201*
the Escapist (comic character), 141
ethics, 103–4, 119
Europe, 23, 90, 160
existentialism, 24
Extravagant Abjection (Scott, D.), 1–2, 31

Faith and the Good Thing (Johnson, C.),
40
Falkon, Felix Lance, 191–93
family, 71, 88
fandom, 67
Fanon, Frantz, 11, 23–24, 29, 31, 44; antiblackness for, 227; assumptions of, 86;
blackness for, 121; comics for, 68–70;
fantasy-acts for, 83; film for, 89–93;
government for, 167; Legman for, 181,
188–89; philosophy for, 125; race for,
122, 179; temporality for, 124; Vidal
and, 96; Wertham and, 176–77, 180;
whiteness for, 122–23

fans: *Black Panther* for, 173–74; gay fan art, 243n6; identification for, 97; scholarship on, 96–97; superheroes for, 161; Superman for, 174
fantasists, 76–77, 86–87
Fantastic Four (comic), 74–75, 115, 128, 138–44, 154–56, 170
fantasy: action and, 84–85; Afrocentric, 206; alternate histories in, 122, 141; as art, 10–11; for Belasco, 215; Black, 36–38, 51; blackness in, 2, 23–24; of black power, 6–7; children and, 16–17, 25, 37–38; in comics, 15, 85–88, 225, 233–37; consciousness of, 24; for critical race scholarship, 12–13; criticism of, 10–11, 39; definitions of, 77–78; desire from, 72–73; against domination, 35; in education, 50; empiricism for, 216; from film, 90–91; identification from, 74–75, 104; of identity, 28–29, 68–69; imagination in, 29–30, 40–41, 52–53, 72; invulnerability in, 115; limitations in, 169; in literature, 13–14; logic of, 24–25; of masculinity, 195–96; Nubia as, 54–56; origin stories in, 171; phantasy, 72; plots, 16–18, 25–26; political, 151; propositions in, 21–22; psychic fantasies, 79; psychology of, 72–73; racial, 12; racism in, 214; for readers, 185; reality and, 31–32, 83; of revenge, 20–21, 105, 107; for Sartre, 229–32; scholarship on, 8–9; sexual fetish and, 15–16; signification in, 196; social justice in, 11–12; stereotypes of, 13–14; from storytelling, 91–92; subjects of, 83–84; typologies, 26–27; of utopia, 36; utopia in, 27; victimization in, 119–20; of whiteness, 95–96, 104, 174–75, 178–79, 182; as world-building, 39–40. *See also specific topics*
fantasy-acts: for actors, 77–78, 85; in culture, 41–46; desire for, 84; erotic, 173–79; for Fanon, 83; politics of, 145–

46; psychology of, 87–88; for readers, 86; reading, 54–56; scholarship on, 30, 34–37; whiteness as, 104
fascism, 182, 184–85
Fawaz, Ramzi, 44, 57, 74–76, 244n25
feminism, 190–91
Fillion, Patrick, *203*, 215; desire for, 46, 192, 195; Space Cadet by, 202, 204, *205*, 206, *207*
film: Africa in, 164; as art, 82; comics compared to, 93–95; criticism, 7–8; for Fanon, 89–93; fantasy from, 90–91; for Hudlin, 100; male gaze for, 96; from Marvel Comics, 146–47; performance in, 110–11; race in, 89; sci-fi in, 154; in Spain, 7, 232–33, 241n2; storytelling in, 159–60; in United States, 147–48; for Vidal, 95–96
Final Crisis (comic), 3, *4*, 62
Franco, Francisco, 7, 9–10, 232–33
Frankfurt School, 27
Franklin (comic character), 98
Future State (McKinney and Martinez), 56, 62

Gaiman, Neil, 173
Game of Thrones (TV show), 151
Garcia, Russell, 192
Garcia Marquez, Gabriel, 41
Garner, Jennifer, 147
gay culture, 9
gay fan art, 243n6
gay porn, 189–94
gender, 26, 184, 190
genitalia, 185–87, 191–92, 195–96, 202, 213–14
Germany, 49
Giordano, Dick, 55–56
Goldberg, Petra, 135
Golden Age comics, 46, 141
Goodwin, Archie, 117–18
government, 18, 156–58, 167

Graham, Billy, *114*, 118
Green Lantern (comic character), 66
Grell, Mike, *131*
Griffith, D. W., 174–75
Guadalupi, Gianni, 153

Haiti, 150
Halperin, David, 45
Hanson, Glen, 192
Hartman, Saidiya, 95, 126–27
Heck, Don, 55–56, 59
hegemony, 14, 32
Hemphill, Essex, 89
Hernandez, Gilberto, 57
Hernandez, Jaime, 57
Hicksville (Horrocks), 124
Hinz, Christopher, *109*
historiography, 126–27
history: of Africa, 143, 158–59; alternate
    histories, 122, 127, 141; of *Black Pan-*
    ther (comic), 132–34, 137–41; of *Black*
    Panther (film), 146–51; of comics, 89,
    98, 119–29, 130–31, 131–37, *136*, 176–77;
    of criminality, 104; effect of, 170–71;
    of *Fantastic Four*, 138–39; of politics,
    26; of sci-fi, 128–29; of slavery, 126–27,
    202; of Superman, 27–28, 95–96; of
    Wonder Woman, 98–99; of *X-Men*,
    134–35
Hitch, Bryan, 192–93
Hollywood, 147
homophobia, 13, 176
homosexuality, 182–84, 194, 219
Horrocks, Dylan, 124
hostility, 79–80
Hot Chocolate (Fillion), 202, 203, 206
House Party (film), 100
Hudlin, Reginald, 100, 117, 146, 159–62
Hughes, Langston, 23–24
human existence, 18–22, 230–32
Hurston, Zora Neale, 1
hypermasculinity, 96–97
hypersexuality, 195, 215–16

identification: for Bersani, 226; for chil-
    dren, 90, 93–94, 177–78; with family,
    71; for fans, 97; from fantasy, 74–75,
    104; with Nubia, 71–72; with queer-
    ness, 85; for readers, 70–71; sequences
    in, 170; with superheroes, 183; with
    whiteness, 68–69
identity: of Batman, 118; consciousness
    in, 22–23; fantasy of, 28–29, 68–69;
    insight from, 67–68; morality and, 107;
    psychology of, 19–20, 29; queerness in,
    49; sexual, 77; of Superman, 118
ideology, 43
imagination: of Africa, 152–53, 167;
    assumptions from, 236; of black-
    ness, 30–31, 175; creativity and, 27; in
    fantasy, 29–30, 40–41, 52–53, 72; of
    genitalia, 186–87; of government, 156–
    58; imaginary races, 136–37; imaginary
    whiteness, 3; inspiration from, 189;
    in Marvel Comics, 156; performance
    in, 234; for readers, 63–64; of self-
    destroying concepts, 230; superheroes
    for, 225; of Superman, 179; of white-
    ness, 92–93, 95, 117, 144
immigration, 95–96
Inglourious Basterds (Tarantino), 122
inspiration, 189, 191–92
In the Wake (Sharpe), 95
Invisible Girl (comic character), 139
involute, 144–45
invulnerability, 115
Iron Man (comic character), 86

Jackson, Rosemary, 10–11, 13–14, 16
Japan, 193–94, 251n34
Jenkins, Patty, 63
Jim Crow laws, 224, 228–29
Jimenez, Phil, 63, 67
Johnson, Charles, 40
Johnson, Daniel Warren, 62
Jones, Gayl, 126
Jordan, Michael B., 162

Joseph, Frederick, 150–51
Julien, Isaac, 46, 216–17
Jungle Action (comic), 98, 132, 142–43, 159. See also *Black Panther*
The Justice League of America (comic), 62

Kael, Pauline, 7–9
Kafka, Franz, 232
Kanigher, Robert, 55–56
Kendi, Ibram X., 6
Ken dolls, 186
Killraven (comic character), 128–29, *130–31*, *131*–34
King Kong (film character), 63–64
Kinnard, Rupert, 192
Kirby, Jack, 93, *93*, 134, 138–41, 154–56, 159
Kushner, Tony, 237

Lacan, Jacques, 30, 34, 81
language, 10, 76–77, 78, 81
The Language of Psycho-Analysis (LaPlanche and Pontalis), 72
LaPlanche, Jean, 72
Larocca, Salvador, 3
Lashley, Ken, 160
Law of Desire (Almodóvar), 8
"Law of the Land" (Temptations), 1
The League of Extraordinary Gentlemen (Moore), 173
Lee, Spike, 100
Lee, Stan, 134; *Fantastic Four* for, 170; Kirby and, 138–41, 154–56, 159; Mr. Fantastic for, *155*; race for, 183
Legion of Super-Heroes (comic), 129, *131*
Legman, Gershon, 46, 180–89, 225–29, 250n11
Le Guin, Ursula K., 37–38, 40
Lennon, John, 37
liberty, 42
linguistics, 10, 76–77
Literary Wonderlands (Miller, L.), 153
literature: Black, 38; comic characters in, 141; comics as, 75–76; fantasy-acts in,

41–42; fantasy in, 13–14; scholarship on, 10–11; world-building in, 35–36
Live Flesh (Strauss), 7
The Lord of the Rings (Tolkien), 232
love, 214–15
Love & Death (Legman), 180–81
Love & Rockets (Hernandez, J., and Hernandez, G.), 57
Lucas, Jorge, *112*
Luke Cage (comic character), 45–46, 66, 117–18, 120, 204
Luke Cage, Hero for Hire (comic), 111, *114*, 115–19, *119*

magical realism, 41
magical substitution, 23
magical thinking, 215
Mahnke, Doug, *4*
Malcolm X, 100
male bonding, 177–78
male gaze, 96, 212
Mandingo (film), 218
Manguel, Alberto, 153
Mapplethorpe, Robert, 65
Markmann, Charles Lam, 181, 242n19, 245n1, 250n23
Martin, George R. R., 151
Martinez, Alitha, 56
Marvel Comics: civil rights for, 140; DC Comics and, 55, 158; film from, 146–47; imagination in, 156; race for, 133–35; after World War II, 74–75. See also *specific topics*
Marx, Karl, 33–34
Marxism, 15
masculinity, 79, 87, 96–100, 105, 190; in costumes, 111, 115, 129; embodiment of, 110, 194–202, *198–201*, *203*, 204, *205*, 206, *207*, 208–10, *209–11*, 212–19, *213–14*
McCartney, Paul, 37
McClennen, Nathaniel, 123–24
McCloud, Scott, 53–54, 65, 123, 233

McGregor, Don, 132–37, 142–43, 159
McKinney, L. L., 56, 62
memory, 83
Mercer, Kobena, 65
metaphysical love, 215
Midnight's Children (Rushdie), 41
Might Avengers #3 (comic), 3
Mighty Thor (comic), 143–44
Migrating the Black Body (Raphael-Hernandez and Raiford), 57–58
military culture, 227–28
Miller, J. Reid, 102–4, 119
Miller, Laura, 153
Miller-Young, Mireille, 191
minorities, 134–35. *See also specific topics*
misogyny, 99, 176
Mitchell, W. J. T., 94–95, 123–24
Moore, Alan, 173–77, 179–80, 187
morality, 107, 119
Morrison, Grant, 62, 129–30, 133
Morrison, Toni, 1, 41, 85
la movida, 7, 241n2, 241n4
Mr. Fantastic (comic character), 155
M'Shulla (comic character), 132–36, 136
Ms. Marvel (comic character), 98
Muhammad Ali, 100
Muñoz, José, 66, 173

narratives, 126
national fantasy, 18
Nat Turner (Baker), 58
Nazis, 87, 182
"The Negro Speaks of Rivers" (Hughes), 23–24
The New Mutants (Fawaz), 74
Nigeria, 45, 151–53, 164, 248n62, 249n72
No Straight Lines (documentary), 192
"Not For Children" (Legman), 180
Nubia (comic character), 52, 86, 88, 90, 243n11; blackness of, 56–58, 59, 60–66; in comics, 48, 49–50, 55, 59; as fantasy, 54–56; identification with, 71–72; for

queerness, 66–67, 78; stereotypes in, 96, 98–99
nudity, 193
Nyong'o, Tavia, 95

Oasis (comic character), 197–202, *198–201*, 208–10, 219
Obama, Barack, 2, 4, 6, 216
objects, of desire, 72–73, 217
Okorafor, Nnedi, 45; *Binti* author of, 151; *Black Panther* for, 162–64, *164–66*, 167, *168*, 169–71; Nigeria related to, 151–53, 248n62, 249n72; *Who Fears Death* author of, 151
One Hundred Years of Solitude (Garcia Marquez), 41
"The Ones Who Walk Away from Omelas" (Le Guin), 37–38, 40
online comics, 191
ontology, 80
origin stories, 171
Oxherding Tale (Johnson, C.), 40

painting, 82
P. Diddy, 100
Peanuts (Schulz), 98
perceptual realism, 32–33
performance, 78, 93, 110–11, 234
perspective, 94–95
Pertinax, Helvius, 8
phantasy, 72
phenomenology, 44, 67–68
philosophy: Black philosophical fiction, 40; in comics, 124–25; existentialism, 24; from Frankfurt School, 27; of human existence, 18–19; of phenomenology, 44; of reality, 22–23
physical love, 215
plots: in *Black Panther* (comic), 163–64, *164–66*, 167; in *Captain America*, 87; in DC Comics, 56; in *Fantastic Four*, 144, 154, 156; fantasy, 16–18, 25–26; for

villains, 138–39; for women, 61–62; in *Wonder Woman*, 60, 62

politics: of Africa, 150–51; of blackness, 11–12; for children, 222–23; of criticism, 13–14; of fantasy-acts, 145–46; history of, 26; of inclusion, 12–13; political fantasy, 18, 151; queerness in, 15; of race, 134; racial, 181; of readers, 187–88; reality of, 29–30; in United States, 41–42

Pontalis, Jean-Bertrand, 72

popular culture, 68

porn comics: blackness in, 194–202, *198–201, 203, 204, 205, 206, 207, 208–10, 209–11, 212–19, 213–14*; gay, 189–94; whiteness in, 46

pornography, 189–96

pornotroping, 116

possibility, 84–85

privacy, 28

projection, 79–80

psychic fantasies, 79

psychic unconscious mind, 81

psychology: of children, 70–71; of criminality, 102–3; of fantasy, 72–73; of fantasy-acts, 87–88; of identity, 19–20, 29; Lacan for, 30; of language, 81; of perceptual realism, 32–33; of possibility, 84–85; of projection, 79–80; psychoanalysis, 13, 33, 70–72, 79–80, 99, 189; psychopathology, 179–89; psychotherapy, 185; of queerness, 53–54; of reading, 52–53; of reality, 37; of repression, 188–89; of revenge, 9; of violence, 226–27

"The Psychopathology of Comic Books" (Legman), 181–89

Pugh, Steve, *109*

punishment, 222–24

"Queer and Now" (Sedgwick), 76–77

queerness: blackness and, 39–40, 57, 66–67, 171; in comics, 45–46, 74–76; in culture, 121; gay porn related to, 189–

94; against homophobia, 13; identification with, 85; in identity, 49; Nubia for, 66–67, 78; in politics, 15; psychology of, 53–54; queer porn comics, 191; queer theory, 78–79; superheroes for, 66–73, 76–77, 180; of *Wonder Woman*, 180. *See also specific topics*

race: blackness and, 78–79, 117–19, 119; in *Black Panther* (film), 100; for children, 178; in comics, 57; critical race scholarship, 12–13; in culture, 19, 102; for DC Comics, 133–35; embodiment of, 100–101; ethics and, 103–4; for Fanon, 122, 179; for Fillion, 215; in film, 89; gender and, 26; imaginary races, 136–37; in *King Kong*, 63–64; for Lee, Stan, 183; in *Luke Cage, Hero for Hire*, 111, *114*, 115–19, 119; for Marvel Comics, 133–35; politics of, 134; privilege for, 162; racial fantasies, 12; racial hierarchy, 177; racial politics, 181; signification of, 95; stereotypes of, 65–66; for superheroes, 95–99, 105, *106*, 107, *108–9*, 110–11, *112–14*, 115–16; of Superman, 99; whiteness as, 97; for women, 131–32

racism: antiblackness as, 176; for children, 224–25; in costumes, 63–64; criminality and, 118; in culture, 63; in fantasy, 214; of Jim Crow laws, 224, 228–29; performance of, 93; in reality, 182; in stereotypes, 116; in United States, 222–23

Radio Raheem (comic character), 208–10, *209–11, 212–14, 213*

Raiford, Leigh, 57

Raphael-Hernandez, Heike, 57

Rapture (Fillion), 205

readers: children as, 178–79, 182–83; closure for, 233; comics for, 64–65, 71–72; of DC Comics, 60; embodiment for, 116; fantasy-acts for, 86; fantasy for, 185; form for, 170–71; identification for, 70–71; imagination for, 63–64;

readers (*cont.*)
for Legman, 225–29; Nubia for, 88; perspective for, 94–95; phenomenology for, 67–68; politics of, 187–88; reality for, 234–35; storytelling for, 65–66; superheroes for, 74, 170; transformation for, 232; white supremacy for, 128
reading, 52–56
Reading Comics (Wolk), 187
realism, 32–33, 41, 138, 193, 251n34
reality: alternative, 229–30; from consciousness, 32; consensus, 27–28, 235; of criminality, 118–19; fantasy and, 31–32, 83; perception of, 44; philosophy of, 22–23; of politics, 29–30; propositions in, 24; psychology of, 37; racism in, 182; for readers, 234–35; of social justice, 51
repression, 188–89
resignification, 41–42
revenge, 9, 20–21, 105, 107, 118
Richie Rich (comic character), 86
Riggs, Marlon, 212
Robin (comic character), 192
Romero, Leonardo, *164–66, 168*
Romita, John, Jr., 159
Ross, Diana, 51, 88
Rushdie, Salman, 41
Rushdy, Ashraf, 126
Russell, P. Craig, 135

sadomasochism, 182–83, 251n34
Salamon, Gayle, 44
Sandman (Gaiman), 173
Sartre, Jean-Paul, 24, 181, 188–89, 229–32
Sassaki, Raphael, 174
scholarship: African American, 38; on antiblackness, 57; on Christianity, 102–4; on comics, 74–76; critical race, 12–13; criticism as, 16; on fans, 96–97; on fantasy, 8–9; on fantasy-acts, 30, 34–37; hegemony in, 14; linguistics in,

76–77; on literature, 10–11; on reading, 53–54; semiotics for, 10; on *Wonder Woman*, 56–58
Schulz, Charles, 98
Schuyler, George, 28
sci-fi, 9, 128–29, 154. *See also* fantasy
Scooby-Doo! Team-Up #5 (comic), 62
Scorsese, Martin, 147
Scott, Darieck, 1–2
Scott, Nicola, 5
Search for a Method (Sartre), 232
Sears, Bart, *108*
Sedgwick, Eve, 44, 76–77
Seduction of the Innocent (Wertham), 44, 68, 180
self-destroying concepts, 230
semiotics, 10
sequentiality, in comics, 123–24
sexism, 176
sexuality: in culture, 26; hypersexuality, 195, 215–16; masculinity and, 79; sexiness, 193; sexual deviance, 184; sexual fetish, 15–16; sexual habits, 19–20; sexual identity, 77; for superheroes, 197–201, *198–201*
Shamoon, Deborah, 193–94
Sharp, Liam, *113*
Sharpe, Christina, 95
Shooter, Jim, *131*
Shuri (comic character), 146, 151, 163, *164–66*, 167, *168*, 170–71
Shuster, Joe, 27–28, 121, 174
sidekicks, 192–93
Siegel, Jerry, 27–28, 121, 174
signification, 82, 95, 196
Simon, Joe, 93, *93*
slavery, 126–27, 160, 190–91, 202
Snipes, Wesley, 105, *106*, 107, 110–11. See also *Blade*
social fantasy, 18
social justice, 5, 11–12, 42, 57
Song of Solomon (Morrison, T.), 41
sound effects, 212–13, *213*

Space Cadet (comic character), 202, 203, 204, *205*, 206, *207*, 209–10

Spain, 7, 232–33, 241n2

spatialization, in comics, 126

speculative fiction, 9. *See also* fantasy

Spicer, Mike, 62

Spider-Man (comic character), 99, 141

Spillers, Hortense, 116

Stain Removal (Miller, J. R.), 102

stereotypes: of Africa, 141–42, 152, 157; of blackness, 1–2, 95–99, 105, *106*, 107, *108–9*, 110–11, *112–14*, 115–16; in comics, 92–93, 93; in costumes, 62–63; of criminality, 105; of fantasy, 13–14; of gay culture, 9; in Nubia, 96, 98–99; of race, 65–66; racism in, 116; of sexual habits, 19–20; of superheroes, 61, 215–16; of villains, 101

Stewart, John, 66

Stockton, Kathryn Bond, 176–77

Storm (comic character), 160–61

storytelling, 53, 65–66, 91–92, 157–60, 183–84

Strauss, Frédéric, 7

Stroman, Larry, 160

Sue Storm (Invisible Girl), 139

Super-Friends (comic), 62

superheroes: anatomy of, 185–86; for Belasco, 208; blackness for, 89–95, 93, 100–104, 119–29, *130–31*, 131–37, *136*, 189–94, 236; for children, 176–77, 184–85; for culture, 117–19, *119*; deconstruction of, 173–74; for fans, 161; for fantasists, 86–87; genitalia of, 185–86, 191–92; identification with, 183; for imagination, 225; involutes for, 144–45; names of, 98; problem-solving for, 163–64; for queerness, 66–73, 76–77, 180; race for, 95–99, 105, *106*, 107, *108–9*, 110–11, *112–14*, 115–16; for readers, 74, 170; realism for, 138; sexiness of, 193; sexuality for, 197–201, *198–201*; stereotypes of, 61,

215–16; transformation by, 235–36; whiteness and, 179–89; white supremacy for, 169, 175. *See also specific topics*

Superman (comic character), 27–28, 87, 120, 246n22; appearance of, 111; Batman compared to, 192–93; eroticism in, 187; for fans, 174; fascism in, 184–85; formula for, 181–82; history of, 95–96; as human, 110; identity of, 118; imagination of, 179; Luke Cage compared to, 115; race of, 99

surveillance, 212

Swamp Thing (comic), 173

Tarantino, Quentin, 122

Tarzan, 60, 62, 69–70, 90–92

A Taste for Brown Sugar (Miller-Young), 191

taxonomy, in comics, 65–66

Taylor, Tom, 5

T'Challa (comic character), 86, 132, 139, 153, 161–63. See also *Black Panther*

temporality, 124

The Temptations, 1, 34–35

Thanos (comic character), 169–70

Their Eyes Were Watching God (Hurston), 1, 47, 49

This American Life (radio show), 223

Thomas, Roy, 141

Thor (comic character), 86

Tillet, Slamishah, 150

Tilley, Carol, 70, 180–81

Tinsley, Natasha Omise'eke, 151

Tolkien, J. R. R., 232

Tomb of Dracula (comic), 105, *106*, 107

Tongues Untied (Riggs), 212

Tony Stark. *See* Iron Man

transformation, 219, 232, 235–36

translations, 181, 242n19, 245n1, 250n23

transphobia, 176

Trump, Donald, 6–8, 42, 150, 177, 221

Tuska, George, 118

unapologetic blackness, 149
unconsciousness, 81–82
United States: antiblackness in, 7–8, 222; Black feminists in, 190–91; *Black Panther* (comic) in, 97–98; Black Power in, 140; Cold War for, 47–48; comics in, 70, 153, 185; culture of, 2, 70–71, 87; education in, 223–24; film in, 147–48; government in, 18; immigration in, 95–96; politics in, 41–42; racism in, 222–23; whiteness in, 156; white supremacy in, 6; World War II for, 117
utopia, 27–28, 36, 41, 179

vampires. See *Blade*
"Venus in Two Acts" (Hartman), 126–27
V for Vendetta (Moore), 173
victimization, 119–20
Vidal, Gore, 90–91, 95–96
villains, 101, 104, 138–39
violence, 225–27
visual arts, 82

Wakanda. See *Black Panther*
War of the Worlds (Wells), 128–29, 130
Warren, Kenneth, 151
Watchmen (Moore), 173–74
Waugh, Thomas, 193
Welles, Orson, 129
Wells, H. G., 128–29
Wertham, Frederic, 44–46, 68–70, 86, 176–77, 180–81
Western culture, 216–17
Whaley, Deborah Elizabeth, 56, 58, 60–61
What Truth Sounds Like (Dyson), 148
"When the Master Commands" (Belasco), 197–202, 198–201
whiteness: blackness and, 102, 132; in culture, 46, 222–23; desire for, 179–89; domination of, 120–21; for Fanon, 122–123; as fantasy-acts, 104; fantasy of, 95–96, 104, 174–75, 178–79, 182; identification with, 68–69; imaginary, 3; imagination of, 92–93, 95, 117, 144; ontology of, 80; in porn comics, 46; privilege of, 28, 95–96, 217–18; as purity, 177–78; as race, 97; superheroes and, 179–89; in United States, 156; white supremacy, 2, 6, 87, 128, 169, 175, 177, 180, 187
Whitewash Jones (comic character), 93, 93, 96
Who Fears Death (Okorafor), 151
"Why 'Black Panther' Is a Defining Moment for Black America" (*New York Times Magazine*), 147–48
Williams, Linda, 218
Willis Stryker (comic character), 118
Williwaw (Vidal), 91
The Wiz (film), 221–22
Wolk, Douglas, 187
women: blackness for, 49–50, 62–63; for Coates, 163; comics for, 55–56; misogyny for, 99, 176; as mothers, 88; plots for, 61–62; race for, 131–32; sexism against, 176
Wonder Woman (comic), 44, 48, 48–52, 55–58, 59; history of, 98–99; for Jimenez, 63, 67; plots in, 60, 62; queerness of, 180. See also Nubia
Wonder Woman (film), 63
world-building, 35–36, 39–40
World War II, 117, 246n22
The Wretched of the Earth (Fanon), 11, 167

X-Men (comic), 128, 134–35, 160

yaoi comics, 193–94
The Young Allies (Simon/Kirby), 93, 93

Zen Buddhism, 30

ABOUT THE AUTHOR

DARIECK SCOTT is Professor of African American Studies at UC Berkeley. Scott is the author of *Extravagant Abjection: Blackness, Power, and Sexuality in the African American Literary Imagination* (2010), winner of the 2011 Alan Bray Prize for Queer Studies of the Modern Language Association, and of the novels *Hex* (2007) and *Traitor to the Race* (1995) and the editor of *Best Black Gay Erotica* (2004). Scott is coeditor of the American Literature special issue "Queer about Comics," winner of the 2018 Best Special Issue from the Council of Editors of Learned Journals.

Printed and bound by CPI Group (UK) Ltd, Croydon, CR0 4YY

09/06/2025

14685794-0003